THE QUEST FOR SECURITY

PUBLICATIONS

under the direction of the
NETHERLANDS INSTITUTE OF
INTERNATIONAL AFFAIRS

2

THE QUEST FOR SECURITY

SOME ASPECTS OF NETHERLANDS
FOREIGN POLICY
1945—1950

by

Dr. S. I. P. VAN CAMPEN

MARTINUS NIJHOFF / THE HAGUE / 1958

PRINTED IN THE NETHERLANDS

TO DAPHNE

You were in some sort a predestined victim... my debt and your long-suffering are all the greater.

DOROTHY L. SAYERS, *Busman's Honeymoon*.

FOREWORD

The foreign policy of the great powers has been studied thoroughly by many historians and students of international affairs. They
have inquired into its deepest motives and have tried to search
its innermost workings. Even so, much remains to be done in
this field.

The foreign policy of the average small state has been neglected, however. The reason for this neglect is not difficult to
find: the small state usually contributes only in a modest way
to the shaping of the international political situation. The
conduct of its foreign affairs does not produce the tragic effects
that occasionally mark the policy of the great powers, when the
happiness, if not the very existence of nations may come to
depend upon decisions taken by a few political leaders.

The concept of the small state is a vague one. Some of the
minor states are weak in material resources, some in manpower,
others again are small in territory. The differences in potential
are so great that attempts have been made to introduce a further
classification. Between the great and the small powers, it was
said, there is a group of "middle powers", such as Canada and
Australia, or Spain, Brazil and the Argentine. They differ
markedly from others like Ireland, Austria or Syria. However,
all attempts at classification are bound to fail. There are no
hard and fast rules by which major and minor powers can be
distinguished. All minor states have their own specific problems
in foreign relations, the nature of which is determined by their
geographic location, their history, the circumstances in which
they came into being and by their economic and social structure.

The international position of many small states of recent
origin is so intimately connected with existing relationships
between the great powers that their foreign policy can be little

more than a series of reactions to the acts of these powers. Other states of minor potential are more or less isolated by their geographic location and thus protected against the direct influence of power politics among the big nations. The diversity is so great that the question may be asked whether it is permissible at all to speak of "the average small state". It is possible, however, to describe an imaginary small state on the basis of those characteristics which are common features of many existing small states.

The average small state is so located geographically that it is close enough to the crossroads of world politics to feel their direct influence, yet strong enough to endure them without being swept away by their flow. Its strength is such that, if attacked by a more powerful neighbour, it cannot be subdued without a considerable effort which, however, would entail grave political risks for the aggressor; and its structure is stable enough to maintain its identity even if temporarily overrun. It often is a state that once belonged to the powers which shaped the political destiny of their part of the world. If so, it was obliged to adjust itself in a long and difficult process to a more modest position. Although no longer powerful and without even the remotest chance of emerging once more as an important political factor, its autonomous existence seems sanctioned by tradition. Its right to independence and the delimitation of its boundaries are not seriously questioned by anyone except in the most violent and revolutionary times. Having been reduced to a less influential position, the small state tends to lay great stress on the rule of law in international affairs. For it, the rule of law, the recognition of moral and legal obligations by all powers, is the best, if not the only substitute for national power. It provides not only the necessary basis for a policy of neutrality in times of war, but it also lays the foundation for a world-wide organization of states that will serve as a regulatory force in periods of conflict and crisis. The typical small state, especially in Europe, sought to avoid entanglement in alliances and the quarrels of foreign nations – to quote the well-known words of America's first president – which formed one of the gravest threats to its independence, until the war of 1939–1945 destroyed the very structure upon which its policy had been based.

The foreign policy of the Netherlands after 1945 seems to provide excellent material for a case-study in the conduct of foreign relations of a typical small state. For a hundred years it had been the leading concept of Netherlands policy to shape the nation's foreign relations in such a way that in case of war between neighbouring states the Netherlands would be able to remain neutral. Only one substitute for neutrality was ever considered: national security through the general acceptance of the rule of law in international relations by all major and most minor powers, if possible by means of a world-wide organization of states. Thus, the Netherlands co-operated with most European and many other powers in the work of the League of Nations. However, the disillusion following the breakdown of the European political system caused the Netherlands to return to a policy of neutrality. The war of 1940--1945 and the subsequent splitting-up of the war-time American-British-Russian alliance made the continuation of such a policy after 1945 a most hazardous undertaking. Yet, the transition from neutrality to alliance was very difficult. It took some time before the leaders of Netherlands foreign policy were willing to concede that the reality of the organizational method of securing peace had fallen far short of the ideal. Netherlands public opinion, never over-optimistic in regard to the efficiency of United Nations methods and practices, was nevertheless for some years reluctant to enter into defensive alliances; many Netherlands people set their hope on a new approach to the problem of national security: European Federalism. For some time there were divergences between governmental policies and public beliefs on this point. Finally, however, general agreement was reached once the overruling advantages of the combination of Atlantic co-operation for defence and European integration for economic development were realized.

The Netherlands Institute of International Affairs thought it worth while to publish a study in English on the political developments sketched in the preceding remarks. The Institute was fortunate, indeed, to find Dr. S. I. P. van Campen willing to undertake the task. The sources which he had to use, were not easy to handle and consisted mainly of documents

presented by the Netherlands Government either to their allies
or to parliament and the debates in parliament. Interviews with
prominent Netherlanders who have participated in the shaping
of their country's foreign policy confirmed the opinion, acquired
by previous experience, that a description of Netherlands
foreign policy based on this material alone, is perfectly justified
from the scholarly point of view. It was considered advisable
not to make use of newspaper-reports or of books presenting
more personal views on the subject, as the method followed
by Dr van Campen has the additional advantage of presenting
an excellent illustration of the process by which Netherlands
foreign policy is made and formulated.

The Netherlands Institute of International Affairs wants to
express its gratitude to all institutions and persons who so
kindly assisted Dr van Campen in his work, and in particular
to the Netherlands Ministry of Foreign Affairs which granted
permission to publish the document reproduced in Appendix 16.
    The Institute hopes to have rendered a service to all
students of international affairs who are interested, not only
in the acts and attitudes of the major powers, but also in the
reflex of these actions and attitudes on the political behaviour
of the average small state.

B. H. M. VLEKKE

Director,
Netherlands Institute
of International Affairs

NOTE

The names and character of the various parliamentary documents quoted in the text may well be somewhat unfamiliar to the foreign reader. All these documents have their place in the legislative process which, in rough outline, may be summarized as follows. A Bill is first discussed in the Council of Ministers, to which it has been submitted by the Minister(s) concerned. The Council of State is then requested to tender its advice, after which the Bill is sent to the Queen; a "Royal Message" (Koninklijke Boodschap), signed by the Queen, is added to it. Next, the Bill is sent, together with the Royal Message and an "Explanatory Memorandum" (Memorie van Toelichting) to the "Second Chamber" (Tweede Kamer) of the States General. *In order to avoid all misunderstandings, it must be stressed that in the Netherlands Constitution the "First Chamber" is the Chamber of revision, and not the "Second Chamber", as the foreign reader might be led to believe from its name.* The Bill is reviewed in the non-public Committees of the Chamber, the findings of which are laid down in a "Provisional Report" (Voorlopig Verslag) which is sent to the Minister(s) and published. In answer to this Report, the Minister(s) submit a "Memorandum in Reply" (Memorie van Antwoord) which is also published and to which, if necessary, a "Note of Modifications" (Nota van Wijzigingen) may be added.

Finally, the Bill is publicly debated in the Chamber and, if passed, sent on to the "First Chamber" (Eerste Kamer) of the States General. The procedure in the First Chamber is the same as in the Second: again the Chamber submits a Provisional Report to the Minister(s) and the latter a Memorandum in Reply to the Chamber. But there is one difference inasmuch as the First Chamber has not the right to move amendments.

If passed by the First Chamber, the Bill receives the Royal Assent, is countersigned by the Minister(s) concerned and published.

Of all these terms only a few will be frequently found in the present work; and these have been abbreviated in the notes as follows:

Explanatory Memorandum   – Expl. Mem.
Provisional Report   – Prov. Rep.
Memorandum in Reply   – Mem. Repl.
Second Chamber   – Sec. Chamber

In conclusion, a word on references. The public debates of the States General are reported in the PROCEEDINGS OF THE STATES GENERAL; whenever these debates have been quoted, reference has been made to the relevant page(s) of these PROCEEDINGS. If, however, the Explanatory Memoranda, Provisional Reports or the Memoranda in Reply are quoted, the name and date of the document in question are mentioned in the notes.

Most of the statements quoted have been made either during the annual Budget discussions on Foreign Affairs or in the course of discussions on special Bills. Unless otherwise stated, notes must be understood to refer to the annual Budget discussions. For example: "Mem. Repl., Sec. Chamber, Nov. 10, 1948" refers to the Budget discussions, but "Mem. Repl., Sec. Chamber, Pact of Brussels, April 5, 1948" to the discussions on the Pact of Brussels Bill.

Finally, in all cases where an official or semi-official English translation of Netherlands Government documents was available, the translated texts have been quoted and reproduced in the Appendices.

CONTENTS

Appendices

ERRATUM

Page 98, line 18: Final Communiqué (p. 225) *read* (p. 255)

INTRODUCTORY REMARKS

At the end of the Second World War in Europe and Asia, the Netherlands people and their Government (which, after almost five years of exile, had returned to The Hague in June 1945) were confronted with a number of problems, two of which, equally difficult and urgent, almost monopolized the nation's attention. There was in the first place the truly enormous task of reconstruction and recovery. Elsewhere in this work, data will be given about the damage which war and occupation inflicted upon the nation; here it may suffice to point out that Holland was one of the most severely hit countries in Europe. Naturally, in these circumstances, Government and people regarded reconstruction and recovery as their paramount concern. Moreover, quite apart from the material damage, it should be realized that the organization of the State too, had been severely affected. There was, for instance, no elected representation of the people; and the temporary States General, soon formed, were restricted in their scope and activities. From the States General downward, similar measures were necessary. All this presented problems of the first magnitude.

Nor was this all. At the same time Holland had to face a crisis in its overseas territories; developments took place in the then Netherlands East Indies, now Indonesia, which threatened the future of the Kingdom as it had been hitherto known. What is commonly known as the Indonesian Question is outside the scope of this work, although this is but the first of many allusions to it, but it must be realized that the conflict which arose out of these developments was hard and bitter; and the Netherlands people showed a keen and highly emotional interest in these events which, indeed, divided the nation in an unfortunate manner. Thus, after five years of occupation, the country had to face problems, all of which in turn were sufficiently pressing and important to claim the whole of the nation's strength and attention.

But of course there were other questions as well which also needed solving. It may well be that they were somewhat over-shadowed by the great issues just mentioned; and perhaps they were, in fact, less spectacular; but it should not be thought that for that reason they were less important. The country's foreign policy formed one of these questions and it is with that policy, and its fundamental problem in particular, that the present work is concerned. If it were asked what exactly must be understood by the expression "fundamental problem", we would reply that in the international community as it was in the past and – despite all efforts since 1918 – still is now, the funda-mental issue of each country's foreign policy is to ensure that country's national security against external attack. Foreign policy obviously has other objectives; but in present circum-stances the maintenance of national security is foreign policy's most fundamental issue with which no other can compare. In other words: the foreign policy of any country must look after the national interests; and the most essential and permanent of these interests is national security.

For many years the Netherlands had ensured – or had tried to ensure – their national security and independence by means of a policy of neutrality which is discussed in some detail in Chapter I of this work. Whatever may have been this policy's theo-retical and practical merits, the Second World War had demon-strated that it had failed in its fundamental purposes and was likely to fail again in the future. Here, then, was another quite important question of the post-war period: what should be the country's policy with respect to the paramount objective of national security? How could and should the nation's safety be safeguarded?

The essential importance of this question is evident. Yet it would seem that the problem did not exactly arouse the nation.

Nothing is more characteristic of this relative lack of interest than the fact that the "fundamentals" of the country's foreign policy were not discussed in the States General until the end of 1946 although there were slight allusions to them when the United Nations Charter was debated in 1945. But on that occasion when Foreign Minister van Kleffens suggested that such problems should not as yet be discussed, the advice was accepted.[1] [2]

It may well be that this lack of active interest was chiefly due to the fact that the prominent questions of Indonesia and reconstruction monopolized the national stage. But it would be rash to overlook in this connexion the well established fact that at no time have the Netherlands people shown any very great interest in problems of foreign policy; the complaints about this are by no means recent. And as will be explained below, the long-standing policy of neutrality did nothing to combat this tendency; on the contrary.

But whatever the degree of national interest or indifference – the problem existed; in fact, it existed – not to speak of pre-war times – from that very day in May 1940 when the failure of neutrality became so convincingly evident. And it became highly topical after the formation in 1945 of a new Government which, unlike the Government in exile, could speak and act for the nation. In the present work, then, the attempt is made to follow the developments of Netherlands foreign policy in this fundamental field from 1945 until such time as a new orientation may be said to have definitely replaced the old one. Such an attempt may of course be realized in several ways; and it is bound to meet with many difficulties. For instance: if, in our opinion, there can be no discussion as to the *character* of foreign policy's fundamental problem, it does not follow that its *extent* can be determined with any degree of precision or accuracy. It is often very difficult to say which things are relevant to national

---

[1] Sec. Chamber, United Nations Charter, Oct. 30, 1945, 141.
[2] Mr. E. N. van Kleffens became Foreign Minister on August 10, 1939 and resigned on March 1, 1946. He was followed by Mr. J. H. van Royen who resigned on July 3, 1946 and who was succeeded by C. G. W. H. Baron van Boetzelaer van Oosterhout, who was in office until August 7, 1948. At that date Mr. D. U. Stikker became Foreign Minister and was responsible for Netherlands foreign policy until September 1952.

security and which are not.[1] Again, it is possible in tracing these developments, to concentrate strictly on the fundamental issue and to refrain carefully from discussing all side issues. But quite apart from the fact that this might prove difficult in view of the vague delimitations of the main problem, too narrow a conception would also seem inadvisable, as we would thus exclude the possibility of illustrating the old truth that decisions in the main issue of foreign policy will sooner or later affect the possibilities and proceedings in other, relatively less important sectors.

Consequently, too strict a concentration on the main issue has been consistently avoided, as will be apparent from the plan on which the work has been based. The first three Chapters, discussing *a*) Holland's traditional policy, *b*) the Netherlands position towards that new element in international relations, the United Nations and its system, and *c*) the Netherlands position in the German problem and their vital interests in that country, are intended to acquaint the reader with some key points of the situation in which the developments we are about to describe, had their origins.

We follow in subsequent Chapters, on a strictly chronological basis, the developments of 1945 and after, first (in the section "General Policy") with respect to the fundamental issue which has been given a wide interpretation so that the policy of the Netherlands Government towards the federalist conceptions regarding the integration of Europe or Western Europe, for instance, could also be dealt with; second (in the section "Germany") with regard to a problem which was obviously closely related to the main issue and in which the Netherlands interests were heavily engaged. Here special emphasis is placed on the question to what extent the Netherlands interests and objectives in the German problem were affected by the developments which Netherlands policy considered advisable or inevitable with regard to its main issue – national security.

Finally, in a concluding Chapter, the developments described are briefly reviewed as a whole, while, in a number of Ap-

---

[1] One recalls the third Marquess of Salisbury's gibe about the military mind which would occupy Mars to protect the Moon.

pendices, certain documents, either of Netherlands or foreign origin, are reproduced in full.

A word on the sources of which use has been made, must not be omitted. Whether or not one can ever hope to write a "definite" version of certain political developments, even as regards the "facts", must be a matter of doubt; but it is certainly impossible as long as the time has not come for publishing the archives of all countries concerned. As much of what is discussed here still belongs more or less to contemporary politics, this was obviously out of the question. The data in this work were practically all taken from Government statements as they were made in the two Chambers of the States General, either in the course of the annual debates on Foreign Affairs, or on the occasion of special events. As this work is chiefly concerned with Government policy, the statements of Ministers have been specially emphasized. But in democratic countries foreign policy is not a matter for Governments alone. Whenever this appeared desirable – for instance, to illustrate parliamentary reactions to Government decisions of great importance (the Pact of Brussels in 1948!) or in those cases where there appeared to be a fairly constant discrepancy between the States General and the Government (European Federalism) – the opinions expressed by groups in the States General have been reproduced at some length. Wherever other sources have been utilized, mention has been made in the text at the appropriate places.

The present account is of course not a history of five years of Netherlands foreign policy; it is not even a history of a special chapter of that policy. Where foreign policy is concerned, Governments are notoriously reticent in their statements to the national parliaments; and the Netherlands Government is probably no exception to the rule. What is given here is not more than a sketch of a certain development which, no doubt, leaves much unsaid of what has, in fact, happened.

It should, moreover, not be overlooked that what may be quite important in a general history of Netherlands foreign policy, need not be so if certain of its aspects are reviewed from a particular point of view. Let us mention some cases in point. In a general history the work of the Netherlands in the United

Nations would be a most important item; but it is not in the present account; hence all mention of such work has been omitted. Again, Benelux was widely applauded abroad during the post-war years; and it was certainly regarded as a very bright element indeed of Netherlands foreign policy. But Benelux was, and still is, an experiment in *economic* co-operation and integration; and even if there had been complete *political* co-operation or integration between the three countries (quod non), it would have been of no importance whatever as far as their fundamental problem of national security was concerned. As was well realized, even the combined forces of Holland and Belgium could not guarantee, in modern conditions, their countries' safety.

Again, the *political* effect of the Marshall Plan was certainly a factor in the developments in which we are interested; and it has not been overlooked. But in our context its *economic* significance calls for no detailed analysis.[1] Our point, therefore, is this. In the present work both Benelux and Marshall Plan occupy a different place than would certainly be the case in a general exposé. Accordingly, whenever Holland, Belgium and Luxemburg co-operated politically – and they did so on very important occasions – the fact has been duly noted and stressed in the text; and so has ERP's political significance. On the other hand, the economic aspects of Benelux have only been briefly touched upon in a Note, whilst some data with respect to the Marshall Plan's salutary effects on Holland's economic and psychological recovery and the specific Netherlands contribution to its realization have been given in another Note.

---

[1] It may of course be said that, had the Western European countries not been saved from economic disaster by General Marshall's initiative, the political history of the post-war years would have been very different from what it, in fact, has been. Whatever the truth in this assertion, it is clear that there is nothing in it which is specifically relevant to Holland.

CHAPTER I

NETHERLANDS FOREIGN POLICY
BEFORE 1945

During the greater part of the nineteenth and twentieth centuries up to the Second World War, the foreign policy of the Netherlands was commonly known as the policy of neutrality or independence. These two terms are not entirely synonymous and they did, in fact, indicate a slight difference in underlying conceptions which shall be referred to later; but generally they have been used indiscriminately.

The very first thing to be noted about this policy is that it was proclaimed and maintained by the Netherlands Government of its own free will; it was a unilateral act; Holland's neutrality was neither instituted nor sanctioned by any international treaty or convention. For this reason alone any comparison with Swiss neutrality or with that of Belgium before 1914 would be misleading. Nor would it be right to mention the North Sea Convention of 1908 in this connexion; on that occasion the participating powers – Germany, France, Great Britain, Denmark, Sweden and the Netherlands – guaranteed the territorial status quo and undertook to respect each other's sovereign rights. This was, of course, quite a different matter and it is significant that Belgium and Norway were no party to that convention. [1] It follows that the Netherlands were entirely free to continue or discontinue their policy of neutrality and it was precisely on account of that feature that some people, particularly after the First World War, preferred to allude to Netherlands foreign policy as one of independence rather than one of neutrality.[2]

---

[1] J. A. van Hamel, *Nederland tusschen de Mogendheden*, 1918, p. 389.
C. Smit, *Diplomatieke Geschiedenis van Nederland*, 1950, p. 273.
[2] Mem. Repl., Sec. Chamber, Nov. 29, 1946, 14.

Upon what was this policy based? In discussing this question, the strategic position of those times should be borne in mind: except for the last two decades before the Second World War, long range air power, with all its consequences, was as yet unknown.

Four centuries of European history had demonstrated time and again that the possession of the Netherlands, the delta of some of Europe's most important rivers, was an essential precondition of continental or world supremacy. This is easy to understand in view of the country's strategic position and its colonial possessions and commercial power.

In fact, the great continental powers could never tolerate any one of them ever establishing themselves here permanently; and as for Britain, she has always considered the independence and inviolability of Holland as a necessary condition for her own security.

This being so, it follows naturally enough that when Holland's power and resources weakened in the eighteenth century, the idea of exploiting this situation was bound to emerge; and in fact, from then onwards, sustained efforts can be observed to attain that position of neutrality which, however, did not become a permanent feature of Dutch foreign policy until after 1839.[1]

Other factors contributed as well. From the beginning of the nineteenth century onwards Holland's position was not without a certain dualism. In Europe it was but a small power; in the Far East, however, it possessed and immense colonial empire. That Holland could defend it against the dominating seapowers was unthinkable; so here, too, neutrality seemed natural, the more so as a similar state of conflicting ambitions as in Europe could be exploited. And for the time being it suited the powers to leave the East Indies in Netherlands hands.

Moreover, it is clear that to a mercantile state like Holland, with its worldwide trade relations, a policy of neutrality, political withdrawal and friendly relations with all powers, must have been singularly attractive. One might go further and say that Holland's very economic position to a certain extent im-

---

[1] England's known willingness to maintain Holland's independence and the other common interests between the two countries explain why intimate relations with Great Britain generally formed an essential aspect of the policy of neutrality.

posed such a policy upon it. And finally, in the course of time, the policy of neutrality assumed all the respectability of a heritage, handed down to successive generations by the wisdom of their ancestors; it had been tested and, it was thought, found good; it was cloaked in sentiments of elevated idealism; and in due course tradition itself became one of the policy's most revered props.

The question might be asked whether such a policy could have ever offered real security. Clearly it could not; it follows from the very character of its bases that this policy, so useful in times of an accepted balance of power, was bound to fail if and when that balance was destroyed. In the event of one of the great powers initiating a policy of expansion, setting itself the definite goal of continental or world domination, the neutrality and independence of Holland could not possibly be respected, because of the very strategic and economic facts upon which, in times of equilibrium, a policy of neutrality could be based.[1] It is therefore difficult to see how the events of May 1940 could have contained an element of surprise – but for one reason. It is well known that Holland's neutrality was not violated during the First World War. Hence the mention made above of a policy "tested and, it was thought, found good". In point of fact, however, that fortunate escape was the effect, not of the policy of neutrality, but of mere chance. On the other hand, the developments of Revolutionary and Napoleonic times – confirmed in 1940 – show that Holland is bound to become involved as soon as the accepted balance of power is disturbed.

Nevertheless, it cannot be doubted that the events of 1914–1918 were widely regarded as a triumphant confirmation of the traditional policy's wisdom; and there was certainly no intention to change course.

Meanwhile the Netherlands had become a member of the newly established League of Nations. The exact status of Holland's traditional policy under the League Covenant forms a difficult and complicated question which need not be enlarged upon here. In the circumstances, the *unqualified* policy of neutrality could

[1] Van Hamel, *op. cit.*, pp. 308, 337.

not be maintained, but on the other hand it must be admitted
that during the years 1920–1936 a certain dualism was always
noticeable and it is probably fair to say that the old policy,
if less conspicuous, was still not without its attractions.

When it became clear that the League had failed, the Netherlands joined certain other powers in stating at Copenhagen,
that application of Articles 10 and 16 of the Covenant could
only be facultative (July 1936).[1] In other words, it was for the
Netherlands Government to decide *a*) whether the Covenant was
violated or not; and *b*) whether, this being the case, application
of sanctions should follow. This meant, of course, a reversal to
the old policy and, from 1936 until the outbreak of hostilities,
the position did not change further. If, then, some qualification
is clearly required for the period of 1920–1936, this is not the
case with respect to the policy of 1936–1940: in the face of the
approaching storm, Holland took its stand on the basis of the
old policy of neutrality.

The inevitable effects of a policy of such long standing on certain trends of thought are particularly noteworthy, as they
tend to linger long after the disappearance of the policy which
contributed to their rise.

Since the eighteenth century the Dutch have been noted for
their inclination to pacifism and their interest in the development
of international law. It would be wrong to say that this grew out
of the policy of neutrality; the name of Grotius and Frederick
the Great's dictum – La Hollande est pacifique par principe et
guerrière par accident – bear witness to this. But neutrality
strongly encouraged such tendencies. And in one sense this was
quite natural: a small and relatively weak power has a tactical
interest in furthering such causes which in themselves are of
course most laudable. But like all things, such inclinations, when
indulged too freely, may be a little dangerous. The importance
and force of international law in diplomacy and international
politics may well be overrated; one's own pacifism may quite
erroneously be regarded as part of a world wide trend – all this
to the ultimate detriment of those holding such optimistic beliefs. In fact, it is difficult not to agree with a Dutch writer who

[1] Belgium, Luxemburg, Denmark, Finland, Sweden and Norway.

warned that such preoccupations are no doubt admirable, but should not be taken too seriously [1]. In Holland, unfortunately, that warning went unheeded all too often.

Even more serious was the fact that such beliefs, added to a policy of passivity and mere observation led to an unmistakable and widespread apathy towards the problems of foreign policy and the military defence of the country.

In short, it is fair to say that under the influence of long-term neutrality the Netherlands became dangerously detached from the realities of the international scene; and although it is no doubt true that, as far as Holland was concerned, the events of 1940 were inevitable, it is equally certain that the country was not so well prepared mentally and materially as might have been expected.

Following the defeat of 1940 and its consequences, the majority of the Dutch felt that neutrality was not only dead but also damned. The arguments for this change in opinion might seem all too obvious; nevertheless, it is not without interest to review them in some detail.

With the great mass of the people it was no doubt the disappointment of having been dragged into the war after all; this seemed argument enough for making a change. But it is difficult to believe that this way of reasoning weighed very heavily with the Government. For, after all, neutrality had never offered any guarantee against war and loss of independence; and the events of 1940 as such provided no reason to forsake the old policy once there was again a stable balance of power.

There were, however, other arguments. It was said that the strategic position showed a fundamental change – which was perfectly true. The emergence of long range air power had created new conditions. The narrow industrial basis of Holland made it impossible to organize a sufficient military defence without the help of others; and in view of the country's exposed position, everything should be ready and arranged before an attack would actually take place. In other words, technical conditions and requirements of modern defence posed these alternatives: either the country prepared its defence in co-oper-

[1] Van Hamel, *op. cit*, p. 395.

ation with others before an attack (which, of course, ruled out neutrality) or no defence would be possible at all; and the latter course was acceptable to nobody.

This line of reasoning was followed by Mr. van Kleffens, at that time Minister of Foreign Affairs, in a speech from London to the Netherlands people on December 28, 1943. The force of these arguments was undeniable, but no more so than it would have been in the Twenties, and certainly, the Thirties. Yet, as we know, in 1936 the Netherlands reverted to full neutrality.

However, the outlook in the early Forties may well have formed the decisive argument. Neutrality, it was pointed out, was a useful instrument provided there was a genuine general peace or at least a global or continental balance of power. But far from this being likely, was there not some justification for thinking that Holland would be confronted by what might be termed a permanent expansion crisis, caused either by renewed aggression by Germany, or of some other great power? Germany would be beaten, no doubt; but Germany had been beaten before; was this sufficient evidence in itself that it would never rise again? Fear of German aggression persisted in Holland for a long time after the war; during the struggle itself this factor must have been even stronger. In later years, it is true, it was gradually realized that Russia was by far the greater danger of the two; but Russia or Germany – the point is that there was very little prospect of an undisturbed equilibrium. On the whole, the developments of 1945–1948 confirm that this, indeed, was the decisive issue in the ultimate discarding of Netherlands neutrality.[1]

---

[1] It may be argued that neutrality and membership of the United Nations cannot be reconciled. In fact, that is what the Government thought in 1945: "…. our obligations as a member of the United Nations cannot be reconciled with a policy of neutrality which, as experience has taught us, can no longer form the basis of our foreign policy in the present day world" (Mem. Repl., Sec. Chamber, United Nations Charter, Oct. 25, 1945, 50.)

On the other hand, speaking at the conclusion of the Brussels Pact in 1948, Baron van Boetzelaer was rather more precise, saying: ,,…. Toutefois, la neutralité n'était ni après la première, ni après la seconde guerre mondiale, mise hors la loi. La possibilité de rester neutre en cas de désaccord entre les grandes puissances en ce qui concerne la désignation de l'agresseur, restait entière. Le Pacte d'union de l'Europe occidentale que nous signons aujourd'hui met définitivement fin à la possibilité de rester neutre quand l'un des cinq partenaires a été la victime d'une agression en Europe …."

(For this speech, see below, The Pact of Brussels, p. 59).

To say that neutrality must go, is one thing; to determine what should replace it, is quite another. During the occupation many articles and pamphlets were secretly published about the subject, but here we shall only mention some extracts of Mr van Kleffens' speech, already referred to, of December 28, 1943. This speech should be regarded, and was intended, as a contribution to discussion and reflection in occupied Holland, for of course the Government in London were neither able nor willing to commit the Netherlands people as long as the German occupation prevented free discussion and consultation.

Mr van Kleffens made, inter alia, the following observations:

".... In any case the choice is between isolation and association with others of good will. You will have to make that choice.

There is certainly no need for me to say much more about isolation. But should your choice be co-operation with others of good will, we would be well advised to make clear with whom we are going to co-operate. Enemy propaganda is already suggesting that Holland is being asked to be included in the British Commonwealth. But reassure yourselves – nothing is asked of us; and if ever anything were to be asked of us, it would not be absorption in the British Commonwealth. The Commonwealth is a community, linked together by the loyalty of all to the Crown – the British Crown. The Kingdom of the Netherlands knows of no bond but to the Netherlands Crown which is exclusively hereditary in the House of Orange. Consequently there can be no question of our Kingdom being absorbed in any other Commonwealth, even in the extenuated form of association through subordination.

But if that kind of association is, in fact, out of the question, there still remains the possibility of co-operation. Should that co-operation, however, be limited to the British Commonwealth? That does not depend on us alone. It also depends on our other partner with whom we have, on account of our position at the brink of the Pacific Ocean, many common interests. I refer, of course, to the United States. As yet it is difficult to say what the position of the United States will be at the end of the War towards political and military co-operation with other powers. It might well be that their position on this subject in South East Asia, where China occupies such a particular place, will not be the same as in Europe. But even if we assume that the United States will be prepared to co-operate with the British Commonwealth and with us – which for us, no doubt, would be most desirable – it seems as yet too early to discuss the form in which this co-operation should take shape. The main point is this: we may expect that bitter experience and deepened perception will have given the United States a proper understanding of the vital stake they have in the effective maintenance of peace – also in Europe. They have seen, for the second time, that a German attack on Holland, Belgium and France is, essentially, an attack on England and they may now be expected to realize better than before that England's fall poses the dagger at America's very heart.

If, in fact, developments were to proceed in this direction, there would emerge in the West a strong formation in which America with Canada and the other British Dominions would function as arsenal, Great Britain as base (particularly for the airforce) and the Western parts of the European Continent – I refer to Holland, Belgium and France – as bridgehead. In this manner we would be dependent, it is true, on the Western powers; but these powers would, conversely, have a need of us. It is difficult to think of a stronger position for our country.

This formidable bloc in the West would find its balance in Russia. Russia which will be covered, after Japan's defeat, by natural boundaries in the North, East and South, must and will continue – as we must and will – to pay full attention to the security of its open frontier vis-à-vis Germany. In this outline nothing emerges more naturally than the necessity of good relations between the Netherlands and the Soviet Union.

If all this could be realized, it might, I am inclined to think, well guarantee a long period of peace. In this system France will have to resume its place among the Western powers. Let us hope that it will arise, purified and strengthened, from the purgatory into which it was hurled three years ago. That Belgium will be on our side, cannot be doubted.

An exposé such as the present one, however objective, is practically bound to show, between the lines, the direction in which the thoughts of the man who is speaking to you are turning. Besides, you have every right to know this. But the Government shall not take binding decisions in the field of foreign policy, as long as the Germans occupy our country, unless such decisions are absolutely unavoidable. For things are not static and it is not always possible to wait until Hitler has been beaten. However, up to now this has not been necessary. Anyhow, I can assure you that these decisions will be left, to the largest degree possible, to the free and well-considered will and desires of a reborn Holland".

The chief interest of these quotations lies in the fact that they clearly foresee the developments which culminated in the Pact of Brussels and the North Atlantic Treaty. In fact, the speech unfolds a programme which, unlike most programmes, was in due course fully realized. In due course – in actual fact not until 1948/1949; for it must not be imagined that either the Netherlands Government or the Netherlands people adopted this programme, this policy of blocs, as the basis of their foreign policy in 1945. On the contrary, as our discussion of Holland's attitude towards the United Nations will show. The time of van Kleffens' programme was to come later; and considered in this light, the period of 1945–1948 may well be regarded as one of transition.

CHAPTER II

THE NETHERLANDS AND THE SYSTEM OF THE UNITED NATIONS

There can be little doubt that developments in the United Nations have been a factor of considerable importance in the shaping of Netherlands post-war foreign policy. For in the view of the Dutch, the United Nations embodied the principle of universal co-operation, a principle of which, in 1945, great things were still expected; and its subsequent collapse was but hesitantly and reluctantly accepted by the Netherlands Government.

On the other hand, the fact that Holland was prepared to give all possible support to a policy of universal co-operation did not mean that there was much sympathy for the system of the United Nations as laid down in the Charter. There certainly was not; and in fact, when the States General discussed the Charter it became clear that they anticipated little good from it; nor have subsequent events shown that they were mistaken in this.

For this reason, and because of the effect which the collapse of universal co-operation had on the course of Netherlands foreign policy, Holland's point of view in 1945 with respect to the Charter should not go unmentioned.

The Netherlands views regarding the proposed structure of the United Nations have been formulated in two documents; in the first, of January 1945, the Netherlands Government presented certain suggestions concerning the Dumbarton Oaks proposals to the Governments of the United Nations and other Governments concerned [1]; the second contained the amendments sub-

---

[1] "Suggestions presented by the Netherlands Government concerning the proposals for the Maintenance of Peace and Security agreed on at the Four Powers Conference of Dumbarton Oaks as published on October 9, 1944".

mitted by the Netherlands Delegation to the San Francisco Conference.[1]

These suggestions and amendments are noteworthy inasmuch as they reflect a way of thinking which was typical of Netherlands foreign policy traditions. On the one hand, they reveal the legal approach in its practical and also, perhaps, impracticable form, and on the other hand, the desire to find constructive compromises for existing differences and contrasting views.

Some points may be noted. In the first place it is considered that the standard of the Charter, viz. the maintenance of international peace and security, is not enough (Suggestions, p. 167). According to the Dutch view "some acceptable standard of conduct in international affairs" must be recognized. The present criterion might put "a premium on pressure brought to bear by stronger on weaker states". What, then, should be the basis of decisions? According to the Suggestions: "a statement .... to the effect that some standard of justice will always be observed"; or in the words of the Amendments: "Insert in Chapter I sub 1 after the words 'To maintain international peace and security' *in conformity with the elementary principles of morality and justice and on the basis of due regard for international law*". In case this was unacceptable, it was proposed to add to the Chapter in question a *statement setting forth the fundamental rights and duties of States*. (Amendments, I).

Thus, the question arises: how to ensure the observation of such a standard? The Netherlands Government felt that this "could not be left to the Security Council (to decide), for if that were done this Council would be allowed to sit in judgment on its own proposals. Nor could it, for practical reasons, be left to the Assembly, or to the arbitrary appreciation of individual member-states". Accordingly, the appointment was suggested "of an independent body of eminent men from a suitable number of different countries, men known for their integrity and their experience in international affairs, who should be readily avail-

---

[1] "Amendments to the Proposals for the Maintenance of Peace and Security agreed on at the Four Powers Conference of Dumbarton Oaks supplemented as a result of the Conference of Yalta, submitted by the Netherlands Delegation to the San Francisco Conference".

The full text of both documents will be found in Appendix 1.

able to pronounce upon decisions of the Security Council whenever an appeal to that effect were addressed to them.... This body .... should pronounce upon the matter solely from the point of view of whether the Council's decision is in keeping with the moral principles referred to above and should render its decision within a set number of days so as to avoid all undue delay and any diminution of the Council's effective and speedy handling of a given case" (Suggestions, p. 168).

The relationship between the great powers and the smaller states – "that very thorny question" – is then dealt with. (Suggestions, p. 168 ff.) It was fully admitted that the great powers should be given a special place in the new organization, but the smaller states should not be without an adequate voice. To that end, the states who, without belonging to the great power class, are in a position to make a substantial contribution to the success of the organization, should, in the opinion of the Netherlands Government, always be adequately represented on the Security Council. Moreover, a provision "that the affirmative vote of at least three of the non-permanent members of the Security Council.... would be required, would go far to allay what would appear to be legitimate apprehensions on this point of the smaller powers".

But this was not all. The Netherlands recognized that in the present state of the international community it was necessary to give a special place to the great powers, although, after all, the Dumbarton Oaks Plan was said to be based on the sovereign equality of all peace-loving nations. But in return the smaller states were surely entitled to ask "that these great powers show in practice that they are conscious of the special duties and responsibilities these concessions place upon them".

Now this point was of course intimately related to the system of voting to be adopted, and in particular to what the Netherlands Government called "the right of free appreciation which may take the extreme form of a right of veto".

As regards free appreciation, it was the view of the Dutch that every member of the organization should undertake to co-operate loyally in applying sanctions *other than those consisting of the use of force;* but every state, great or small, should be free to decide whether or not it wished to participate in the application of armed force. No state, the Dutch believed, could be expected to promise to apply armed force "against adversaries unknown in advance, in the company of unknown partners and in unknown circumstances".

But this was a relatively simple question compared to that of the right of veto. The Netherlands Government thought that if there was to be a right of veto at all, it could only be one with regard to measures of coercion; and they considered that it should be restricted to cases of coercion by force.

However, it was not anticipated that any small power would claim such a right of veto; and as regards a great power, two different cases might be imagined: either it was not a party to a dispute or it was. In the former case, the Netherlands Government could not understand "why a great power should have a right of veto with regard to questions with which that great power is only remotely concerned" (Suggestions, p. 171). As regards the latter case the position of the Dutch Government was as follows. They fully admitted the right of any great power to say that it will not join an organization which gives authority to its members in certain circumstances to use force against it; neither did they deny that coercion of a great power by armed force might be an operation of very great magnitude. Still, in their view, there were only three grounds on which the right of veto might be claimed (Suggestions, p. 171). Of these the third calls for special comment. The veto may be claimed because a power needs a safeguard against possible conspiracies of others. This argument is rejected, for is there any power, "which need fear that it may become a victim, *as a result of its adhesion to the Dumbarton Oaks Plan*, of a conspiracy of others, so that reservation of a right of veto with regard to themselves is necessary for member states? To the Netherlands Government it seems difficult, at any rate, to see in what measure such a contingency is, in point of fact, less likely to arise, if a right of vetoing coercion is conceded to a power in its own cause than if it is not conceded. It affords no real protection" (Suggestions, p. 172).

The peculiar manner in which this aspect of the problem was

presented is noteworthy and the conclusion might well be questioned [1]; but it is clear, at any rate, that the Dutch admitted of no grounds on which the veto might be claimed and they made their position perfectly plain: ".... it is difficult to see what advantage or attraction the Plan would have for the Netherlands if a right of veto were granted to great powers in their own cause.... If this Government may express a hope, it is that the right of veto in a power's own cause be not insisted on by any state".

The Charter in its final form, as agreed upon at the San Francisco Conference, was indication enough that the efforts of the Netherlands Government had not been particularly succesful. On the other hand, when, in 1945, the States General were asked to approve Netherlands membership of the United Nations, the debates showed that the Government's position was generally supported. There was little hope that the United Nations would prove to be a "League of Nations with teeth"; and such features as the preponderant position of the great powers, their right of veto and the absence of any means to enforce social and economic decisions were generally disliked.

In his reply, Mr. van Kleffens readily agreed that the Charter showed many questionable aspects and there was certainly no reason to entertain illusions. However, without a universal organization like the United Nations, anarchy would once again reign among the community of states; with such an organization there was at least a possibility of something better, something that might avoid future conflicts or contribute to their peaceful settlement. At any rate, the Charter as submitted was the best that could be hoped for; it embodied the principle of co-operation, as opposed to international anarchy on the one hand and a supra-national authority on the other.[2]

The smaller powers, Mr van Kleffens said, really did their

[1] "Adhesion to the Dumbarton Oaks Plan" had nothing to do with the real problem. The point is whether or not there was a conspiracy against a certain power. One might deny this; but if the power in question maintained there was, it must be conceded that the veto power would give protection against such a conspiracy, *in so far as its effects within the United Nations were concerned*. Were the United Nations to assume an important place in international relations, the protection would be accordingly great. Did the words "it affords no real protection" really imply that the Charter was expected to be brushed aside and that the United Nations would never assume importance in international relations?

[2] Mem. Repl., Sec. Chamber, United Nations Charter, Oct. 25, 1945, 49.

best at San Francisco; but in the end they preferred agreement to nothing at all. They no doubt sacrificed much more than the great powers; but they achieved certain results.[1] For example, the Charter now stated that international disputes should be adjusted or settled "in conformity with the principles of justice and international law" – an addition without which the Netherlands would have found it difficult to join the new organization. Without that definition, the door would be open to arbitrariness and opportunism; and the Charter would have been a mere legal consecration of power politics.[2]

The Foreign Minister made it clear that he, too, regretted the preponderant position of the great powers, but it had to be accepted; as for the limitation of national sovereignty, this was, in his view, the inevitable reverse of a policy of collective security. "For this reason, we must accept the principle of a majority decision, while reality demands, regrettably enough, that we resign ourselves to the preponderant position of the great powers and their right of veto".[3] He then recalled the efforts to establish a revision agency for the decisions of the Security Council. These had been unsuccessful; it had been the general feeling that this would result in an undesirable accumulation of commissions and agencies. Furthermore, the proposals regarding a permanent commission for peace and security had met with no better fate. The powers of this commission would be limited to those which the General Assembly would on occasion delegate to it, or to such subjects as might be submitted to the Assembly under Article 11, par. 2 and Article 15, par. 1. Thus the commission which was to number eighteen members, would be in a position to discharge some of the Assembly's functions during those periods in which the latter (in which all member-states are represented) did not sit. In proposing such a commission the object of the Netherlands was to give the Assembly a further opportunity to participate in the work of maintaining and promoting international peace. But for the time being nothing came of them, for although the Netherlands Government might well consider the whole question strictly

[1] Van Kleffens in Sec. Chamber, *idem*, Oct. 30, 1945, 144.
[2] Van Kleffens in First Chamber, *idem*, Nov. 7, 1945, 20.
[3] Van Kleffens in First Chamber, *idem*, Nov. 7, 1945, 19.

constitutional in the sense of the Charter, it touched one of the most delicate aspects of its system: the relations between the General Assembly and the Security Council.[1]

So much for the general aspects of the Charter. But of course many other points were raised during the debates, a few of which are of special interest in the light of after events. For instance, the question of regional arrangements and regional groupings.

It was suggested to the Government that the Netherlands, in view of their strategically exposed position in Europe and South East Asia, might well need re-insurance in the form of a Western European regional pact. Such a Bloc, it was said, might not only strengthen Holland's position, but also that of Western Europe which, thus organized, might well give a lead to the world. This continent was in a most vulnerable position; it was therefore likely to understand the advantages of collective security and act accordingly. Furthermore, was there not some reason to believe that in Western Europe the solution might be found for the social and political problems of our time – a solution based on the two principles of economic regulation and freedom of thought? [2]

Traditional caution characterized the Government's reaction to these propositions. In the first place, they told the States General that they disliked the word "bloc" – they preferred to speak of "groupings". Such groupings, they believed, might come and not in Western Europe alone. This should not be a matter of regret provided there were suitable arrangements to avoid conflicts between them. And this was what the San Francisco Charter could and should do. In fact, the Charter was the essential basis for such groupings, without which Holland, at any rate, would never participate in any of them. For, however admirable their original aims, it was well known that such combinations, instead of promoting international peace, could well endanger it. Holland was not against the principle of regional pacts, but they should not be directed against a given friendly state or group of friendly states. To avoid such dangers, the Charter was essential.[3]

[1] Van Kleffens in Sec. Chamber, *idem*, Oct. 30, 1945, 143.
[2] First Chamber, *idem*, Nov. 7, 1945, 31.
[3] Van Kleffens in Sec. Chamber, *idem*, Oct. 30, 1945, 142/143 and First Chamber,

As regards Holland's position in Western Europe, the Government felt that in any circumstances an alliance with *one* great power would be most inadvisable; such a situation might be dangerous for a small nation.[1]

Holland's attitude towards the United Nations in 1945 may be summed up as follows. The Charter, in its final form, was considered unsatisfactory and although the Government had tried to improve it, their success had been small. They accepted the Charter, without any fond illusions about the future, because they preferred agreement, however unsatisfactory, to nothing at all; and in this they followed the traditions of Netherlands policy.

On the other hand, the United Nations represented a policy of universal co-operation; without it, there would be international anarchy once again, a state of affairs which, for the peace and security of small nations like the Netherlands might have the most serious consequences. In spite, then, of the Charter's imperfections, the Netherlands Government was resolved to support the principle of universal co-operation to the fullest possible extent. In accordance with this point of view they approached the question of regional groupings with the greatest caution. It was considered essential that such groupings would be placed under the Charter and as regards a Western European Alliance or Bloc, a non-committal attitude was adopted. An alliance with one great power in any circumstances was rejected; a certain freedom for manoeuvring was obviously considered essential.

---

idem, Nov. 7, 1945, 20. See also "Suggestions presented by the Netherlands Government", January 1945 (Appendix 1): "Nothing, in fact, would seem to them more dangerous for the peace of the world than regional groupings which, however good the intentions which gave rise to their formation, may at any time be set against each other or against any given state for want of proper and adequate co-ordination" (Provisional Remarks, I).

[1] Van Kleffens in First Chamber, *idem*, Nov. 7, 1945, 32.

CHAPTER III

THE GERMAN PROBLEM

To say that Netherlands policy towards Germany did not operate in a vacuum is surely stating the obvious. Since the occupation of the Reich, the German problem was more than ever before, a truly international one.

In the Declaration of Berlin of June 5, 1945, the representatives of the United Kingdom, the United States, the USSR and France were stated to have assumed sovereign powers in Germany, on the authority of their respective Governments. At the same time, an occupational zone was established for each of the powers mentioned and an Allied Control Council was set up.

Moreover, at Potsdam certain directives were agreed upon, which need hardly be recalled. Suffice it to mention that during the occupation, Germany was to be treated as one economic unit, to which end a common policy was to be followed regarding the most important economic problems; in the field of finance, transport and foreign trade, central German bodies were to be introduced under the direction of the Allied Control Council. In the political field, the powers' aim was the decentralization of power.[1]

However, as is well known, the central German authorities never materialized and the Allied Control Council found it impossible to implement the decisions taken at Potsdam.

In 1945 the German problem presented itself in two distinct and equally important aspects:

a) the future political status and organization of Germany and/or parts of Germany, with the related problem of preventing renewed German aggression;

---

[1] The Declaration of Berlin of June 5, 1945 will be found in Appendix, p. 2; the Potsdam Protocol in Appendix 3.

b) the future economic status of Germany, its economic relations with other countries, with the related problem of reparations and restitution.

Both aspects of the question were of equally great importance to the Netherlands.

As regards the first, however, the Netherlands Government refrained during 1945 from submitting to the great powers any official statements as to the policy which, in their judgment, should be followed; but they did inform them that, in connexion with the Declaration of June 5, 1945, Holland should have the fullest opportunity of participating in all consultations concerning future policies in Germany, and in particular, the demarcation of the western boundaries of Germany or of any parts of it. In fact, Holland urged this request upon the powers on numerous occasions, not only in 1945, but also in later years.

As for the second aspect of the problem, the situation was in a sense much more complicated. The Potsdam directive, according to which Germany was to be treated as a single economic unit, to which end "common policies shall be established with regard to import and export programmes for Germany as a whole", came to nothing; and the natural result was that the Allies organized the foreign trade of their zones in such a way as seemed most suitable to their own interests and purposes. For Holland this was a most serious matter. The Dutch had, in fact, to deal with four different zones; trade and transport between the zones were greatly hampered, and apart from the question whether or not the occupation authorities were aware of Netherlands interests, they certainly showed very little consideration for them.

And yet, these interests were both extensive and of long standing. During the period 1930–1939, some 20–30% of total Netherlands imports came from Germany: in the same period 15 to 20% of total Netherlands exports went to Germany. "In 1938 more than 50% of these figures originated from the agrarian sector".[1] Germany, in short, was, and still is of great importance as a débouché for Netherlands agrarian produce.

[1] Note on the situation with regard to the German problem, presented to the States General by the Netherlands Minister of Foreign Affairs, July 19, 1949, 16 (hereafter quoted as Note on German problem).

But that was not all. The Netherlands balance of trade with
Germany had always been a passive one; and the resultant gap
on the balance of payments was traditionally made good by
a) revenue from Netherlands services rendered to Germany;
and *b*) revenue from Netherlands investments in that country.[1]

The services rendered consisted mainly of shipping, and activities connected with the transport of goods destined for
Germany via Netherlands ports. All this constituted a most
important source of revenue and foreign currency. Netherlands
investments in Germany have always been considerable, thereby
illustrating the close relations between Dutch and West German
industry. Even before the war developments with respect to
these Netherlands interests in Germany had not been entirely
happy. Of course, there was always a certain competition between Dutch and German shipping interests, as far as Rhine
traffic was concerned; and the same is true of the North German
and Netherlands/Belgian ports. During the years of the great
depression, however, the German government embarked upon
a policy of discrimination against Netherlands shipping. As a
result Dutch ships were partly driven off the Rhine; but not
only off the Rhine, for before the war Netherlands ships served

---

[1] The following figures may illustrate the nature and importance of the economic
relations between the Netherlands and Germany.

Balance of Payments of the Netherlands
with Germany in 1938

Transactions
(In millions of guilders)

	With Germany	With All Countries
Exports	143	1083
Interests and dividends	41	317
Shipping	45	153
Transit traffic, Rhine shipping, harbour costs, etc.	54	79
Other invisibles	33	92
	316	1724
Imports	317	1466
Interests and dividends	—	134
Other invisibles	34	108
	351	1708

(Dr. H. M. Hirschfeld, "The Economic Relations between the Netherlands and
Germany", *The Statist*, January 31, 1948).

and used all rivers and waterways in Germany – in fact, they went and traded everywhere. The Rhine was navigated by Dutch vessels as far as Basle, the Dortmund-Ems Canal as far as Emden; they went to Berlin via the Mittelland Canal, they were seen on the Oder, Weser and the Elbe. These activities represented economic interests of importance; and the discrimination applied by Germany before the war was naturally resented.

The Netherlands investments in Germany did not fare much better. Here, too, the Germans followed a discriminatory policy with resultant damage to Dutch interests. That the Germans did everything in their power to liquidate Netherlands capital interests in Germany during the war, need hardly be pointed out. The Netherlands Government estimated that securities to a total amount of R.M. 600.000.000 were transferred to Germany. And it was considered that only a "fraction of this sum" could be recovered.

On the other hand, it was considered that the residue of Netherlands investments in Germany after the war still amounted to some R.M. 1.669.000.000, of which R.M. 1. 300. 000. 000 were in the three Western zones.[1]

So much for the situation prior to 1945. After the war the shipping position worsened considerably. The division of Germany was responsible for the fact that the whole Elbe region became closed territory to Netherlands shipping (and, for that matter, West German shipping). In other words, part of the normal outlet of shipping activities had gone and this, of course, led to overcapacity. Another factor will be found in the position of the North German ports. The division of Germany had been a bad blow to them: their natural hinterland became inaccessible. From the point of view of Dutch shipping and trade interests all this was most unfortunate. The occupation authorities who had taken the place of the former German Government wanted to save foreign currency: the occupation was costly enough and they had to think of the British and American taxpayers; it is also possible that they were not quite aware of the extent of the Netherlands interests involved; but whatever

[1] Note on German problem, 19/20. All figures based on 1938 values.

their motives, they wanted to use German ports to the fullest possible extent and they resumed more or less the old German policy of discrimination.[1] There is no need to go into the details of these policies; it is enough to mention the application of differential railway charges and special canal dues.

Naturally enough, such measures were much resented in Holland.

Enough has been said to show the great importance of the German hinterland to the Dutch national economy. To Holland, the future economic status of Germany, and the character of its economic relations with other nations were matters of the greatest interest. No one realized this better than the Dutch themselves: and apart from the issue of security, the position of Germany as an economic partner of Holland will be seen to have been the prime consideration in this country's German policy of 1946 and after.

The question of reparations and restitution might, of course, have had certain negative effects on the future economic strength of Germany; that was one aspect of the matter and one, moreover, of special interest to the Dutch. But on the other hand, Holland, after the experiences of the war, felt entitled to compensation on a large scale. In fact, in 1944 already the Netherlands Government in London, having received reports about extensive destruction and damage in Holland, issued a Statement (October 28, 1944) in which they reserved the country's rights, "in particular that of formulating its considered opinion and claims after its liberation"; and the Governments of the United Nations were informed, that "the people of the Netherlands may reach the conclusion.... that if in their case some substantial measure of reparation is to be made by the invader, a suitable part of adjoining Prussian territory should either be ceded to the Netherlands (provision made for the absorption by Germany of the Prussian inhabitants) or brought into the Dominion and

---

[1] It is of course true that there was a chaotic state of affairs in Germany; nor was there any co-ordination in occupation policies. Also, it may be doubted whether all echelons of occupation personnel had an equally profound understanding of the structure of the German economy.

economic orbit of the Netherlands in some other manner, on a provisional or permanent basis".[1]

In 1944 the Government could do no more; but towards the end of 1945 they were able to submit to the powers a provisional estimate of Dutch claims.[2] The total amount to be claimed was no less than Fl. 25.725 million (1938 values) or some Fl. 45.000 million (1945 values).[3]

How, and to what extent, was this claim realized? At Yalta, it will be recalled, it was laid down that Germany was to make good all damage for which its aggression had been responsible; and this fundamental decision was further elaborated at Potsdam in July 1945. There it was decided that Russia and Poland would be compensated by reparations from the Russian Zone in Germany and out of German assets in Finland, Bulgaria, Hungary, Rumania and Eastern Austria; in addition to which Russia would be entitled to an extra share of industrial e-quipment in the Western Zones. The claims of all other allied powers were to be met by reparations from the Zones occupied by the United States, Britain and France, and out of German assets outside Germany, with the exception, of course, of the countries just mentioned.

It will be observed that no decision was taken regarding the manner in which these reparations were to be divided between the allied countries concerned. This problem was discussed at the Paris Conference on Reparations at the end of 1945, which was followed by the Agreement of January 14, 1946.

The Netherlands Government were not in a position to influence the contents of the Paris Agreement in one way or another. In fact, the Agreement was practically written by the three inviting powers (the United States, Great Britain and France) and then submitted to the Conference which could do little

---

[1] See for full text of Statement, Appendix 4.

It will be noted that in this Statement the right to annex certain parts of German (Prussian) territory is based, not on political or strategic, but on economic grounds: compensation by way of annexation.

[2] "Memorandum of the Netherlands Government containing the claims of the Netherlands to reparations from Germany", 1945. In Appendix 5 the full text of this Memorandum will be found.

[3] Specification: Material losses, Fl. 11.425 million; loss of production during the war, Fl. 4.000 million; forced deliveries to Germany, Fl. 6.000 million; and loss of production after May 7, 1945: Fl. 4.300 million. See Appendix 5, Summary.

more than either approve or reject it. For their part, the Netherlands Government accepted the Agreement.

One reason for their attitude was the fact that they were
particularly interested in a satisfactory settlement with respect
to German assets in the Netherlands. The Paris Agreement,
however, contained no definite directives on this point; further
discussions between the interested countries were therefore necessary. By accepting the Paris Agreement, Holland made sure
that she would take part in these conversations which ultimately resulted in the Agreement relating to the Resolution of
conflicting claims to German enemy assets of December 5, 1947.

The Paris Agreement of 1946 mentioned two categories of
German reparations: Category B, which included industrial and
other capital equipment removed from Germany, merchant
ships and inland water transport; and Category A, embracing
all forms of German reparations except those included in Category B. On the basis of these categories, each of the participating
powers was granted a certain percentage share of the total
value of Categories A and B. In the case of Holland, these
percentages amounted to 3.90 and 5.60 respectively. Nothing at
all was laid down as to the definite extent of the reparations;
and it was finally agreed that the goods made available by the
Allied Control Council in Berlin, would be apportioned by the
Inter Allied Organization for Reparations which was set up for
that purpose in Brussels.

Was Holland satisfied with the percentages obtained? Of
course, these percentages were only of relative importance;
essential was the total amount of reparations which, in the end,
would be available for distribution. And only the occupying
powers, it will be recalled, had any right of say with respect to
the nature and volume of German reparations. The Netherlands
Delegation naturally tried to obtain higher percentages; but no
agreement with the other participating powers could be reached
on this point. Nor is this very surprising in view of the fact
that practically all countries, with the exception of the United
States, the United Kingdom and France, considered the percentages granted to them too low. And as will appear from
subsequent Chapters, Holland received but a fraction of what
it had originally claimed.

CHAPTER IV

1946: GENERAL POLICY

The annual debates in the States General on Foreign Affairs of 1946 took place at the end of the year; and on that occasion – for the first time since 1940 and, more remarkable, since the country's liberation in May 1945 – the Government stated the general principles and lines of their foreign policy. The gist of their various statements was as follows.

Once again, neutrality was rejected. Its basis – the equilibrium policy of the powers as it was known before the war – was gone; neutrality could no longer guarantee the country's security.[1] In these circumstances it should be Holland's policy to support the principle of collective security; it should, therefore, support the United Nations, in spite of its many structural imperfections. In fact, universal co-operation, it was said, was Holland's first objective in international relations. But was this enough? This the Government denied; the United Nations, after all, was still in its infancy. Accordingly, participation in regional arrangements might well become desirable in the future; but there was obviously a distinction between the cultural and economic aspects of such regional co-operation and its security aspects. As regards the former, the Government stressed the importance of voluntary, economic co-operation, as, for instance, demonstrated in Benelux.[2] Regional arrangements of this kind, on a voluntary basis, were desirable and should be warmly supported. But the position was different as far as security arrangements were concerned. It had been stated in the States General that Holland was little more than a bridgehead of the allied political system in Europe.[3] The Government denied this;

[1] Mem. Repl., Sec. Chamber, Nov. 29, 1946, 14.
[2] For economic aspects of Benelux, see Note on Benelux, p. 158.
[3] Mem. Repl., Sec. Chamber, Nov. 29, 1946 ,14.

it was not true in 1946 and whether or not it would be true in the future depended entirely upon the manner in which the German problem would be solved. In the Dutch view, a satisfactory solution should fulfil two conditions: *a*) German aggression should be made impossible once and for all; *b*) the German economy should be allowed to re-establish itself gradually.[1]

Now if the great powers were to reach agreement in this sense, Holland would be the neighbour of a militarily weak Germany.[2] In that case there was little reason to fear that the Netherlands would become a military bridgehead in Europe for certain powers; for, after all, Holland's security would then be assured by the United Nations, by a Four Power Agreement on Germany, and finally, by the fact that Germany would be disarmed.[3] Thus, the German problem formed the crux of the European problem.[4]

Certainly, the Government did not deny that for such a solution the great powers would have to show a greater measure of mutual trust than had been the case hitherto. But in November 1946 it was considered premature to assume that the disagreements between the powers were insurmountable; and certainly, at that time, the Dutch were not prepared to make this assumption. On the contrary, they felt that, given the position and the interests of the country, it was their duty to contribute in the greatest measure possible to establishing correct and satisfactory relations between the four great powers.[5]

In these circumstances, Holland was not likely to show much enthusiasm either for the idea of a Western European Bloc or for that of a Federal Europe. Blocs, the Government thought, were unlikely to improve the international climate. They might provoke the formation of other blocs; as a result, not only states, but whole groups of states might confront each other.

[1] See also: Netherlands Memorandum of January 14, 1947, below pp. 45ff and 50.

[2] Hence Holland's interest in the proposals of the United States Government to keep Germany disarmed for at least 25 years (Mem. Repl., Sec. Chamber, Nov. 29, 1946, 15).

[3] The Netherlands Government wished to participate in such a European security system which, although dependent on four power agreement, should not be exclusively based on the co-operation of these four nations. See Memorandum of January 14, 1947, below, pp. 45 and 242.

[4] Mem. Repl., Sec. Chamber, Nov. 29, 1946, 15.

[5] Mem. Repl., Sec. Chamber, Nov. 29, 1946, 15.

As for a Western European Bloc in particular, they believed, in the first place, that close co-operation between France and Germany was, as yet, little more than a dream; and they further considered that the inclusion of Germany, or Western Germany, in a Western European Bloc was neither possible nor desirable.[1] Apart from the fact that it was rather premature to act as if final decisions about Germany's future status had already been taken, the Government doubted very much whether such a Western European Bloc could really play – as had been suggested – a conciliating rôle between the great powers. In point of fact, it was the opinion of the Netherlands Government that, if such a group of states were formed (Germany, the enemy of yesterday, participating), this would only lead to a serious deterioration in the international situation.[2] And neither did they believe that an immediate start should be made with the realization of a European Federation. As a political entity, Europe did not exist without the USSR and the United Kingdom; on the other hand, if these powers were included, the geographical conception of "Europe" became a very loose one indeed, for both nations were not only European, but also world powers. And if, for the sake of argument, it were maintained that Europe could exist politically without either the USSR or the United Kingdom, would this not mean that the way would be clear once again for renewed German efforts to attain domination, in view of the fact that Germany would undoubtedly be the most powerful nation in such an amputated Europe?[3] The Government therefore felt that as yet there was little to say for either a Western European Bloc or a European (or Western European) Federation. But at the same time they made it clear to the States General that they would never hesitate to give up, on a basis of reciprocity, such sovereign rights as might be necessary for the establishment of international agencies charged with the organization of limited and well defined aspects of international activities.

What did these statements amount to? Let us first restate the fundamental issue of Netherlands foreign policy in 1945 and

[1] Mem. Repl., Sec. Chamber, Nov. 29, 1946, 15.
[2] Mem. Repl., Sec. Chamber, Nov. 29, 1946, 15.
[3] Mem. Repl., Sec. Chamber, Nov. 29, 1946, 15.

after. In the first place, it should be decided whether or not neutrality be definitely rejected. If so, would this imply the adoption of a policy of regional alliances? Or should the country seek entirely new means to guarantee its security, as, for instance, the conception of a federal Europe? Or should it put its trust in a policy of collective security and universal co-operation, in other words, in the United Nations and await further developments in the international situation?

In the Government statements of 1946 three positive elements will be noted: first, neutrality is firmly rejected; second, continued support for the United Nations; third, support for the principle of voluntary economic and cultural co-operation in regional arrangements. As far as the political and military aspects of such regional arrangements were concerned, the Netherlands attitude was clearly one of awaiting further developments. The German problem was regarded as the crux of the European problem; without greater certainty as to whether or not the great powers would reach agreement, further decisions had better be postponed. If they reached agreement, well and good; if they did not, the policy of universal co-operation would break down, and with it, the system of the Charter; in that case the security of the country would clearly require other measures. But for the time being, the final outcome of the four power deliberations should be awaited; and meanwhile, all ideas of blocs or a European federation were obviously inopportune.[1]

Some of the reasons for this attitude are not difficult to understand. It was clearly not to the country's interest to take any steps, or promote any ideas, which were likely to strengthen the already emerging division between Eastern and Western Europe. Again, it might be asked what security value could be attached to regional military arrangements without effective participation of the United States? In the case of a four power treaty, the United States would be automatically involved, but what was the position in the opposite case? [2]

[1] Mem. Repl., First Chamber, March 12, 1947, 7.
[2] The emphasis on the danger of renewed German aggression is noteworthy – see, in this connexion, above, p. 12.

CHAPTER V

1946: GERMANY

As far as economic relations between Germany and Holland were concerned, very little progress was made, from the Dutch point of view, during 1946. In fact, at the end of that year, the Netherlands Government had to inform the States General that the volume of trade between the two countries was still most unsatisfactory; the occupying powers persisted in their discriminatory policies against Netherlands shipping interests and Netherlands ports; little or no consideration was shown to Holland's interests in the field of agrarian exports to Germany. Travelling facilities between Germany and Holland were still restricted; business men of the same nationality as the powers in occupation were believed to be given preferential treatment. In short, from the Dutch point of view, the position was very bad indeed and the occupation authorities showed little of the co-operation to which Holland felt entitled.[1]

It is, of course, true that during that same period the position of the German economy itself showed considerable deterioration. The burden on the occupying powers was heavy; Britain felt the strain; and these developments led to the proposals of the United States Government of July 20, 1946, aiming at an economic merger of the allied zones in Germany. The British accepted them, but the French and the Russians did not. Both acceptance and refusal should be regarded in the light of the economic structure of the zones in question, *and* of the international situation. The merger was not brought about until December 4, 1946 with the conclusion of the so-called Byrnes-Bevin Agreement. This Agreement, it will be recalled, said that the primary responsibility for the course of affairs in the

[1] Mem. Repl., Sec. Chamber, Nov. 29, 1946, 17, 18, 19.

merged zones was to rest initially with the Joint Export-Import
Agency (JEIA) which started its activities in January 1947.

The work of JEIA need not be discussed here; it is undoubtedly true that certain difficulties in the field of foreign trade were
gradually removed. For their part, the Netherlands Government
promoted the formation of the "Nederlandse Trust Maatschappij
voor de Handel met het Buitenland" (Netherlands Trust Company for Foreign Trade) which was to act as the counterpart of
JEIA in the Netherlands.[1] All this might augur well for the
future; but the fact remained that the actual position at the
end of 1946 was far from satisfactory.

So much for the immediate difficulties in the economic relations
between Holland and Germany. But as has been made clear
above, these difficulties, aggravated as they might be by the
inevitable consequences of the war, reflected a fundamental
clash of interests which existed already before the war. This
state of affairs must be borne in mind in considering the Memorandum concerning "the demarcation of the future Netherlands-
German frontier and related problems" which the Netherlands
Government addressed to the Council of Foreign Ministers on
November 5, 1946.[2]

It will be noted that at the very beginning of this Memorandum, the Netherlands Government allude to their Statement
of October 28, 1944; and in point of fact, it is of some interest
to compare the two documents. The 1944 Statement clearly
suggested that "a suitable part of adjoining Prussian territory
should either be ceded to the Netherlands. . . . or brought into
the Dominion and economic orbit of the Netherlands in some
other way, on a provisional or permanent basis".

Since then, two years had elapsed; and in November 1946 the
Netherlands Government had changed their position: "It has
become clear that the damage inflicted on the national economy
has reached such proportions that adequate compensation in

---

[1] The Netherlands Trust Company was to act as the central agency of Netherlands
trade and industry in their efforts to re-activate Netherlands-German trade relations.
Its main task was the exploration of possibilities in this respect and to do all that was
necessary in view of the demands of the occupation authorities regarding trade with
Germany.

[2] The full text of this Memorandum will be found in Appendix 6.

the form of an allocation of German territory will not be practicable, in view of the extent of the annexations that would be involved.... the solution of the problem should mainly be approached on different lines. In this H.M. Government have also been led by the consideration that the people of the Netherlands are traditionally opposed to annexation; besides, the Netherlands Government are unwilling to urge a solution which might harbour the seeds of a future conflict and of German irredentism, which in its turn might develop into a danger to peace and security in Europe".

Whether or not these were the true reasons for this change in attitude – of which more below – the fact remained that the territorial claims were to be limited to "certain frontier rectifications" while indemnification for the losses and damages sustained would be sought "in the economic sphere primarily". Thus, "annexations" were replaced by "rectifications". Was this more than mere juggling with words? This, of course, might be denied, on the principle that things are what they are, not what they are called. Nevertheless, the proposed rectifications (see Annex II of the Memorandum) were without any military significance, their economic importance, certainly in terms of either the national damage, the national wealth, or the total population extremely small – in short, these "rectifications" were something entirely different from what was desired and envisaged in some quarters during the war.[1]

Now some of the motives for this shift in attitude have been mentioned in the Memorandum; but there were other reasons as well. In fact, it might be said that, given the position and the interests of the Netherlands and the developments in the international situation, the change in policy was inevitable. To illustrate this point, the policy of some of the great powers in the German problem should be recalled. What, for instance, was the basic objective of French policy toward Germany? The answer is extremely simple: it was security and nothing but

[1] Those in Holland who, in 1944 and 1945, advocated the annexation of German territory, justified this on the ground of either compensation, or Holland's need of living space for its growing population, or considerations of military security (idea of the barrier). With many writers – for there is a whole Dutch "annexation" literature – all three motives were of course present.

security. To attain this, the French aimed at *a*) the elimination of the German war potential, i.e. the industries and industrial resources of the Ruhr; and *b*) the neutralization of those German regions and territories which might serve as a "zone de passage" or "une base de départ" in a new attack on France or the Western powers in general. The word "neutralization" had been chosen advisedly; for pure and naked annexation was to be avoided. Elsewhere in this work more will be said about this [1]; but here the point is that the security factor was absolutely paramount in the French way of thinking; and whether the proposed arrangements with respect to the Ruhr, the left bank of the Rhine and the Saar would be economically feasible, was a consideration of quite secondary importance. Security was the thing that mattered. Now, the British and Americans, although far from being in perfect agreement about all aspects of the German problem, never went to the same length as the French. Both powers, no doubt, saw the security factor as one meriting all possible attention, but at the same time they were not prepared to allow the economic factor to be so completely overwhelmed by considerations of security. This is no doubt partly due to the fact that the economic structure of the British and American Zones was different from that of the French and Russian Zones; but, apart from that, considerations of international politics, originating in the slowly emerging problem of the relations between Russia and the Western powers were certainly not less important. In short, in the British and American way of thinking, the security factor was neither paramount nor exclusive. The economic factor, i.e. assuring Germany a certain minimum level of existence, was supposed to be at least equally important.

The alternatives confronting the Netherlands ran somewhat along the lines just mentioned. Holland could of course claim far-reaching annexations which, apart from offering (perhaps) additional security against German aggression, would probably profit the Netherlands less than they would harm Germany. On the other hand, Holland could refrain from such a policy on the principle that a decisive weakening of the German hinterland

[1] See below, p. 48.

would be a most unwise policy for any Netherlands Government
to follow, whilst, as for security, the country was anyhow in a
dependent position.

In these circumstances and with such alternatives, the point of
view represented in the Memorandum of November 5, 1946
was a logical one for Holland to adopt. No doubt, the French
would have supported Netherlands demands for large-scale annexations; and it is certain that they *did* support the reduced claim
to rectifications; but as against that, the words spoken by Mr
Byrnes at Stuttgart in September 1946 cannot have failed to
carry considerable weight with the Dutch: "The United States
will not support the encroachment on territory which is indispu-
tably German or any division of Germany which is not genuinely
desired by the people concerned". In fact, it would not have
been surprising if the Netherlands had refrained from *all* territorial claims; neither can the Netherlands Government have
expected that their claims would be complied with integrally.

As regards the economic desiderata (see Annex I of the Memorandum), no further comment is really necessary, in view of
what has been said above regarding the character of the economic
difficulties between Holland and Germany.

In conclusion, a word about the question of Netherlands
participation in the military occupation of Germany. Several
Members of the States General were in favour of it; so were
the Government; but there were obvious difficulties. In the
first place, agreement would have to be reached with other
powers concerned about the extent of Dutch participation and,
even more important, the demarcation of the territories to be
occupied by Netherlands troops. This was by no means a simple
question; even among the Western allied countries there was a
certain measure of mutual distrust. In the second place, were
sufficient Netherlands forces available for this purpose? Holland's military commitments in 1946 were considerable – due to
developments in Netherlands East Indies; moreover, the state
of the country and financial considerations imposed certain
limitations on the number of troops to be called up. So, in point

of fact, the planned participation in the military occupation was not realized because in 1946 the necessary forces were not available. For the rest, the Government had to make it clear to the States General that participation in the *occupation* did not imply participation in the *government* of Germany; that was a different question altogether.[1]

[1] Mem. Repl., Sec. Chamber, Nov. 29, 1946, 19.

CHAPTER VI

1947: GENERAL POLICY

As we have seen in the previous chapter, the question of the relations between the great powers was no doubt a most important determinant in the evolution of Dutch foreign policy. On this everything depended: not only the outcome of the German and European problem, but also the fate of the United Nations and the policy of universal co-operation to which the Dutch were so attached.

However, the events of the year 1947 were to show that agreement between the powers was a rapidly vanishing possibility. There was, in the first place, the London meeting in January 1947 of the Deputies of the Foreign Ministers who had to prepare the ground for a Four Power Conference which was to take place in Moscow in the spring. The problem to be dealt with was Germany. But this Moscow Conference, like its successor, the London Conference of November and December 1947, ended in complete failure: no agreement could be reached on the political or economic unification of Germany.

Secondly, there was General Marshall's Harvard speech of June 5, 1947, followed by the Three Power Conference of Bevin, Bidault and Molotov of June 27 at Paris. Marshall's conception was one for the whole of Europe; nevertheless, Russia refused to participate and it forced its satellites (Czechoslovakia!) to follow its example, a decision finalized by the refusal of the Commander in Chief of the Russian Zone to submit information to the Committee of European Co-operation.[1]

All these developments pointed to one conclusion: disagreement between the great powers was almost complete. It was a conclusion which was bound to have great – but not necessarily immediate – consequences for Dutch foreign policy.

[1] See further: Note on the Marshall Plan, p. 153.

So much, at this stage, for the international scene. What were the reactions of Netherlands policy?

At the beginning of the year its general pattern was, of course, not different from that defined in the States General in 1946: universal co-operation, and in Europe, a Four Power agreement under the United Nations.[1] In November 1947, however, when foreign affairs were once again discussed in the Second Chamber, it became clear that the Government's attitude was changing *slightly*. They repeated that universal co-operation remained their first objective and they certainly would do nothing that might further deteriorate the relations between the great powers; they welcomed closer co-operation between such states as might be regarded, on account of geographical situation or affinity of culture or interests, as congenial partners – although they referred, in saying this, in the first place to Benelux which was the "cornerstone of their foreign policy".[2]

But at the same time they made it clear that these principles would only be maintained as long as the international situation did not show *fundamental* changes (as opposed to *gradual* ones which of course occurred continually). For instance, "should, contrary to our hopes, the division of Germany into western and eastern parts assume a more or less definite character, the Government would feel impelled to reconsider their whole policy in Europe".[3] It is obvious that the Government were more than a little doubtful about the future, but at the same time they refused as yet to discuss alternative policies.[4] Even more important, they persisted in their negative attitude with respect to all ideas about European Federalism or a Western European Bloc.

The debates of 1947 reflected the growing importance of these ideas; and the Government obviously considered it desirable to enlarge upon their statements of 1946. They said that there was nothing in the United Nations Charter, or, for that matter, in international law which was at variance with

[1] See also Section III of the Netherlands Memorandum of January 14, 1947, below, pp. 46 and 240.
[2] Mem. Repl., Sec. Chamber, Nov. 13, 1947, 9.
[3] Mem. Repl., Sec. Chamber, Nov. 13, 1947, 14.
[4] Mem. Repl., Sec. Chamber, Nov. 13, 1947, 14.

the idea of a Federal Europe. The question was, however, whether or not this conception could be realized. Naturally, they preferred unity to chaos in Europe; neither did they deny that modern problems could not be solved by purely national remedies, but only by way of international co-operation; and they readily admitted that Europe should do everything possible to conciliate existing contrasts and conflicts. But how should this idea of a European Federation be realized? If co-operation between the various European states were to be confined to certain well defined aims and objectives, it could be decided in each case whether or not there was sufficient reason for participation. The fact that the Netherlands played their part in the realization of the Marshall Plan and that Benelux did everything possible to promote greater economic unity – vide their invitation to the powers for economic talks in Brussels –, all this went to show that the Netherlands Government were not at all adverse to European co-operation where possible and desirable.

But a European Federation in the sense of a new international community of a political character, with general objectives, not only in the economic, but also in other fields, was quite a different matter and the Government felt that little good could be expected from it. For one thing, in the present circumstances, such aims were too idealistic; for another, such an idea went counter to all modern trends. What is modern Europe? Could anybody indicate its frontiers, especially in the East? Could it be said that modern Europe was a political or economic unit in the present day world? It might be granted that the theoretical aim was nothing less than a real Pan-Europa; but in point of fact things were different, for all such ideals and movements were bound to degenerate in practice into a Western European Bloc, which in the long run could not be but harmful to universal international co-operation.[1] On these grounds – and not because all idealism was foreign to them – the Netherlands Government felt that they should not support such ideas and they very much preferred that all attention be directed to the United Nations, in which the conception of universality had been realized.

[1] Van Boetzelaer in Sec. Chamber, Nov. 20, 1947, 444.

Thus was the Government's point of view. Whether or not it was justified, or consistent with their own expectations about the future, is a question which need not detain us here; it is a fact that the States General did not completely agree with them, as will be apparent from the foreign affairs debates in the First Chamber which did not take place until February/March 1948.

The Dunkirk Treaty between France and Great Britain was also discussed. Some Members of the Lower House suggested that closer relations with these two countries were desirable in which connexion they stressed the "open" character of the Dunkirk agreement.[1]

But the Government once again showed little enthusiasm for the idea. They doubted whether the Dunkirk agreement was really an "open" one. In fact, they felt sure, considering the treaty's text and the words spoken by Bidault in the National Assembly, that it was not. It was of course possible that the French Government were prepared to conclude similar a-greements with other countries, including Belgium and Holland; but in that connexion the Government reminded the States General of what they had always said about regional agreements and arrangements. The Dutch did not want a system of bilateral agreements. Since 1944 they had maintained that what was required were regional treaties under Article 52 of the Charter. Moreover, was it advisable for the Netherlands to enter into such agreements without knowing beforehand to what extent the United States would participate in a European security system? What security value, either against a German attack, or against that of another power, could be attached to treaties like the Dunkirk one?

Apart from all this, the Netherlands preferred to wait on general grounds; Foreign Minister van Boetzelaer made this clear enough: "However, in the first place it seems necessary to me to wait and see whether the near future will produce

---

[1] In connexion with the Treaty, Bidault, speaking in the French National Assembly, said: ,,Chacune des clauses du traité franco-britannique en voie de conclusion a été offerte à chacun de nos grands alliés, en vue de savoir s'ils le préféraient à celles qui nous lient actuellement à eux. La porte est donc ouverte et le Gouvernement l'a ouverte aussi à nos alliés belges et hollandais en vue de négociations économiques et politiques, comme à nos alliés de longtemps . . . ." February 28, 1947.

some measure of clarification of the political situation in Europe"
(Second Chamber, November 20, 1947). Thus, here too, both
general and special reasons counselled avoidance of all hasty
reactions to Bidault's overture. Moreover, Holland's reluctance
met, it may be assumed, with full understanding in other
capitals.

It is true that during 1947 Holland actively participated in the
work necessary for the realization of the Marshall Plan; and the
political implications of these activities cannot be denied. Yet,
viewed as a whole, 1947 was, as far as the general problem of
Dutch policy was concerned, a year of waiting, a year of growing
doubts about the ultimate probability of four power agreement,
a year of dwindling hopes although they had probably, prior to
the failure of the London Conference, not entirely gone. It is of
course possible that the Government had already drawn their
private conclusions from the failure of the Moscow conference;
at any rate they did not say so; officially they stuck to their
waiting attitude.

It is interesting to note that their reluctance to take decisions
– a policy in itself – was not always properly understood in
parliamentary circles and was sometimes mistaken for their
having no policy at all. However that may be, after the debates
of November 1947 things were to enter a more active stage. The
year 1948 would witness decisive developments in Netherlands
foreign policy – the period of transition was coming to an end.

CHAPTER VII

1947: GERMANY

During their meeting of November 1946 in New York, Bevin, Byrnes, Bidault and Molotov decided that their Deputies should meet in London (January 1947) in order to prepare a peace treaty and to study the various desiderata and suggestions of other Governments concerned with respect to the German problem. Accordingly, the views of the Netherlands Government were made known to them, *a*) by a Memorandum on Allied Policy with regard to Germany, of January 14, 1947 and *b*) by a Netherlands Delegation which, during a hearing on January 28, 1947, elucidated the Dutch standpoint in some detail. Finally, a supplementary Memorandum regarding the Dutch territorial and economic claims, chiefly of a technical character, was brought to the Deputies' notice on January 25, 1947.

Let us first consider a few points of the Memorandum of January 14, 1947 – its full text will be found in Appendix 7. Holland's dual objective in the German problem is clearly stated in the very first paragraph: security for Germany's neighbours and, for Germany itself, recovery of its prosperity in so far as this was essential to the prosperity of Europe and the world. This formula is very much like the one stated in the States General in 1946. However, if the objectives are quite clear, the question remains: in what manner were they to be realized?

The Dutch views on the political aspects of the problem were as follows (cf Memorandum, I and III). If security is to be real and permanent, binding agreements between the Allies and "also the promotion and development of political relations.... inside Germany, calculated to further a peace-loving policy" are necessary. As to the binding agreements, Holland expressed its satisfaction that the discussion of a draft of a long term treaty, aiming at the demilitarization and disarmament of Germany had been placed on the agenda of the "ensuing Moscow Conference". Now the Netherlands Government expected two things from such a treaty. In the first place, it should be a regional agreement under Chapter VIII of the United Nations Charter. But there was more. The Dutch felt that although co-operation between the four great powers was absolutely essential for an effective European security system, it was not right for such a system to be based on their co-operation alone: "the Allied States neighbouring on Germany should be enabled to partake in such a system. That the great powers consider the co-operation of other powers in the maintenance of peace and security desirable and necessary, does not only follow from the Charter of the United Nations, but also from the Declaration of Moscow of 30th October 1943".[1]

So much for the desired security system which, it will be observed, was quite consistent with the general pattern of Netherlands policy of that period. As for the future political relations in Germany, the Netherlands Government thought that application of the principles of Potsdam – decentralization of the political structure and development of local responsibility – should result in the organization of Germany on a federal basis. Not a federal state; rather a confederation of states; and in view of the German inclination to centralization, it was considered imperative" to complete the organization of the Laender, and to have that organization firmly established in the Laender themselves by constitutional laws before central German ruling bodies are formed, notably where bodies vested with political authority are concerned". The future (central) German Government, moreover, should have derived powers only, delegated by the Laender; and certain powers should never be delegated at all.[2]

These measures, of course, should be accompanied by parallel measures in the economic sphere. Deconcentration of economic

[1] Memorandum, III.
[2] Memorandum, I.

power in Germany was, in the opinion of the Netherlands Government, the answer to the problem. Decentralization alone might not be enough; and in that connexion it was pointed out that there is, or may be, a difference between "socialization" and "nationalization".

There was reason enough to stress the point: at that time the British were busy nationalizing at home and they played with the idea of following the same policy in their German zone.[1] Moreover, the English in particular had always used and defined these terms very loosely indeed. So the Netherlands Government impressed the point on their Allies more than once, for "the danger is by no means imaginary that important industries in the various German Laender will be nationalized in an identical way and that thus, behind the screen of decentralization, an unparalleled monopolistic organization is in fact set up".[2]

We must now refer to the status of the Ruhr-Rhine regions which, on account of their strategic and economic importance, have always occupied a very special place in the German problem. The Netherlands suggestions will be found in Section I of the Memorandum. They are based on the assumption that consistent political decentralization of Germany and deconcentration of economic power in Germany are accompanied by effective demilitarization and disarmament; in that case, it is said, no measures for the Ruhr-Rhine regions were necessary "which differed *completely* from the general project".[3] And in fact, the suggestions required nothing more than a separate regime for the industries of the Ruhr, sanctions in case of infringements, an allied occupation at a certain number of strategic points, while as regards the Saar, decisions should be related to the desiderata of other powers: "in this connexion the Netherlands Government refer to their Memorandum of November 5, 1946"[4].

Now it is obvious that on these points the Memorandum of January 14 referred to, and considered the merits – or demerits – of other policies which had been proposed with respect to

[1] *Cf.* Ernest Bevin, House of Commons, Oct. 22, 1946.
[2] Memorandum, I.
[3] and [4] Memorandum, I.

Germany, without indicating them, however, in so many words.[1]

In short, the international background should be borne in mind. The policy of the French, British and Americans in this field has already been referred to above; at this stage it may be of interest to discuss these matters in somewhat greater detail. The objectives of the French were roughly the following:

a) as regards the Ruhr: an *international* regime; the Ruhr should be separated from Germany and should be open, in the economic field, to *all* nations. The French considered this separation from Germany, i.e. from any central administration in Germany, no matter whether this would be the future German one or the then Allied Control Council in Berlin, as absolutely essential. This demand of theirs should have the highest priority; and as far as they were concerned, there could be no question of central German bodies before the status of these territories was settled and decided.[2]

b) as regards the left bank of the Rhine: a permanent military occupation; the region should belong neither to Germany, nor to France; its organization should be that of one or more states, whose governments would be free to manage their own affairs – it being of course well understood that they had to accept foreign garrisons and should promise not to work for a return to Germany.[3]

c) as regards the Saar: permanent French occupation; its mines should be transferred to France and the region as a whole should be part of the French economic orbit.

These French proposals, may it be repeated once again, were based on considerations of security, security against Germany and also, perhaps, against other powers. All other considerations were quite secondary.

It has already been observed that the British and Americans never went so far as the French in this respect. The security and economic factors were equally important to them and although the French might think the internationalization of the

[1] "It is now a generally accepted thesis that as regards the economic arsenal constituted by the Ruhr, special measures of security are required. However, difference of opinion exists as to how these measures should be applied in practice" (Memorandum, I.).

[2] B. H. M. Vlekke, *Tweespalt der Wereldrijken*, 1953, pp. 303, 332.

[3] In 1946 (Constituante, 15/17 January) Bidault hinted that autonomy within Germany might be acceptable as far as the Rhineland was concerned.

Ruhr an eminently reasonable proposal[1], the British and Americans rejected the possible economic effects of such a step.

What if the Ruhr developed into a more or less prosperous region, encircled by resentful Germans living in a poverty-stricken Germany? Would not such a situation create, once again, the very danger of war it was supposed to prevent? In point of fact, these political proposals might have economic consequences which, in turn, were likely to defeat the original political objective.

Accordingly, what the British wanted was a central government for Germany, armed with as few powers as could be harmonized with the principle of economic unity; the political structure should be that of a "Bundesstaat", in which the components should have a preponderant position; local patriotism and responsibility should be stimulated. As regards the Ruhr, control was certainly desirable, but this might be realized either by nationalization of the Ruhr mines and industries, with supervision by the Allies, or by transfer of mining and industrial properties to the Allies who, in that case, would have to assume the exploitation and management of these works.

In other words, the British opposed a "corpus separatum" for the Ruhr; they certainly rejected the establishment of independent states in the Rhine region: both Ruhr and Rhine should be part of the German federation. A military occupation of the left bank for an unlimited period on the other hand, was acceptable to them and they had no particular objection to the French demands in the Saar question.

Finally, as regards the position of the United States, the Stuttgart speech of Secretary Byrnes of September 1946 gave a clear answer to the French demands. The Americans no doubt had no fundamental objections – as yet – to military occupation of the

---

[1] Russia might well agree to the French projects, for they would open the Ruhr to her. This possibility was of course not likely to increase British-American enthusiasm for the French plans. On the other hand, here was one more reason why the French wanted to avoid too intimate a co-operation with the British and the Americans. In fact, the guess may be hazarded that the French tried to "sell" their Ruhr project by stressing its security value both to the Russians (against America and Britain) and to the Anglo-Saxon powers (against Germany). Later, at Moscow in 1947, the true Russian programme for Germany became apparent (a strongly unified and centralized state, economically tied to Russia by excessive reparations), after which the French realized the illusionary character of all their manoeuvrings. *Cf.* Vlekke, *op. cit.*, 445.

Rhineland, nor against supervision of Germany, and the Ruhr and Rhine regions in particular; but American policy, like that of the British, admitted of no "corpus separatum" which was the essential point of all French plans. The French point of view with respect to the establishment of central German bodies was equally unacceptable.

Such, in very brief outline, was the position of the Western powers at the end of 1946. Their policies were neither absolute nor fixed but, on the contrary, flexible and apt to change. Only a minute analysis could do justice to all the changes, the shifts in accent, the shades in opinion which occurred during the first few years after the war. Nevertheless, it is fair to say that throughout all these developments the rift between two kinds of policy remained clearly noticeable. One aimed at security against Germany first and last and demanded, up to a certain degree, that country's dismemberment; the other, apart from security, was concerned with the economic future of Germany (and thus, of Europe) and was, moreover, increasingly aware of the fact that all action in the German problem was bound to influence the future position of the Western powers vis-à-vis Russia. For many years to come Western policy was to be handicapped by this fundamental contradiction in its basic aims. As the years went by, the French objectives proved to be unattainable; but the French Government retreated only step by step.

It is against this background that the Memorandum of January 14, 1947 must be considered. It states the *dual* objective of Netherlands policy in the German problem, it declares that a "certain measure of German recovery is essential to the continued recovery of her neighbours" and it gives the views of the Netherlands on all points which, before or at the time of its publication, were regarded or discussed as crucial aspects of the German problem. The Memorandum did not state or indicate the views of other powers, but it did, by implication, discuss them and reject some of them.

Section II of the Memorandum dealt with the economic and financial aspects of the German problem. Many of its observations will recall the Memorandum of November 5, 1946, in which, however, only points of direct interest to Holland were discussed; here the economic question as a whole is reviewed. Three points are of special interest: the insistent reference to a future European economic co-operation (paragraphs 1 and 2); the rôle of the security factor in the economic discussion (7, 8, 9 and 10) and finally, the interesting suggestion with respect to the rôle of labour "in the decision about major problems" (10).

Finally, in Section IV, the cultural and spiritual aspects of the German problem were dealt with; the last paragraph concerning those German territories which were affiliated with Holland in some way or another may be thought to be of special interest.

Thus, the Memorandum of January 1947, together with that of November 1946 gave the Deputies a fairly complete picture of the Netherlands objectives in the German problem.[1] Moreover, on January 28, 1947, a Netherlands Delegation, consisting of Jonkheer H. F. L. C. van Vredenburch, (Head, Political Affairs Department, Foreign Ministry), the Government Commissioner Dr H. M. Hirschfeld and Mr T. A. Lamping, had an opportunity to elucidate the points made in the documents. There can be little doubt that, apart from elaborating the various Netherlands suggestions, they reiterated Holland's wish to be fully consulted and to participate in the deliberations and decisions concerning Germany.[2]

The Moscow Conference for which the Deputies in London had been preparing the ground, took place in March and April 1947; and, in the words of the Netherlands Government, it "failed to reach any agreement on the German problem. Although it was found possible to achieve agreement on many points with regard to the form and character of the German Government to be established, this was by no means the case as

---

[1] It has already been mentioned that the Netherlands Government submitted an "Additional Memorandum with regard to the Demarcation of the future Netherlands-German frontier and Related Problems" to the Deputies of the Foreign Ministers. This document, being mostly of a technical nature, has been omitted here, with the exception of Section II, Economic Desiderata, which gives further interesting information on the points mentioned above. (Appendix 8).

[2] Apart from communications to the powers via the usual channels, the Netherlands Government had again insisted upon this point in paragraph 2 of the General Observations of the Memorandum of January 14, 1947.

far as the economic unification of the zones was concerned, for
the Soviet Union stated two conditions for any such unification,
viz. compliance with its wish for four power control of the
Rhur region and payment of a sum of $ 10.000.000.000 as
German reparations to Russia. This sum was to be withdrawn
from German production in the form of goods. These conditions
were regarded as unacceptable".[1]

The Netherlands Government were not, of course, present in
Moscow. Nor were they invited to the following meeting of the
Council of Foreign Ministers which took place in the autumn of
1947 in London. In these circumstances the Governments of
Holland, Belgium and Luxumburg decided to submit a Joint
Note to the Foreign Ministers.

This Joint Note is of some interest, not so much on account
of its contents, but because this was the first public joint démarche of *Benelux* in the German question. In other words, here
we meet with an instance of *political* Benelux co-operation which,
as we shall see, was not confined to this case, but maintained and
developed not only in the German problem, but in Western
European affairs as well.

There is no doubt that from the end of 1945 onwards the
three countries were in constant consultation over the German
problem. Considering the manoeuvrings of the great powers,
particularly in the Ruhr-Rhine question, it was obviously necessary for Holland, Belgium and Luxemburg to work together,
or even better, evolve, if possible, a common policy. By acting
together they might hope to make their influence felt. There is,
however, some reason to believe that during 1946 they did not
succeed in reaching *complete* agreement.[2] No doubt, the three
Governments were of one mind in insisting upon full consultation, but it may be doubted whether Belgium was completely
happy with the Netherlands Memorandum of November 5, 1946
or whether there was unanimity about the future organization
of Germany. However that may be, it was not until November
1947 that the three countries did actually present a Joint Note
to the great powers.

[1] Note on German problem, 2.
[2] Mem. Repl., Sec. Chamber, Nov. 29, 1946, 17; Van Boetzelaer in Sec. Chamber,
Dec. 6, 1946, 691; and Mem. Repl., First Chamber, March 12, 1947, 9.

Nevertheless, the results were not encouraging: the Benelux powers were not present at the London Conference, nor were they fortunate enough to receive a reaction from the powers to their Note. The Conference itself ended, once again, in complete failure: no agreement could be reached on either the political or the economic unification of Germany.

The question of four power agreement was, as we have seen, the governing factor in Holland's general policy; but it was equally important for the Dutch position in the German problem: For it must always be remembered that Holland's German policy started from the concept of Germany as one economic unit, within frontiers to be determined by the peace treaty. The Memoranda of 1946 and 1947 showed this beyond all possible doubt; and it was again pointed out on a later occasion.[1] In other words, the Netherlands territorial and economic claims were based on the assumption that such a peace treaty could be concluded. This, of course, pre-supposed four power agreement, but the failure of the various four power conferences and specifically of the London one at the end of 1947, made it abundantly clear that such agreement was not likely to be achieved. As far as Holland was concerned, the consequences of this fact were all too clear.

In the first place, it could be assumed that the political structure – a confederation–, proposed in the Memorandum of January 14, stood no chance of realization. On the contrary, a more or less permanently divided Germany was to be expected; and in view of the growing rift between the Western powers and Russia, it was only natural to assume, further, that the Western powers would do everything in their power to bring and keep Western Germany within the western orbit.

Western Germany in this connexion, it is clear, really meant its public opinion. In these circumstances, could it be expected that territorial claims, even of minor frontier adjustments, would be complied with? Hardly. Again, the Western powers could be expected to do everything to make Western Germany, as soon as possible, independent of dollar or sterling assistance. Was it likely, then, that the Netherlands economic demands

[1] Note on German problem, 2.

would be granted? In short, it might be said that once the political crisis round the German problem had set in, Holland's chances of securing compliance with its demands were greatly reduced; and the longer this crisis lasted, so much the worse for these demands.

That was the position which Holland had to consider at the end of 1947. In November, i.e. prior to the failure of the London Conference, the Government had already spoken of the need to reconsider their whole policy in Europe, if the division of Germany into western and eastern parts should assume a more or less permanent character.[1] But what was true of "the whole policy", was even more true of Holland's German policy; 1948 would show how far the "reconsideration" of Dutch demands upon Germany was to go.

As regards the normal economic relations between Germany and Holland, 1947 was little different from 1946 – in other words, the position remained unsatisfactory. Some progress, it is true, was made in the course of bilateral negotiations with the various German Zones; in fact, these conversations resulted in a monetary agreement with Bizonia and monetary and trade agreements with the French and Russian Zones. While, before the agreement with Bizonia, Netherlands imports from the Bizone had to be paid for in dollars, which implied that they were limited to coal and wood, the innovation of a so-called "off-set account" made it possible to overcome this difficulty to a certain extent. Nevertheless, there was as yet no question of normal trade relations; the total volume of trade remained small; for, after all, the crucial point was not so much the system or means of payment, but rather – and this was especially true of the Bizone – the limits which were imposed on the delivery of goods and the rendering of services. In these respects the situation with regard to the French and Russian Zones was much more satisfactory, because the trade agreements concluded with them were based on the principle of balanced quantities.

Mention has already been made of the "Nederlandse Trustmaatschappij voor de Handel met het Buitenland". This Company published, in the beginning of 1947, a list of commodities in which it was allowed to trade with the Bizone. This list – which

[1] See above, p. 41.

had been prepared in close consultation with JEIA – was chiefly interesting on account of the fact that it made no mention of vegetable produce. Now these were, as we have explained, an important item in normal Netherlands exports to Germany; and it was of vital importance to Holland that the allied authorities should recognize this fact. It is probably fair to say that this very question was responsible for the long delay in concluding a trade agreement with the Bizone – which did not take place until 1948.

Holland had no objection to the raised level of German production. The Netherlands Government considered that this step would contribute to the recovery of the German economy which, in turn, was an inevitable pre-condition for an increase in the total volume of trade between Holland and Germany. The Government did not agree that this raised level in itself created a potential danger of war. Another question was, however, whether or not the increase in production would prove detrimental to some aspects of the Netherlands economy. Should it do so, the Government would, of course, not fail to act. They had already taken steps with the British and American Governments to defend the interests of Netherlands proprietors of mines in Germany, of the Netherlands industries of consumption goods and finally, of Netherlands shipping. The shipping question was especially important. In January and July 1947 there were talks between the Dutch and the British and American occupation authorities; these talks resulted in a Report and Recommendations which may be summarized as follows:

the military authorities agreed to transfer a volume of 1.700.000 tons of commodities from North German to Netherlands and Belgian ports. The total value involved amounted to $ 4.900.000. In view of the various reparations which would be undertaken by the Germans, a final claim of $ 3.800.000 resulted from this arrangement, which amount was to be dealt with as a deferred claim on goods to be exported from Germany. This agreement was announced officially; but it was, after all, not accepted by the occupation authorities. In their opinion the agreement demanded too great a sacrifice from the Zones; in October 1947 a further meeting took place in Berlin, without satisfactory results. On that occasion the Governments of

Belgium and Holland informed the occupation authorities that neither of the two Governments felt themselves any longer bound by the abortive agreement of July 1947 which, in their opinion, had not been particularly favourable to their countries. Moreover, they failed to see how the whole principle of this agreement could be reconciled with the objectives of the Marshall Plan. In fact, they considered that the services which Holland and Belgium rendered to the Zones should be regarded as a normal export item, to be paid for in the normal manner via the existing clearing arrangements. But the occupation authorities did not accept this point of view. And yet, was it not obviously unreasonable to demand payment in hard currency for all commodities exported from Germany while subjecting at the same time services exported to Germany to treatment the nature of which has been indicated above? In this connexion the Netherlands Government reiterated once again that they were invariably opposed to all forms of discrimination.

And here the matter rested, as far as the year 1947 was concerned. Once again, Netherlands efforts had met with very little response.[1]

---

[1] Mem. Repl., Sec. Chamber, Nov. 13, 1947, 13 ff.

CHAPTER VIII

1948: GENERAL POLICY

The year 1948 opened under the shadow of the London Conference whose failure was soon to bear fruit in the form of great
changes and far-reaching developments on the international
scene. Not only in Germany, where the British and Americans
made the first moves towards establishing a West German State,
but also in Western Europe as a whole: on January 22, Mr Bevin,
speaking in the House of Commons, re-introduced the theme of
the relations between the Western European nations:

".... I believe that the time is ripe for the consolidation of Western
Europe. First in this context we think of the people of France. The time
has come to find ways and means of developing our relations with the
Benelux countries. I mean to begin talks with those countries in close
accord with our French allies. Yesterday our representatives in Brussels,
the Hague and Luxemburg were instructed to propose such talks in concert
with their French colleagues. I hope *treaties* will be signed with our near
neighbours, the Benelux countries, making, with our treaty with France
an important nucleus in Western Europe.

We have then to go beyond the circle of our immediate neighbours; we
shall have to consider the question of associating other historic members
of European civilization, including the new Italy, in this great conception".

The British Foreign Secretary made it clear that he was not
only concerned with Europe as a geographical conception.
Europe, after all, had extended its influence throughout the
world. In Africa, Britain shared great responsibilities with France,
Belgium and Portugal; and, in South East Asia, with the Dutch.

The organization of Western Europe should not be without
economic support; but that involved the closest co-operation
with the Commonwealth and the overseas territories of France,
Belgium, Portugal and Holland. Their raw materials, food and
resources could be of mutual advantage to the territories concerned, to Europe and to the world.

Mr Bevin wanted not only to develop economic co-operation between the Western European countries, but also the resources of their overseas territories; and the ultimate aim should be the establishment of a system of priorities which, in his opinion, would produce the quickest and most lasting results for the world. Finally, he hoped that other countries with dependent territories would do the same in association with Great Britain, thus organizing a mighty effort that would stretch through Europe, the Middle East and Africa to the Far East.

This startling and significant departure of no uncertain implications well illustrated the recent far-reaching changes in the international situation. As for Netherlands foreign policy, The Hague's first reactions to Mr Bevin's speech made it clear enough that here, too, a change of opinion had taken place. Did not Baron van Boetzelaer state on February 13 that Bevin's proposals should be seriously considered, later adding that the "constructive thoughts" of the British Foreign Secretary had been "most welcome" to the Netherlands? [1] No doubt the Netherlands Government thought, as will appear from the detailed discussion of the Brussels Pact below, that there were many aspects about which further negotiations were necessary, but the fact remains that their attitude towards Bevin's speech was a positive one; in short, the change between November 1947 and February 1948 was obvious. Nor were the reasons far to seek. Surely, from the Netherlands point of view, the failure of the London Conference in December, i.e. the definite breakdown of four power co-operation, represented, in the terminology used by the Government in November, a change of quite *fundamental* importance in the international situation.

That alone, as we have seen, was reason enough for Holland's changing course, particularly so as the world situation was obviously deteriorating: at that time the danger of a third world war was, in the opinion of many, anything but a remote possibility. Nor should we, as far as Holland was concerned, ignore the accumulated importance of various other facts and events, such as the political implications of the Marshall Plan, or the procla-

[1] Mem. Repl., First Chamber, Febr. 13, 1948, 5; First Chamber, February 24, 1948, 182.

mation of the Truman Doctrine which had shown that the
United States were aware of their stake in European security
and ready to act accordingly, or finally, the relatively small
value of the Security Council in action which had, once again,
confirmed already existing impressions that other measures to
ensure national security were indispensable.[1]

In short, the time had come for that "reconsideration of their
whole policy in Europe" of which the Netherlands Government
had already spoken in November; and in such circumstances
they approached the negotiations which on March 17, 1948
resulted in the conclusion of the Pact of Brussels – a pact which,
for Holland, marked the end of a period of transition.

THE PACT OF BRUSSELS

Mr Bevin spoke in the House of Commons on January 22; and
within a week the Governments of Holland, Belgium and
Luxemburg met to discuss the implications of the British
initiative. In fact, during their conference in Luxemburg of
January 29–31, they reached agreement on the principles of a
common Benelux policy, thus initiating a political co-operation
which was successfully maintained during all subsequent negotiations. The principles agreed on were no doubt known to the
British and French when the latter at long last submitted actual
proposals to the Benelux countries on February 19.

Let us first consider the position of Benelux. They were in
perfect agreement with Mr Bevin as regards the fundamental
objective: the consolidation of Western Europe. But they felt
that agreements modelled on that of Dunkirk would be of very
little use for this purpose. For one thing, the Dunkirk Treaty
of March 1947 – these dates are important! – was clearly directed
against a possible re-emergence of German aggressive policies;
but the course of events since then made any such allusions to a
German danger somewhat hypocritical. For another, multipli-
cation of the Dunkirk treaty would simply mean the creation of
a network of bilateral agreements; and to this, as we have seen,

---

[1] That not even the combined forces of Holland and Belgium were able to guarantee national security and independence, was, of course, well recognized in both
countries.

Holland and the other Benelux powers were opposed. Such a system would be ineffective; and it might produce impressions in other parts of the world which were at variance with the intentions and aims of the contracting nations. Hence, multilateral regional agreements, based on Articles 51, 52, 53 and 54 of the Charter were felt to be preferable. The fact that the Inter-American Defence Treaty of Petropolis of September 2, 1947 resulted from a similar way of thinking, was no doubt of some influence in this question; [1] far more important, however, were the well known views of the Netherlands Government that only the United Nations Charter could afford the means to avoid tension and conflicts between regional groupings. Other powers might well object to treaties similar to that of Dunkirk, but surely not to regional arrangements *as foreseen and justified under the Charter*.[2]

It might of course be argued that other powers, far from protesting against treaties of the Dunkirk type, were actually likely to prefer them to a system of regional co-operation. But that was not the view of the Netherlands Government. Bilateral treaties, expressly referring to Germany, did not correspond to realities and were moreover hypocritical, whereas a regional system, *aiming at the consolidation of Western Europe, directed against no power in particular*, met actual needs perfectly.

It follows that the Netherlands and the Benelux powers in general desired that due priority be given to the economic and social aspects of the proposed system of co-operation which should be completed by arrangements for mutual military assistance in case of aggression. Benelux considered that the recovery and the consolidation of Western Europe was primarily a question of economic co-operation; the new arrangements should reflect this point of view. Furthermore, that in these economic tasks the co-operation of Germany could not be missed, was nowhere better realized than in Holland. Finally, the Netherlands Government supported, as a matter of course, the British position as to the full utilization of overseas territories in the planned Western European system of association.[3]

[1] Expl. Mem., Pact of Brussels, April 2, 1948, 6.
[2] There was, of course, nothing in the Charter to exclude bilateral treaties against the danger of renewed German aggression.
[3] First Chamber, February 24, 1948, 182.

But this was not all. What Mr Bevin had proposed was clearly a system of solidarity and co-operation. Now, if the Benelux Governments were to assume obligations, they clearly should have rights as well. It was therefore incomprehensible to them that while asked to participate in a system of solidarity and co-operation, they were not granted the right to be associated in the deliberations and decisions regarding a problem which was equally essential to all of them – Germany. Accordingly, Benelux felt that without such association the proposed arrangements would be of little importance to them.[1]

Such were, in substance, the policies on which the Benelux Governments agreed. The conference referred to took place at the end of January. A second Benelux meeting was convened on February 5, 1948 in Brussels where it was decided to send a collective Note to Great Britain and France, in which these powers were to be given a comprehensive picture of the conceptions of Benelux. However, according to Baron van Boetzelaer's statement on February 24 in the First Chamber, this Note was not handed to the British and French Governments until February 19 – i.e. on the same day that the Benelux countries received the proposals of London and Paris. Whence the delay? Was it due to difficulties arising out of the Benelux demand to participate in the London talks on Germany which started on February 23? It is certain that this desire of the Benelux Governments was the source of many difficulties; it is equally certain that the three countries were not prepared to waive their claim.[2]

However that may be, on February 19 the Benelux Note was

[1] Mem. Repl., First Chamber, Febr. 13, 1948, 5, 7; First Chamber, Febr. 24, 1948, *passim*. There were, of course, problems which were not equally essential to all Benelux Governments – Indonesia for instance. There is no doubt that this matter was discussed during the Pact of Brussels negotiations; and also afterwards – see further the debates on the Pact of Brussels in the States General, below pp. 68ff and 87.

[2] The Conference of the United States, France, Great Britain and the Benelux countries on Germany of February 23–March 6 and April 20–June 1, 1948 in London, and the vexations in connexion with the Benelux demands are discussed, below, 1948: Germany, p. 90ff. According to van Boetzelaer (First Chamber, Febr. 24, 1948, 183), the telephonic invitation to participate in these talks was not received until the evening of February 23. That Benelux pressed their demand in London, Paris and Washington to be included in the discussions on Germany, is confirmed by the Note on Germany, 3.

duly submitted to Britain and France and on the same day
these powers presented, as a basis for further talks, projects for
treaties, similar to that of Dunkirk, to the Benelux Governments.[1] Thus all three negotiating parties – Benelux, France and
Britain – had formulated their point of view; and it was evident
that there was a wide area of fundamental disagreement.

Britain and France did not readily accept the ideas of the
Benelux countries. This was, to a certain extent, understandable:
for if, on the one hand, these conceptions were more or less
consistent with previous political thinking in the Benelux
countries and particularly in the Netherlands, they implied, on
the other hand, a much wider interpretation of Mr Bevin's
speech than Mr Bevin himself intended or approved; and they
were difficult to reconcile with the previous policies of the
French.

And yet, in spite of the British-French predilection for bilateral treaties, it was the multilateral, regional principle of
Benelux which was ultimately accepted as the basis of the
Brussels Pact. This was partly due to the political events,[2] and
particularly the Russian coup in Czechoslovakia, which meanwhile had taken place. The Russian coup was certainly not such
an important event in the genesis of the Brussels Pact as has
been assumed at times. This much should be clear from the
chronological order of events.[3] Yet the *form* in which the closer
co-operation between the Western European nations was finally brought about, was no doubt strongly influenced by the
events in Prague. These made, it will be recalled, a tremendous
impression and there can be little doubt that as a result, conceptions in France and Britain about the form of Western
European co-operation evolved in the direction of the Benelux
proposals.

The Benelux countries conferred again in Brussels on February 29, 1948; and this conference was followed by discussions of all five powers during which some remaining points,

[1] Van Boetzelaer, First Chamber, Febr. 24, 1948, 182; Expl. Mem., Pact of
Brussels, April 2, 1948, 6.
[2] Expl. Mem., Pact of Brussels, April 2, 1948, 6.
[3] Whether or not the British had any inkling of coming events either in Czechoslovakia or elsewhere when Mr. Bevin launched his initiative of January 22, is, of course,
quite another matter.

such as the question of automatic assistance in case of ag-
gresion against one of the contracting parties, ways and means of
mutual consultation and the problem of the special reference to
Germany in the Treaty were more or less successfully disposed
of. On these and other points the Netherlands Government made
the following comments when they submitted the Brussels Pact
to the States General.[1]

As regards the question of automatic military assistance, the
Benelux countries had been reluctant to assume obligations of
automatic assistance in case of aggression against one of the
contracting powers *anywhere in the world*. This point of view,
the Government declared, implied a certain disadvantage for
the Netherlands, for in March 1948 the East Indies still formed
part of the Kingdom. This was, however, made good to a certain
extent by the stipulation of Article VII concerning consultation
"with regard to any situation which may constitute a threat to
peace, in whatever area this threat should arise".[2]

The Netherlands Government would have preferred that no
country in particular had been singled out in the Treaty as a
potential aggressor. Other powers had insisted upon this. The
Government stated, however, that this should not be regarded
as an obstacle to future co-operation with "German territories",
provided of course that the latter conform to the guiding
principles of the Treaty. The words of the Preamble: "to
associate progressively in the pursuance of these aims other
States inspired by the same ideals and animated by the like
determination" should, therefore, be interpreted in this light.[3]

The Netherlands Government, furthermore, regarded the
Consultative Council as one of the most important features of
the Treaty. In their view the Council should be seen as an
"advisory body" to the Governments concerned. The Council,
it was considered, was of special interest to the Benelux countries,
because it made it possible to discuss any situation anywhere in
the world which might constitute a threat to the peace – which
was particularly important in view of the limitations of Article
IV; and because it offered Benelux an opportunity to raise its

[1] The text of the Treaty will be found in Appendix 9.
[2] Expl. Mem., Pact of Brussels, April 2, 1948, 6, 7.
[3] Expl. Mem., Pact of Brussels, April 2, 1948, 6.

voice regarding international measures taken by the other contracting powers, i.e. Britain and France, and which, in the opinion of Benelux, might endanger the peace. In other words, via the Council, Benelux might influence, to a certain extent, the policies of the great powers.[1]

The Netherlands Government considered that the Treaty applied also to those territories overseas over which the contracting parties exercised sovereignty, or for whose foreign relations they were responsible.[2] Finally, it was pointed out that the arrangement of the various articles of the Treaty had been intentional. Thus, the paramount importance of the social, economic and cultural aspects of the new system of co-operation was stressed once again.[3]

The Treaty was signed at Brussels on March 17, 1948 and in his speech on that occasion Baron van Boetzelaer emphasized the *special* importance of the Pact as far as Netherlands foreign policy was concerned. He spoke of "la gravité de cette décision, qui, sous certains aspects, marque un tournant dans la politique traditionnelle de mon pays"; in fact, in the context of the present work, the whole speech is of great interest; its full text was as follows:

,,La signature du Traité régional concernant l'Europe occidentale marque une date très importante dans l'histoire du Royaume des Pays-Bas. Au dix-neuvième siècle les Pays-Bas ont suivi une ,,politique de neutralité", ou plutôt, puisqu'il ne s'agissait point d'une neutralité permanente, garantie par les Grandes Puissances, une ,,politique d'indépendance". Les Pays-Bas considéraient la neutralité comme la directive de leur politique internationale, parce qu'ils étaient d'avis que cette neutralité contribuait au juste équilibre entre les Grandes Puissances européennes, et parce qu'ils étaient convaincus que de cet équilibre dépendait la paix en Europe. Cette politique d'indépendance fut, en principe, abandonnée lors de l'entrée des Pays-Bas dans la Société des Nations et par sa participation à l'Organisation des Nations Unies. Toutefois la neutralité n'était, ni après la première, ni après la seconde guerre mondiale, mise hors la loi. La possibilité de rester neutre en cas de désaccord entre les Grandes Puissances en ce qui concerne la désignation de l'agresseur, restait entière. Le Pacte d'Union de l'Europe occidentale, que nous signons aujourd'hui met définitivement fin à la possibilité de rester neutre quand l'un des cinq partenaires a été la victime d'une agression en Europe; il garantit, d'autre part, l'assistance par tous les moyens, militaires et autres, dans le cas où

[1] Expl. Mem., Pact of Brussels, April 2, 1948, 8.
[2] Mem. Repl., Sec. Chamber, Pact of Brussels, April 20, 1948, 17.
[3] Expl. Mem., Pact of Brussels, April 2, 1948, 6.

nous mêmes aurions été attaqués. Le Gouvernement de la Reine est convaincu que la participation des Pays-Bas à ce Traité trouvera un accueil favorable auprès d'une très large majorité de la population néerlandaise. On ne peut fermer les yeux aux modifications radicales de la situation en Europe et dans le monde entier. On est convaincu du danger qu'une agression dirigée contre le territoire européen de l'un de nous entraînerait pour les autres, et de la menace qu'une pareille attaque signifierait pour la culture européenne toute entière. On se rend compte de la communauté de nos intérêts ainsi que des liens économiques, sociaux et culturels, qui nous unissent déjà. On comprend que l'union n'a qu'un but purement défensif. En effet, elle ne se dirige contre aucun autre Etat, européen ou non-européen; au contraire, elle vise à collaborer dans toute la mesure du possible avec tous les autres Etats en vue du maintien de la paix et de la sécurité internationales. Elle forme, d'après les mots de M. Bevin, un ,,nucleus'', un noyau, auquel une fois qu'il s'est formé et consolidé, d'autres Etats, inspirés du même idéal, pourront se joindre. Dans cet ordre d'idées la création du Conseil Consultatif dans lequel nous voyons l'instrument d'une mise en oeuvre pratique des dispositions du Traité, nous paraît présenter un intérêt primordial. Cette tâche doit, à notre avis, être entamée sans délai. C'est seulement de cette manière qu'on pourra éviter que le Traité ne reste qu'une belle façade, au lieu de devenir une construction réelle, solide et durable. Nous saluerons avec joie le jour où le cercle des participants à notre union régionale sera élargi, mais nous sommes d'avis qu'il s'agira en premier lieu d'approfondir l'union avant de viser à son élargissement.

La tâche du Conseil Consultatif, telle que nous la préconisons ne fait nullement double emploi avec celle du Comité de Coopération Economique Européenne, au contraire, elle appuie et favorise le travail de ce Comité, parce que les résultats d'une collaboration plus étroite, rendue possible par la plus grande communauté d'intérêts d'un cercle plus restreint des participants, pourra être très utile à la réalisation des buts de la communauté européenne toute entière. Le Gouvernement des Pays-Bas est convaincu que les deux organisations pourront se développer l'une à côté de l'autre dans un esprit de parfaite harmonie.

La sphère d'application du Traité a été géographiquement limitée. Ceci n'exclut pas que les conditions économiques des territoires d'outre-mer, avec lesquels des liens spéciaux unissent les Hautes Parties Contractantes, pourront être prises en considération pour autant qu'elles affectent l'échange des produits avec les territoires européens. D'autre part, le Gouvernement de la Reine a constaté avec satisfaction que tout en restreignant l'assistance automatique au cas d'une agression en Europe, le Traité ouvre la voie à une consultation au sein du Conseil Consultatif sur toute situation pouvant constituer une menace contre la paix en quelque endroit qu'elle se produise. En vue des relations qui existent entre les Pays-Bas et les territoires d'outre-mer, cet article du Traité pourrait, le cas échéant, obtenir une importance considérable. Abstraction faite de ce cas spécial, mon Gouvernement exprime l'espoir que ces stipulations seront interprétées d'une manière aussi large que possible. Si les pays du Benelux lient leur sort à celui des Grandes Puissances, il nous semble justifié d'insister à ce qu'ils puissent faire entendre leur voix quand il s'agira de prendre des décisions qui pourront constituer une menace de la paix mondiale.

Les brêves observations que j'ai eu l'honneur de vous présenter font preuve de la satisfaction avec laquelle les Pays-Bas saluent la signature du Traité de l'Union de l'Europe occidentale. D'autre part, je ne vous ai pas caché que nous nous rendons compte de la gravité de cette décision, qui, sous certains aspects, marque un tournant dans la politique traditionnelle de mon pays. Le Gouvernement de la Reine a la ferme conviction que la décision qu'il a prise est celle que le souci pour l'honneur et le bien-être du Royaume des Pays-Bas lui prescrivent. Que la bénédiction du Tout-Puissant soit acquise à notre oeuvre".

"Le Gouvernement de la Reine est convaincu que la participation des Pays Bas à ce Traité trouvera un acceuil favorable auprès d'une très large majorité de la population néerlandaise....". How in fact was the Treaty received in the Netherlands? In view of the event's significance it is obviously of interest to discuss this aspect of the matter in some detail.

The Treaty was fully discussed in the States General; and considering the debates as a whole, it was evident that there were three lines of argument, two of which were really fundamental. The first rejected the Pact and regretted that the traditional policy had been abandoned; the second agreed in principle, but was somewhat critical of the Treaty's form and some of its features; and the third warmly supported the Pact, but considered that it was only a beginning: it should be followed up by positive supra-national policies.

That the Brussels Pact meant a definite break with the past, was, of course, well realized on all sides. The Government themselves stressed that as long as the United Nations could not guarantee the nation's security, it was clearly Holland's duty, in the present circumstances, to protect itself against aggression by way of complementary arrangements. The great majority of the States General supported this point of view, but the applause was not general [1] and the opposite view was stated in somewhat extremist fashion in the First Chamber.[2] That statement, for all its obvious fallacies, must be regarded as

[1] There is no need to dwell on the opinions of the Communist Party and its representatives in the States General. Their position towards the Pact, which they considered a bloc with inimical intentions towards the Soviet Union, was similar to that of their friends in other countries.

[2] The speaker was a Catholic Senator, although he did not speak for the Catholic People's Party in this question. His views, however, were shared by small sections of public opinion and the press.

highly interesting, for it showed not only to what extent Netherlands neutrality had been the product of mercantile considerations, but it raised also for the first time the spectre of Germany's
neutrality in a future war, and it finally advocated a concept of
neutrality which was to become highly fashionable in later
years.

The break with the old policy, it was contended, should be
regarded as a matter for "profound" regret. Thanks to neutrality,
Holland had escaped the horrors of the First World War; and
if "Switzerland and the Scandinavian countries" had not deserted neutrality, then why had the Netherlands? The alternative which now had to be faced was nothing less than total war.
There was every reason to believe that, as far as the Netherlands
were concerned, the formal danger of war had been increased
by this Treaty. Holland would now be drawn into the conflicts
of the great powers; and the position of Great Britain, in particular, should be considered in this connexion. Was it not true
that that country was only partly a European power? The
British interests were world-wide; serious clashes between
Britain and other powers occurred in all parts of the world: the
inference was obvious.

Furthermore, what would happen if the five powers should
become involved in hostilities and Germany remain neutral?
Was it not true that in such a situation Germany was likely to
regain its dominant position, not to mention the enormous
profits which German mercantile interests would be bound to
make? The Brussels Pact was fraught with danger.

What, then, should have been Holland's policy? Not, it was
admitted, the policy of neutrality as it had been known before
the war; a new concept of neutrality should be developed. In
this connexion, reference was made to what Switzerland had
allowed during the late war, with respect to overflying aircraft,
and Sweden with regard to transport of German military forces
over its territory – acts and facts which, before the war, would
have been regarded as violations of neutrality, but nowadays
merely as events which neutral states were unable to stop or
prevent.

Accordingly, the policy of the future could not be total war;
it should rather concern itself with the further development of

truly modern concepts of neutrality, suitable to those states which were wise enough to reject the folly of total war and which preferred a policy of playing safe to being destroyed. "The conclusion is: new forms of neutrality or atomic destruction and downfall. That, Sir, is the reality; and for me, as a merchant, it is that reality which is the ultimate factor".[1]

Needless to say, this point of view was decidedly rejected, not only by the Government but also by the large majority of the States General.

We now come to the opinions of those who, while agreeing in principle with the Pact and the policy it represented, found much to criticize in it. Only a few important points can be discussed here.

One piece of criticism should be mentioned because it is quite characteristic of the Netherlands approach to problems of foreign policy. In both Chambers much was made of the fact that the Preamble of the Treaty made no mention of the name of God. The same point was made in 1945 with regard to the United Nations Charter but then, it was admitted, the position was somewhat different in so far as many religions besides Christianity were represented in the United Nations. But in the case of the Brussels Pact there was, according to a great number of Members, no possible excuse for the omission. This aspect of the Treaty was regarded as vitally important.

The other points touched on the field of practical politics. During the debates a certain distrust of the policies of Great Britain was clearly noticeable in many quarters. These feelings, which were also widespread among the Netherlands people as a whole, must be explained in the first place by certain events in the common history of the two countries.[2] But more recent developments had done much to aggravate them. Certain aspects of British policy in the Indonesian question were keenly resented in the Netherlands. It was felt that measures such as the British

---

[1] First Chamber, Pact of Brussels, June 23, 1948, 667 ff.

[2] It was asserted that England had always injured Holland in the past, even when an alliance united the two countries. „Netherlands History" – or at any rate a very dubious interpretation of it – was supposed to support such sweeping statements! (Prov. Rep., Sec. Chamber, Pact of Brussels, April 15, 1948, 13).

embargo on deliveries of military goods and material or the economic policy followed in Singapore, could not be reconciled with a system of co-operation and solidarity as proposed by Mr. Bevin and presumably realized in the Pact of Brussels. The British embargo was regarded as an anti-Netherlands act.[1]

The Government, while insisting that the various interests in question were not of equal weight and importance, made it plain none the less that they largely shared these sentiments. They said that if one of the contracting parties followed an economic policy detrimental to the development of the overseas territories of another party to the Pact, such a policy could and should be discussed in the organs established by the Treaty. In fact they, too, considered that obstructive policies of one party directed against the overseas interests of another were quite incompatible with the letter and spirit of the Pact. So much for the general point. As to the difficulties in question, the States General were informed that they had been discussed with the other powers concerned and there was some hope that the situation would improve in the near future.[2]

A further interesting point was made during the debates in the First Chamber. The Government had stressed the fact that regional groupings, as realized in the Brussels Pact, had been foreseen in the United Nations Charter. It was, however, pointed out to them that according to Article 53 of the Charter, the Security Council might "utilize such regional arrangements or agencies for enforcement action under its authority". The question thus arose: was it really desirable, in view of the "rather peculiar conceptions of justice and security, which of late had come to the fore in the Council", to hand it an extra weapon, over and above those ex Article 43? [3] The Pact, no doubt, limited the Netherlands obligations in the military field to Europe; but Article 53 knew no such limitations. France and Britain, it was said, were in a different position; they had the

[1] Prov. Report, Sec. Chamber, Pact of Brussels, April 15, 1948, 14; and the debates.
[2] Van Boetzelaer in Sec. Chamber, Pact of Brussels, April 23, 1948, 1642; Mem. Repl., Sec. Chamber, Pact of Brussels, April 20, 1948, 18.
[3] First Chamber, Pact of Brussels, June 22, 1948, 659. This remark was obviously a disparaging allusion to the conduct of the Security Council with respect to Netherlands policy in Indonesia which was fiercely resented in Holland.

right of veto; but the Benelux powers were quite dependent on the Security Council. In other words: what Britain and France in regard to their extra-European interests might be unable to attain within the framework of the Pact, might become possible to them via the Security Council on the strength of Article 53 of the Charter.

Consequently, as far as the Benelux countries were concerned, this situation called for great caution.

To this point Baron van Boetzelaer did not reply in detail; he said, however – and this applied no doubt both to this and previous criticisms – that it would be wrong to distrust other powers' policies. In fact, the Pact of Brussels had been concluded to *increase* sentiments of mutual trust.

Some Members felt that the Pact was very vague as regards the question of the possible aggressor. The Government's position relative to the express mentioning of Germany in the Preamble was generally approved; but for this very reason it was felt that a greater measure of outspokenness in Article IV would not have been amiss. It was regretted that the Dunkirk Treaty was not abrogated by the Brussels Pact. The Dunkirk agreement, after all, was clearly directed against Germany and the Brussels Pact echoed this in the Preamble and Article VII. But what was the Pact's ultimate aim? The economic reconstruction and consolidation of Western Europe. Now this was not likely to be furthered by such unnecessary references to Germany which, moreover, went counter to what might be called the "European spirit". But this was not all. It was of course true that the Netherlands "policy of independence" could not be continued in its old form, but did this imply that we had to follow France and Britain in every respect? Was not the reconstruction of Germany a vital Netherlands interest? We should therefore resist all forms of discrimination – also in the Brussels Pact. It should be open to all powers willing to conform to the principles of Article III. On these grounds, too, it should not be referred to as the "Western European Union" or "Western European Treaty". This would be incorrect, *a*) because of the overseas territories, *b*) because it was nowhere said that only Western European powers could accede to the Pact and finally, because it was a dangerous illusion to think that the aims of the Pact could be realized by the Western European powers alone. A "European policy of independence" was quite as illusionary as its Netherlands equivalent had proved to be.[1]

Consequently, accession of other powers to the Pact should be encouraged; nor should the possibility of complementary arrangements between the five powers of Brussels and other nations – particularly in the military field – be overlooked.[2]

Van Boetzelaer readily admitted that the term "Western European Union" did not reflect the true character of the Pact. With much that had been said he was in agreement; he, too, saw the Pact as a nucleus, further development of which was no doubt desirable; but it was necessary to concentrate first on the organization and consolidation of what had been achieved in Brussels. The experience with Benelux had shown conclusively that this might require considerable time. Premature expansion of the Pact might have dangerous results. Certainly, he did not deny that complementary arrangements in the military field were desirable and indeed, necessary; but at that moment (April 1948) he could not say what might be expected in this respect.[3]

Let us now turn our attention to those not inconsiderable groups in the States General who thought that the Brussels Pact was nothing but a beginning. They regarded the Treaty as nothing less than the constitution of a Western European Union; and they were eager to proceed at once with the construction of the whole edifice they had in mind.

These opinions were, of course, closely allied with, and influenced by, the various conceptions of European federalism. It will be remembered that when federalism was last discussed in the States General, the Netherlands Government showed very little enthusiasm indeed for these ideas. However, that was in November 1947; since then great changes had taken place; and in fact, it was no doubt true that Netherlands public opinion

[1] Prov. Rep., Sec. Chamber, Pact of Brussels, April 15, 1948, 13, 14.
[2] Prov. Rep., Sec. Chamber, Pact of Brussels, April 15, 1948, 14; Second Chamber, Pact of Brussels, April 22, 1948, 1635.
[3] Mem. Repl., Sec. Chamber, Pact of Brussels, April 20, 1948, 18; Sec. Chamber, Pact of Brussels, April 23, 1948, 1643. The Netherlands Government were aware of the essential importance of the United States rôle in any (Western) European security system. The difficulties lay elsewhere.

was taking a keener interest in the ideals and possibilities of federalism than ever before. It was, therefore, symptomatic of these international and national developments that, when the First Chamber discussed foreign affairs in January and February 1948, many Members blamed the Government for having neither understood nor supported the ideals and aims of federalism. The Government's opinion, in a few words, was that a policy of universal co-operation, commonly referred to as the "One World" policy, was preferable to European federalism which as a whole could not be realized, while partial realization might have dangerous consequences. This point of view was severely criticized. In the first place, the "One World" policy, it was said, was not very successful really, nor was it true to say that universal co-operation could not be reconciled with European federalism. In fact, these two ideals, far from being opposed to each other, were complementary. Neither could it be maintained that overseas relations formed a serious obstacle to regional federation. The Government's attention was drawn to what might be termed "pluriformity of federalism" and it was pointed out that this might be of particular importance to those powers which, sooner or later, would have to place their relations with their colonial possessions on a new footing. For instance, one conceivable solution might be that the old colonial powers, on the one hand, federate with each other; and on the other hand, each of them with their colonies overseas. Thus, far from being a source of difficulties, federalism might actually contribute to solving one of the most vexatious post-war problems.[1]

The Government had contended that a Western European Federation would really mean a Western European Bloc. This was denied; a Western European Federation, it was argued, might be described as a club of friends, with other than purely military objectives for the common good, directed against no other powers. A bloc, on the other hand, was little more than a defensive or offensive alliance between certain powers. Such a bloc might be necessary or it might not; but to say that a Western European Federation would be nothing more than a Western European Bloc was surely unwarranted.[2]

[1] First Chamber, Febr. 19, 1948, 172.
[2] First Chamber, Febr. 19, 1948, 173.

Finally, it was thought that the Government did not pay sufficient attention to the general political situation. Everybody was agreed that Europe should not be a satellite of either the United States or the Soviet Union. But to avoid this, Europe would have to change its existing organization: here, too, federation was the only practical solution. And was federalism not equally necessary for the success of the European Recovery Program? For, after all, the Program clearly required supranational economic co-operation in certain well defined fields; did the Government really think that all this could be achieved in a community of sovereign and equal States as we had known it in the past?

But Baron van Boetzelaer was obviously not convinced.[1] He pointed out that discussions on this subject were not facilitated by the fact that "federalism" was an extremely loose term – often very loosely used, too; it was never made clear what exactly was referred to. For instance, if people discussed "European federalism" did they refer to Europe with Britain and Russia, or Europe without Britain, or Europe without either Britain or Russia, or Western Europe with Britain or finally, Western Europe only? This was not mere quibbling with words; that these questions could be asked at all, illustrated the existing confusion in this respect.

On the whole, Baron van Boetzelaer said, the Government saw no reason to modify their point of view. They could not agree that the "One World" policy and the conception of regional federations were complementary, nor could they accept the proposition that if the "One World" conception was not for the time being realizable, a start should be made with regional federalism. Here again the question, what does the term federalism mean? was most pertinent. For, after all, many forms of regional groupings could be imagined which, far from promoting the "One World" idea, were likely to harm universal co-operation in a serious, perhaps even fatal manner. The basis of such arrangements was the important thing.

The Foreign Minister doubted whether "pluriformity of federalism" was likely to work successfully in the reality of inter-

[1] First Chamber, Febr. 24, 1948, 183 ff.

national relations, although he admired the theoretical merits of this conception; and as to the presumed fundamental difference between a Western European Federation and a Western European Bloc, he felt bound to confess that he did not believe this difference to be so great as had been suggested to him.

In general, he thought, the champions of federalism were inclined to see things too simply; complicated problems could not be reasoned away by slogans; and it was a sign of political realism to maintain – as the Government did maintain – that federalism might have most undesirable consequences. Did this imply that they were against regional co-operation? Not at all; the Charter sanctioned it and their proposals to Britain and France of February 19 in connexion with Mr Bevin's speech, were based on the Charter. But they did believe that "all regional co-operation not fully justified by political, economic and cultural considerations and affinities, was likely to do the cause of international organization more harm than good". And about one thing there should be no doubt: the coming co-operation between France, Britain and Benelux could not be regarded as the formation of a bloc; but no more could it be considered as a form of federalism.[1]

Clearly the Government showed no sign of changing their attitude; but the "federalists" had no intention of giving up and the Brussels Pact gave them an opportunity to resume the attack. That the Pact could not yet be regarded as a form of federalism they readily admitted; the point was, however, whether or not it should become one. They thought it should; for what, after all, were the facts? Firstly, the Pact was stated to have an economic, military and social character. Secondly, it was stated to have been modelled to a certain extent on the Treaty of Petropolis, a treaty which was alleged to have "established a truly federal union with permanent organs, invested with power or at least authority".[2] The Brussels Pact, too, spoke of organs; it was therefore assumed that the Benelux powers at least aimed at a federal union with permanent organs. If this assumption was correct, then, it was demanded, these organs should be activated as soon as possible.

[1] Van Boetzelaer in First Chamber, Febr. 24, 1948, 184 ff.
[2] Sec. Chamber, Pact of Brussels, March 18, 1560.

Once again it was pointed out that, as regards the possibilities of federalism, Netherlands public opinion had progressed a good deal lately; and although it no doubt could be maintained that at the moment purely military co-operation was the paramount need, many Members felt that the need for transfer of national authority to permanent political, military and socio-economic organs was no less urgent. In other words: there should now be realized a real community of democratic States in a federal system, in which national authority should be transferred to one or more supra-national organs with well defined and concrete objectives, particularly in the military, monetary and social fields.[1]

It is to be observed that there was no demand for a Western European Parliament; the important thing was the establishment of the agencies as defined above. Whether these should embrace the sixteen powers of the Recovery Program, or for the time being, only the five nations of the Brussels Pact, could be decided later.[2]

The Members who expressed these views were obviously supporters of what has been commonly termed the functionalist approach.[3] However, they took pains to emphasize that only in

[1] Sec. Chamber, Pact of Brussels, March 18, 1565.

[2] Sec. Chamber, Pact of Brussels, March 18, 1561.

[3] The differences between the "functionalist" and the "federalist" approach (to Europe's unification), although not easy to determine accurately, may be roughly defined as follows. The "functionalists" emphasize the idea of inter-national, inter-governmental, specialized authorities; the "federalists", aiming at the political integration of the European states, advocate general, supra-national, political institutions, such as federal parliaments, with a federal system of election, federal political parties and the like. Even proposals for federal assemblies may be regarded as typical of the "federalist" approach. Nevertheless, if we consider the Resolution of the Second Chamber of April 23, 1948 (below, p. 77) and particularly the comments thereon made on February 3, 1949 (below, p. 119) and finally, the Resolution of the Second Chamber of February 8, 1949 (below, p. 119), it is clear that, as far as the States General were concerned, "functionalists", too, accepted the transfer of a certain measure of national authority to the specialized agencies mentioned above. Nor must we overlook the fact that, at least in democratic systems, this is likely to be followed sooner or later by agencies of control, i.e. political institutions. It may be thought, therefore, that in practice the two approaches differ more in their starting point and emphasis than in their ultimate results. On this assumption one can understand the statement made in the Second Chamber (below, p. 119) that the two approaches are complementary, rather than opposed to each other.

From the point of view of a national government, however, the choice between the two approaches is not one of tactics only, for in the case of the federalist one the fundamental question of the delimitation of national government and its authority must be faced and solved at the outset of the federal experiment. Hence the predilection of various pragmatically inclined governments for the functionalist approach

a federal system could the functionalist approach be ultimately successful. Federalism alone could create the international basis of law and authority which was necessary for a well-working supra-national functionalism. It might be asked: How far should we go? This, it was stated, should be left to the future; but the mere fear of losing "sovereign" rights should never be an obstacle to further progress.

These were the most radical opinions of the Debates. Supra-national political institutions were not mentioned, although one Member observed that the authority with which the agencies might be invested, should be a democratic one – i.e. a reasonable influence of the populations concerned was necessary. But on the whole the demands were all of the functionalist type.

Naturally there were differences in emphasis. Some Members stated roundly that the military aspect of the problem was paramount to them and they stressed, in connexion with the term "aggression" as used in the Pact, the great importance of the internal security factor. Others, however, underlined the economic aspects of the Treaty: they neither considered nor desired to consider the Pact as a camouflaged military convention. Accordingly, they wished that all efforts should be directed towards the establishment of one Western European economic structure, independently of what was being done by the sixteen powers in that field.

It is probably unnecessary to add that these demands were not generally supported in the States General. Some Members had no objection to the principles of federalism as such, but they were opposed to a federal system in which socialist influences might be dominant. Others felt that for the sake of military and military-economic co-operation they should be prepared to travel the road of supra-national agencies, but they made it clear that such a policy should be limited to that aspect of the matter. In this connexion it is of interest to note that one or two Members were in favour of a common Western European General Staff and even a common Western European Army.

The Debates about these aspects of the Brussels Pact resulted

which allows for greater latitude in this respect. (See also the statement of Mr. Stikker of December 1948 on this subject, below, p. 84ff).

finally in a number of motions, the following of which is particularly relevant to the present discussion:

"The Chamber,
  in view of its Resolution of March 19, 1948 [1] relative to a permanent association of States and the Government's policy in this question,
  considering that this permanent association may be realized in various specialized authorities in which authority must be granted to supra-national organs, particularly in the field of monetary, economic and social policy and in that of defence;
  of the opinion that such measures may further developments – within the United Nations – in the direction of a community under the rule of law of democratic States, federally joined,
  invites the Government to promote, together with the Governments of the States with which they are now co-operating on a new basis, the speedy establishment of such specialized authorities ...." [2].

What was the Government's reaction to these propositions? To begin with, they made it clear that the Pact of Brussels was the expression of the co-operation between *absolutely sovereign powers*.[3] Minister van Boetzelaer stressed the significance of the Consultative Council, of the International Secretariat and of the Permanent Military Committee, but he added that "during recent negotiations" it had become clear that the Governments concerned preferred to abstain from making any complete and detailed blue-prints for the future growth of the Pact organization.[4] In other words, the development of a Western Union should be left to time and the future. The establishment of supra-national agencies in particular presented a problem which, the Government felt, could not be profitably brought up now. To invest the Consultative Council with binding supra-national authority would be quite unacceptable; the Council should remain a consultative and advisory body. Baron van Boetzelaer considered it probable that various agencies with well defined objectives might be established within the framework of the Consultative Council; but whether such agencies would be invested with binding authority was again doubtful. He reiterated that federation was only justified if and when the peoples concerned acquired an emotional

---

[1] The Resolution of March 19, 1948 stressed the necessity of a permanent association of States to ensure the peace and security of the Netherlands and Europe and approved the Government's policy in the negotiations for the Pact of Brussels.
[2] Sec. Chamber, Pact of Brussels, March 19, 1948, 1594.
[3] Van Boetzelaer in Sec. Chamber, Pact of Brussels, March 18, 1948, 1564.
[4] Mem. Repl., Sec. Chamber, Pact of Brussels, April 20, 1948, 18/19.

relationship to the greater entity envisaged; if and when the peoples concerned were prepared to make sacrifices for the common good of the whole federation; but as long as this was not the case, the establishment of a federal authority, and renouncement of national rights and power in favour of such a federal authority might well lead to domination of the greater powers over the small ones.

Baron van Boetzelaer stated that the Government would certainly take into account the sentiments expressed in the Debates; but they did not act alone: other powers might have different conceptions.

The Government repeated that they had no objections to supra-national agencies with well defined objectives, wherever possible and desirable; and they believed that in this manner the ideals of federalism were best served. Accordingly, the motion quoted above would be acceptable to them, provided the words "as far as possible and desirable" were inserted between the words "in which" and "authority".

Now, the word "possible" regarded possible constitutional difficulties in other contracting countries; but the insertion of the word "desirable" was of course quite a different proposition. There is really no need to say more: these insertions made the Government's position, once again, all too clear; but the change, although its significance was regretfully realized, was duly made; and in this form the motion was carried with a large majority (80 for, 6 against). Thus ended one more assault of the federalist forces. The Brussels Pact, as such, was not to fulfil their hopes and ambitions.

Before turning to other events of 1948 in the field of General Policy, it should be pointed out that the problems of Netherlands general policy now assumed quite a different character. Hitherto, we were mainly concerned with a period of transition; but with the conclusion of the Brussels Pact that period, in principle, belonged to the past; and from now on the main questions to be dealt with regard the new policy's implementation and consolidation. Since March 17, 1948, furthermore, Netherlands foreign policy in Europe had, to a certain extent, become part of a greater whole: first, that of the Western European powers' foreign policy, later, that of the Atlantic powers. These common policies are well known; to follow them in detail is unnecessary. Accordingly, only such events and developments will be mentioned in which Netherlands policy, either by force of circumstance or on account of principle, differed from the general line of their Allies. But such divergences – which were extremely few – must of course be seen against the background of the general policy of the Western powers.

As regards the implementation of the Brussels Pact, this question had at least three aspects – military, economic and social. In the economic field, as we have seen, the Netherlands Government had been asked to press for the establishment of one Western European economic structure and this, independently of what was done within the framework of the European Recovery Program. At a later date, however, it was suspected that the economic aspects of the Pact were being neglected. As a matter of fact, this impression was not in accordance with the facts; but it was understandable that such conclusions were arrived at. Before the end of 1948, two conferences of the ministers of Economic Affairs and of Finance of the Brussels Pact powers had taken place; and the Consultative Council, during its session of July 19 and 20, 1948 in the Hague, had again emphasized the necessity of economic co-operation.

It will be remembered, however, that in Article I of the Treaty a warning was inserted against the unnecessary duplication of international agencies; and, as we know, Holland in particular was invariably opposed to all such agencies not urgently required. The truth was that most of the necessary work could be done in OEEC in Paris; and so it came about that the economic committees of the Pact showed few signs of life. But it would be wrong to conclude from this that the economic aspects were neglected.[1] The committees in the social field were no doubt more active, and before long their deliberations were to result in a number of conventions.[2]

As far as the military question was concerned, everything had to be organized from the very beginning inasmuch as there were

[1] Mem. Repl., Sec. Chamber, Dec. 13, 1948, 14/15.
[2] During the Seventh Session of the Consultative Council (November 4/5, 1949) the five powers signed two conventions regarding social security and medical assistance.

no existing agencies to fall back on. The full story of these military developments would of course carry us too far, but a few points should be mentioned, as they illustrate some of the difficulties of Netherlands policy.

In the first place the powers had to consider the fact that some of them had military commitments in parts of the world not covered by the Pact.

In Holland's case, large forces were tied up in Indonesia; Britain (Palestine, Malaya) and France (Indo China) were in pretty much the same position. Still, the percentage of Netherlands forces not available for the purposes of the Pact was considerably higher than that of either Britain or France. The result was a weakening of military potential in Europe. In the view of the Netherlands Government, this unsatisfactory situation which would have to be remedied as soon as possible, was *one more reason for solving the Indonesian question with all possible speed*.[1] But it was also considered whether Holland should not make an extra sacrifice in order to contribute to the Pact's forces in such a measure as was obviously expected from it.

Then, as now, the Netherlands production of modern military material was not sufficient to meet reasonable defence demands. Accordingly, deliveries of arms and munitions were requested.

Here again the Indonesian affair produced unfortunate complications. It will be recalled that at the time of the conclusion of the Brussels Treaty, the British embargo on the export of military material to Indonesia had been severely criticized. None the less, the embargo had not been lifted; on the contrary, it had been extended. Of course, it might be argued that this embargo need not prevent Holland receiving arms necessary to her defence in the framework of the Brussels Pact; but in practice things were different. Accordingly, it was the position of the Netherlands Government – which had, as we know, protested against the embargo – that the quantities of arms delivered should be such that the defence of *Holland as a whole, i.e. including its military commitments overseas*, could be duly organized. In other words, they contended for the principle of equal treatment of all partners to the Pact of Brussels – and, for that matter, the North Atlantic Treaty.

[1] Mem. Repl., Sec. Chamber, Dec. 13, 1948, 15.

During these military discussions the United States and Canada were represented by observers – a fact which Netherlands policy welcomed.[1] Thus, two powers were present who were not members of the Brussels Pact; and this leads us to the question of the expansion of the Brussels Pact and the beginnings of the North Atlantic Treaty.

As we have seen, the Netherlands Government always considered the Brussels Pact as a beginning: "…. un noyau auquel, une fois qu'il s'est formé et consolidé, d'autres Etats inspirés du même idéal, pourront se joindre". But in saying this, Baron van Boetzelaer had made it clear at the same time – and he did so again in the States General – that all undue haste in expanding the Pact should be avoided. His reasons were twofold: one was that there should be time for consolidation, the other, that certain forms of expansion might actually result in a weakening of the Pact. There were, in fact, countries who might be willing to accede; but their accession would only extend the obligations of the other parties to the Pact, without adding anything at all to their military potential. The Italian Republic was a case in point.

On the whole, therefore, the Netherlands, at the time of the Pact's conclusion, were against its premature expansion.

The relations of the Pact powers to the United States and Canada were in quite a different category. Netherlands policy had always been alive to the essential rôle of the United States in any closer association of Western European powers. Both Government and States General, as we have seen, fully understood that the backing of the United States was necessary to make such an association a political, i.e. in this connexion, a military reality.

The Pact of Brussels had been concluded, it is true, without there being more than a moral certainty that the United States would in fact lend support; but of course the Truman Doctrine and E.R.P. were indications of a highly satisfactory character.

Moreover, on the very day of the Brussels Pact ceremony, March 17, President Truman in a statement to Congress, recommended measures which, in his judgment, were best calculated "to give support to the free and democratic nations

[1] Mem. Repl., Sec. Chamber, Dec. 13, 1948, 14.

of Europe and to improve the solid foundation of our own national strength". And the Vandenberg Resolution of June 11, 1948 made it possible to translate the words of Mr Truman into facts.

On July 6, 1948 the United States Government opened discussions with the diplomatic representatives of Canada and the Brussels Pact powers in Washington. During these talks the following points were examined: the general political situation in Europe, the security of the Western European powers and the means to maintain their security, the possibilities of a common defence and finally, ways and means of associating the United States and Canada with the existing security system. The suggestions formulated in Washington were subsequently examined in the Permanent Commission of the Brussels Pact in London. The Commission made a project of a treaty which was again discussed in Washington. Meanwhile, in October the Consultative Council of the Brussels Pact approved, in principle, the conclusion of a treaty with the United States and Canada; and also approved of consultation with other powers about participation in the coming talks in Washington. That Netherlands policy welcomed these developments, will be clear. For, once the certainty was obtained that the United States were prepared to accept full responsibility in a system of common defence and security, not only in the field of military deliveries but also in that of military action, any objection to the principle of a wider association had lost its justification.

It was clear that this wider association was not to be realized within the framework of the Brussels Pact, but in an altogether new treaty. To the Netherlands Government this was a point of minor importance; the main thing was to achieve the best results as quickly as possible. The Brussels Pact, after all, had served its purpose: it proved to be the beginning of a wider association.[1]

On the other hand, Holland was not prepared to welcome to this association all states which, on account of their strategic situations or other considerations, might well be regarded as likely candidates. When the Consultative Council took its decision referred to above, the following countries were stated

[1] Mem. Repl., Sec. Chamber, Dec. 13, 1948, 14.

to have been considered for inclusion: Norway, Denmark, Iceland, Ireland and Portugal.[1] The omission of Spain, in view of the invitation to Portugal, calls for comment. In December 1948 the Government had already pointed out that country's special position. They conceded that Spain's strategic position was such, that without its participation, the efficiency of European defence could not be maximized. Nevertheless, the country's political regime made its participation in the common defence, for the time being, inadvisable. The position of Spain, the Government added, was being closely watched by the Western powers, but the time had not yet come to draw any definite conclusions.[2]

And here the matter rested as far as 1948 was concerned. Thus, the course of events led to a considerable expansion of the Brussels Pact principle; but that wider association was to be embodied in a new treaty and a new organization. Netherlands foreign policy supported these developments; for they brought the realization of what the signatories of the Brussels Pact had foreseen and desired: a wide association in which one of the most powerful states assumed its share of the common responsibilities.

Once again, the subject of federalism must be mentioned – not in order to repeat the old arguments, but to refer to some aspects which were either new or assumed a new importance.

It would be wrong to underestimate the significance of this question. Of the many interesting features of the year 1948 not the least was the fact that large groups in the States General were consistently pressing the Government to go further on this road than the latter were prepared to go. Even at the end of 1948 the Netherlands Government showed every sign of persisting in their well known attitude.

But meanwhile new events had taken place. In May 1948 various movements working for European unity had organized a European Congress at the Hague, which had declared itself in favour of:

[1] Expl. Mem., North Atlantic Treaty, May 19, 1949, 8.
[2] Mem. Repl., Sec. Chamber, Dec. 13, 1948, 15.

a) the establishment of a European Parliamentary Assembly; and

b) a Charter of Human Rights with a European Court of Justice.

It had also presented, in a number of resolutions, proposals for the political, social and economic development of Europe.

When the Foreign Ministers of the Brussels Pact powers met in The Hague in July, 1948, Bidault referred to the Hague Congress; and at their October meeting in Paris the five Governments agreed that the time had come for them to concern themselves actively with the increasing insistence on greater unity in Europe. As a result, a commission was created which was requested to examine the possibilities in this field and report accordingly.

It will be seen, then, that circumstances had, at long last, induced the Governments concerned to take a step which later was to result in the creation of the Council of Europe. That, however, belongs to the events of 1949 and will be discussed subsequently. What concerns us here is the question: what did the Netherlands Government say at the end of 1948 concerning these projects? There is, in the first place, no reason to suppose that the Netherlands objected to the establishment of the commission mentioned above. On the other hand, the Netherlands Government did not give any instructions to the members they appointed to the commission; nor were these members quite in agreement with respect to the course to be followed.[1] The proposals of the Netherlands members, therefore, were not made on the instruction of the Government and it is consequently noteworthy that at the end of 1948, the Government, on the whole, persisted in the attitude they had adopted on earlier occasions. Mr. Stikker [2] stated in December that he preferred the functionalist approach to any other approach to federalism. The establishment of a federal European Assembly had been spoken of, but it was not clear how this Assembly was to be composed, it being obviously no body of government representatives. Was it intended that the national Parliaments would

[1] Sec. Chamber, Febr. 4, 1949, 1186/1187.
[2] See above, p. 3, n. 2.

appoint the members of the Assembly? The Government considered these questions most important.

On the other hand, what was the character of this new organ? If it were to be a purely advisory council of persons acting in a private capacity, it was felt that there really was no need to add yet another international council to the many which existed already and often did excellent work. If, however, the Assembly were to be invested with a supra-national authority, binding for all countries concerned, "some objections to such a course should be seriously considered". For instance, was it not possible in that case that the influence of national public opinion which, in the present circumstances, might have a considerable effect on the course of international developments, would be seriously curtailed?

Again, the question of the delimitation of the powers and authority of the national governments on the one hand, and of the European Assembly on the other, might produce serious complications. If it were intended that the European community had a foreign policy of its own and that, in other words, questions of trade policy, of nationality and armaments were to be settled in a European community – as opposed to a community of sovereign states – then the Government felt bound to state that such ideas had no relation whatever to reality.

Or again, if it were supposed that each Government remained responsible for their foreign policy but that, at the same time, the European Assembly was empowered to take binding decisions in the field of foreign policy – would such an arrangement not produce a situation which, from the practical point of view, would be quite unworkable? Who would accept responsibility for foreign policy, if that policy might at any given moment be obstructed by decisions of a European Assembly, on the composition of which the national governments were to have no influence at all?

This was the gist of Mr. Stikker's statement [1]; it will be observed that he exposed the fundamental difficulties in a more exhaustive manner than had been done hitherto. For the rest, the Government said they were perfectly ready to adhere to the terms of the Resolution of April 23; but they were careful in reminding the

[1] Mem. Repl., Sec. Chamber, Dec. 13, 1948, 13.

Chamber of the precise character of that Resolution – in other words, of the reservations made therein! [1]

It must be admitted that this statement was not exactly encouraging. Nevertheless, in 1949 the Government were to show a slightly more forthcoming attitude, as will be clear from the decisions of the five powers of January 28, 1949 which we shall discuss in a following chapter.

Thus we have come to the end of our discussion of General Policy in 1948 – a year, it will be conceded, of the greatest significance in the history of Netherlands foreign policy.

A period of hesitancy, of uncertainty was brought to an end; the great decision was made; the Netherlands had thrown in their lot with the Western powers.

It is clear that the seemingly irreconcilable parting of the ways between the Western powers and Russia was the decisive factor in this reorientation. The Government statements of 1946 and 1947 show that the Netherlands accepted this state of affairs with the greatest reluctance, but once the fact was faced that the policy of universal co-operation had collapsed, that agreement between the four great powers was impossible to achieve, the reorientation followed immediately; and its consequences were generally accepted with good grace. Generally; but there were exceptions.

Nothing indicates the change better than the tenor of the Government's statements about the general principles of their foreign policy at the end of the year. The problems of the closer association with the other Western European powers are stated to be the main preoccupation of the Government. The process of consolidating and developing this association may be a difficult one; and it is certainly less spectacular than the activities aiming at a universal co-operation, but the results are stated to be more tangible and more rewarding.[2] The essential difference of this statement, compared with those of 1945, 1946 and 1947, is obvious.

Equally different is the treatment of the rupture between the great powers. These bad relations are to be regretted; and the

[1] Mem. Repl., Sec. Chamber, Dec. 13, 1948, 13.
[2] Mem. Repl., Sec. Chamber, Dec. 13, 1948, 10.

Netherlands, like the other Western European powers, would rejoice if these differences could be solved in a satisfactory manner. But – and this again is an interesting departure of preceding attitudes – the whole question is viewed in the light of the well known proverb: what cannot be cured must be endured. For the time being Netherlands policy saw no solution to the problem; the Government could only note the facts and take their measures accordingly.

No doubt it could be considered that the new orientation was not without its disadvantages to the country. In this connexion we should speak of one further aspect of this question, an aspect which has only been slightly alluded to above. It will be remembered that when the Brussels Pact was debated in the States General, some bitter remarks were made about the British attitude in the Indonesian affair. In fact, in evaluating the significance of the Brussels Pact and the reorientation in Netherlands foreign policy, it must always be borne in mind that the Kingdom also had overseas territories. And it might be argued that in concluding the Brussels Pact, Holland allied itself with powers which adopted in the Indonesian problem a kind of neutrality which was harmful to Netherlands interests, or, even worse, a policy of downright obstruction and sabotage. Now, the remarks made in April 1948 were rather moderate in character; but later, when proposals for a still closer association were discussed in the Consultative Council of the Brussels Pact, the comments were rather more outspoken. It was pointed out that it seemed a dubious privilege to enter into closer association with those powers which had consistently worked against Netherlands interests in the Far East; and not only in the Far East, also in the Security Council. "Britain supports a resolution inimical to our interests; France does not raise her voice; only our faithful friend Belgium has the courage to speak for us".[1] The Government were asked whether it was not more urgent for them to co-operate with states with similar interests in South East Asia – in other words, whether co-ordination in S.E. Asia was not more important to Holland than a Western European Bloc? Furthermore, could one really believe in the significance of a Western European Bloc without co-ordination in S.E. Asia?

[1] Sec. Chamber, February 1, 1949, 1125.

What was the value of the Netherlands – or, for that matter, of France – if the overseas territories were lost? [1]

These quotations indicate the nature of the problem which the Government no doubt considered when the great decision of March 17, 1948 was taken; and they also indicate the sentiments and the point of view of those who felt that the Brussels Pact, this reorientation in foreign policy, was no unmixed blessing. It is to be observed that *these* critics were not moved by any mistaken belief in the merits of the old neutrality policy.

But Netherlands policy consistently rejected the implied consequences of such views. It was maintained that the ultimate interest, i.e. the security of Western Europe and, thus, of the Netherlands, should prevail. All co-operation with other powers demanded certain sacrifices. It was true that neither the United States nor Britain supported Holland in the Indonesian affair; in fact, they obstructed Holland's policy. It was true that both countries showed little understanding for Netherlands claims upon, and Netherlands interests in, Germany.

As against this, it was an undeniable fact that the security of Western Europe was safeguarded only by the power of the United States. Thus the question arose: what was, from the point of view of Netherlands interests, the decisive factor? The obstruction in Indonesia and Germany, or protection in Europe? The Government's answer was: the security of the territory in Europe: *"Our first task is to see to it that our own country is protected in the best manner possible"*; and from this point of view they never wavered. [2]

---

[1] The sharp character of these comments – as opposed to the more moderate remarks of April 1948 – is partly to be explained by the fact that meanwhile a new States General had been elected, but even more by the events of December 1948: the Netherlands Government had again clashed with the Security Council on account of the second police action in Indonesia. Tempers were high; and Members were more outspoken than ever before under the influence of these developments.

[2] Stikker in Sec. Chamber, Febr. 4, 1949, 1182.

CHAPTER IX

1948: GERMANY

After the failure of the London Conference in December 1947, the Governments of France, Britain and the United States considered that they could not go on having one abortive conference after another; a number of political and economic problems in Germany had to be settled, and if this could not be done with Russia, it should be done without her. Consequently, they decided on a three power conference in London to discuss the line of action which should be followed in the new circumstances.[1]

As we have seen, the Netherlands Government were well aware of the effects which the breach between the great powers might have as far as their aims and objectives in Germany were concerned. With renewed vigour, therefore, they insisted that they should be included in the coming talks. There was, of course, nothing new in this insistence; in fact, they had so insisted on many earlier occasions and always with a singular lack of success. But the Brussels Pact negotiations afforded Holland and the other Benelux countries an opportunity of pressing their demands again in more favourable circumstances. There is certainly no doubt that they made the fullest possible use of this opportunity. However, the question was difficult and a source of irritation. At long last, the Benelux Governments received an invitation on February 23, 1948 – but to what exactly were they invited?

According to a State Department Press Release of February 20, 1948, it was hoped that "the Benelux Countries will be afforded an opportunity to present their views". This meant nothing more than a simple hearing and there was no reason why this should be acceptable to the Netherlands. After all, they had had a hearing before, in 1947; and it is doubtful

---

[1] Note on German problem, 3.

whether the experience called for a repetition. In fact, on February 24, Baron van Boetzelaer warned that Benelux insisted on full participation in the discussion of all problems, with the exception, of course, of those which were the direct responsibility of the occupying powers.[1] It is easy to understand, however, that "participation" of Benelux might create difficulties in other quarters. It might provoke Russia; other "middle" powers might well insist that what was granted to the Benelux countries should be granted to them; finally, what would be the policy of Benelux in the Conference? – an interesting question, considering the fact that the three great powers were not in complete agreement about what should be done with Germany!

All this strongly suggests that the Benelux Governments had to fight for their demands; but they gained their point, for in the words of the communiqué of March 6, they took part "on an equal footing, in the discussions of all items on the agenda, except those dealing with administrative matters which are the direct responsibility of the occupying powers controlling the three occupied areas". From February 26 onwards, a joint Benelux delegation, headed by the Netherlands Ambassador in London, Jonkheer Michiels van Verduynen and including Dr. H. M. Hirschfeld, Netherlands Government Commissioner, participated in the work of the Conference.

The London Six Power Conference, the importance of which for Holland's German policy may well be compared to that of the Brussels Pact for the country's general policy, took place from February 23 until June 1, 1948; and its work was accomplished in three distinct phases. The first, from February 23 until March 6, was given over to general discussions, after which the Conference adjourned until April 10; during the intermission a number of working parties assembled in Berlin to examine various aspects of the problems discussed, such as the relations of the Benelux powers to the Military Governors in Germany, the economic co-operation between the Bizone and the French Zone, the administrative, economic and financial aspects of an eventual fusion between these two Zones, the future political organization of Germany and finally, the

[1] First Chamber, Febr. 24, 1948, 183.

safeguarding of the rights of foreign owners of the coal and steel industries in the Ruhr and elsewhere in Germany.

These working parties submitted their reports and conclusions to the Conference which met again on April 19; and after protracted negotiations, a Final Report was signed embodying a number of recommendations to the Governments concerned, which are commonly known as the London Resolutions. This Report was not made public, but its principal features were mentioned in the Final Communiqué of June 7, 1948 [1]

The Netherlands entered the Conference with certain objectives which covered a number of problems, the following of which may be mentioned first, as they were, in fact, equally important to *all* Benelux countries:

a) association of Benelux with Allied policy towards Germany;
b) the political and economic organization of Germany;
c) the question of the Ruhr;
d) the protection of foreign interests in the Ruhr and elsewhere; and
e) reparations.

Most of these questions, and the Netherlands views on them have already been discussed; but as regards the Netherlands capital interests in Germany and reparations, some further details about developments since 1945/1946 may be of assistance.[2]

The Netherlands capital interests were, as we have seen, still quite considerable and their maintenance and protection claimed the constant attention of the Government. In 1949 they told the States General that they had taken numerous steps in this matter in Berlin, London, Washington, Paris and Moscow; but the results had been disappointing.[3] As far as the capital interests in the Russian Zone were concerned, the position was

---

[1] There was also an interim Communiqué at the end of the first session of the Six Power Conference, dated March 6, 1948. Both Communiqués will be found in full in Appendix 10.

[2] See also above, p. 26ff.

[3] Note on German problem, 20.

"most precarious": "the nationalizations carried out there, as well as the manner in which the Occupying Authorities have arranged control of Allied property in that zone, still makes it impossible to obtain an accurate view of the position of the Netherlands interests, despite the great deal of attention devoted to this subject by the Netherlands Military Mission in Berlin. Practically all Netherlands owners in this zone are in the unsatisfactory position that they are not permitted to exercise their rights of ownership".[1]

That was perhaps only to be expected; but the situation in the Western zones also left much to be desired. The Government made it clear that the Western occupation authorities paid little or no attention to the rights of Netherlands owners in their zones. The right to dispose of their property had not been fully restored to them; bank balances of Netherlands subjects were still blocked and could not even be used for new investments. Netherlands industrial interests in the Ruhr were threatened. In short: "The Government regard the continuation of these restrictions which are not applicable to Germans, as a flagrant example of discrimination".[2]

From these statements (which, although dated July 1949, give a pretty fair description of the situation in the beginning of 1948) it will be clear that the Netherlands Government had every reason to welcome frank discussions with the Western powers, and the Six Power Conference made this possible. For Holland, the important question was whether or not the Western occupying powers would agree to an arrangement for the transfer of the proceeds of capital emanating from Netherlands investments in Germany. That such an arrangement should cover *old* investments, was, of course, essential.

As to reparations, it must be said that the value of goods allocated to the Netherlands remained quite small. In fact, up to November 1, 1948, it amounted to 27.145.410 R.M. (1938 values); to which should be added the German assets in Holland at the time of the liberation – some Fl. 170.000.000.—.[3]

[1] Note on German problem, 20.
[2] Note on German problem, 20.
[3] Mem. Repl., Sec. Chamber, Dec. 13, 1948, 18.

It is clear that these amounts were of no importance really, when compared to the claim of roughly Fl. 25.000.000.000 which had been submitted in 1945 by the Netherlands Government. The explanation of these disappointing developments must be sought in the whole course of events in and around Germany which finally resulted in a much smaller number of manufacturing plants being available for reparations.

As to the recovery of stolen property, "important results have been reached, although. . . . only a small part of the total plunder could be recovered. In all, goods to the value of some Fl. 200.000.000 (1938 value) have been returned to the Netherlands. Moreover, the country recovered about Fl. 200.000.000 of monetary gold".[1] Nevertheless, here too, the Government intended to make full use of the Conference to discuss these matters with the occupying powers.

The Benelux powers were equally concerned with all these questions; but there was an additional problem in which the Netherlands – as opposed to Benelux as a whole – were particularly interested. Holland had formulated demands upon Germany, both territorial and economic, which went beyond those submitted by either Belgium or Luxemburg. The Netherlands Government had never received a satisfactory reaction to these claims from the Allies; accordingly, the Government went to the Conference determined to press for a decision in this matter. For they clearly realized that the London meeting was likely to provide the last opportunity for presenting these claims with any chance of success at all.[2]

Thus it will be seen that the Netherlands objectives at the Conference did not deviate from the views formulated in the 1946 and 1947 Memoranda; and in fact, Baron van Boetzelaer confirmed that these documents were the basis of the directives given to the Netherlands delegates.[3]

The degree of success or rather, the relative failure of the Netherlands in London and, for that matter, the whole Conference, cannot be fully appreciated unless considered in the light of the then prevailing world situation. For it was that situ-

[1] Note on German problem, 15.
[2] Stikker in First Chamber, April 21, 1949, 518.
[3] Van Boetzelaer in Sec. Chamber, March 18, 1948, 1563.

ation – and very little else – that formed the decisive factor in the developments of the Six Power meeting. Time and again, Netherlands ministers, in explaining the events of London, have sorrowfully stressed the importance of that factor.[1]

It is not our purpose to discuss the London meeting in detail. But a few words about these general aspects are necessary. The Conference, itself the product of the conflict between the four great powers, showed very quickly that the rift between the West and Russia had become the dominant feature of the international situation; it had, in fact, assumed an overwhelming importance. As a result, the Conference witnessed a clash between two opposing views within the West; to a certain extent it was the old controversy, previously referred to when we spoke of a basic contradiction in Western policy towards Germany. But the circumstances were different from those of 1946.

The two opposing views can be briefly summarized as follows. The first, represented in its radical form by the United States, contended that the breach with the Soviet Union imposed the duty upon the Western powers of bringing Western Germany into their orbit and of keeping it there. It was therefore in their interest to refrain from all measures likely to harm Germany and to evoke anti-western bias in that country. The Western powers, it was held, could not afford to deal harshly with Germany, nor could they, for obvious reasons, afford to lose much time arguing about this.[2]

In general terms: this view accepted the rift between the West and Russia as the ultimate fact of the international situation and considered, consequently, that all moves, all calculations should be weighed in the light of their effect upon the balance of power between the Western powers and the Soviet Union. Whatever might be said and, indeed, has been said of this policy, it was at least a consistent one.

Those who supported the opposite view – France, for instance –

[1] Van Boetzelaer in Sec. Chamber, March 18, 1948, 1563 and April 23, 1948, 1642; Mem. Repl., Sec. Chamber, Dec. 13, 1948, 19; Stikker in Sec. Chamber, Febr. 4, 1949, 1183; Mem. Repl., Sec. Chamber, frontier rectifications, April 1, 1949, 5; (Prime Minister) Drees in Second Chamber, *idem*, April 6, 1949, 1411; Stikker in First Chamber, *idem*, April 21, 1949, 517.

[2] The Prime Minister (Sec. Chamber, *idem*, April 6, 1949, 1411) referred to this aspect of the question in particular.

did not deny that the rift, with its possible consequences, was a serious matter; but that did not allow them to forget that Russia was not the only potential aggressor. To draw Western Germany into the Western orbit, was a most laudable objective. No doubt Germany should be treated less harshly than might have been necessary and, indeed, justified in other circumstances; great concessions should be granted; but certain minimum demands in the field of economic and military security could not be abandoned. Thus, the fundamental cause of the clash was a difference in appreciation of what the rupture between the great powers might ultimately imply. Was it so fateful in its consequences that, as some contended, everything else had to give way? Or was there still room, as others thought, for other objectives?

Much of all this recalls, no doubt, the controversies of 1945 and 1946; but much had changed since then. For one thing, the Russian factor, although far from being overlooked then, had not yet assumed that overwhelming and menacing importance which is so characteristic of the spring of 1948. For another, the French had dropped many of their original demands and objectives; but this had not narrowed the gap between them and the Americans and British; for the latter's policy, as we have seen, had also moved away from their original positions. Nor is all this difficult to understand if we bear in mind what happened in the years before the opening of the Six Power meeting. Furthermore, as the Conference met it witnessed the Russian coup in Czechoslovakia; after that event, tension rose perceptibly everywhere: the situation in Italy and Vienna gave rise to much anxiety. It is true that the Berlin crisis occurred after the end of the Conference, in the summer of 1948; but the Berlin crisis, like the coup in Prague, did not come quite unexpectedly. In fact, the Berlin affair was not produced by the London Resolutions. It was, in the first place, caused by the breakdown of the Four Power Conference of December 1947. A Russian riposte was no doubt fully expected; and it would have been surprising had the Western powers not thought of Berlin as a likely place for this riposte to take place.[1]

---

[1] We cannot, of course, discuss the possible influence of the Zhdanov group which, it has been alleged, was responsible for this riposte in its aggressive form (Cf. Borkenau, Der europäische Kommunismus, p. 490 ff.)

Nor must we, in considering the evolutions of American-British policy, overlook the economic factor. Both countries had spent immense sums on Germany; according to the data of the Netherlands Government, goods to a value of $ 2.000.000.000 had been imported into Germany up to the end of 1948, at the expense of the British and American taxpayers. Can it be surprising that the British and American Governments now desired to place the German economy on a basis where it could meet its requirements without foreign support? But this implied, of course, opposition to all demands which would have an opposite effect, however slight.[1]

So, under the influence of power and circumstance, the chief antagonists had all moved away from their original positions, but instead of coming nearer each other, it appeared from the London Conference that their conceptions differed as much as ever.[2] This, of course, became particularly clear over questions such as the political organization of Germany.

Such points as the time factor, or the distribution of power between the central government and the various Laender, or the composition of the Constituent Assembly (elected or appointed members?) could only be settled after long and difficult negotiations; and the relevant sections of the two Communiqués clearly show what kind of compromises were eventually agreed upon: the French point of view had to give way. As to the Ruhr question, the same impression prevails. In short, the Conference was a battlefield of conflicting opinions; and its results – compromises painfully arrived at – were only accepted by the French with strong reservations and were more or less disliked by all.

Bearing in mind the nature of the opinions expressed in the Memoranda of 1946 and 1947, it need hardly be pointed out that the developments in the Conference confronted the Netherlands with more than one dilemma. Netherlands policy had never supported the original French demands; nor was Holland in the

[1] Note on German pioblem, 9.

[2] It is not impossible that the disagreements of the Six Power Conference might have been avoided, had the United States been in a position to extend the necessary guarantees to the Western European powers, not only against the Russian, but also against the German danger. In this connexion the importance of the presidential elections of November 1948 must not be overlooked, particularly as a Republican Administration was generally expected to come into office.

position to do so. But if the views of the Netherlands Memorandum of January 14, 1947 with respect to the political organization of Germany and the Ruhr-Rhine question are compared with the results of the 1948 Six Power meeting, the supposition may be hazarded that on more than one occasion the Netherlands delegates must have felt tempted to support the French position in the Conference. However that may be, it is clear that Holland had to make more than one concession in London – but they were not alone in that position. Yet, here was one more reason why the question of the Netherlands claims should now be discussed and decided, the more so as this matter could not be dissociated from the question of the German Government and the German Constituent Assembly. From the Netherlands point of view it was, therefore, clearly necessary that decisions should be taken before the Constituent Assembly met.

It is, however, evident that the Dutch claims met with no encouraging response. In fact, the opposite was true. The Final Communiqué gives only a slight indication of what happened; but when the question of the Netherlands-German frontier was discussed in the States General in April 1949, the Netherlands Government freely disclosed the difficulties with which their delegates had had to contend. Both Britain and the United States considered the Dutch claims most inopportune, *a*) on political grounds, which will be clear after what has been said above; and *b*) on economic grounds, for they felt that, quite apart from what they had already spent on Germany, with the establishment of ERP all economic claims upon Germany should now be dropped. For, after all, who were to shoulder the cost of granting such claims? Either the occupying powers or the United States via ERP! In short, for both political and economic reasons America and Britain were not prepared to fulfil the Dutch claims in toto. Then to what did they, after all, assent?

In this respect the Final Communiqué is only too clear. The words "minor provisional territorial adjustments" leave little room for doubt. In the first place, it is to be noted that not a word was said about economic claims. Thus it follows – and this was later confirmed by the Netherlands Government – that, although the Netherlands territorial and economic claims should have been regarded as an inseparable whole, the economic demands were either dropped or reserved for later discussion, presumably at the final Peace Conference. As it was clear that this Conference was still a long way off, the fact had to be recognized that the economic claims had come to nothing.

The term "minor territorial adjustments" clearly implied that only purely technical "anomalies" were to be considered. The Netherlands Memoranda had attached great importance to the correction of the Netherlands-German frontier in various technical respects; but some of the proposed rectifications could not be described as "minor".

The Communiqué's reference to minor adjustments was therefore significant: not even all technical claims were granted; in fact, those with respect to the Eems and the Dollard – both most important – were refused.[1]

The Netherlands delegation was naturally disappointed; and it is perhaps not without significance that according to the Final Communiqué (p. 225) "the delegations have agreed to SUBMIT for the consideration of their Governments etc" – the word "recommend" does not appear!

Before summing up the final results of the Conference, as far as Holland was concerned, the following points may be briefly mentioned:

a) the association of Western Germany with the economic life of Western Europe was welcomed by the Netherlands Government. The Memorandum of January 14, 1948, Section II, already considered this as most desirable. And at the Paris Conference of July–September 1947, the Netherlands delegation had also insisted on Germany being included in the Organization for European Economic Co-operation.

b) as regards the security problem, the following words of the Final Communiqué were of special interest. Under "General Provisions" it was stated that "the Governments concerned should consult if any of them should consider that there was a danger of resurgence of German military power or of the adoption by Germany of a policy of aggression". It is clear that the

---

[1] See for particulars regarding the demarcation of the frontier in the Dollard and the Eems estuary, Netherlands Memorandum of November 5, 1946, Annex II (Appendix 6).

"Governments concerned" referred to the United States, the United Kingdom and France. It would seem therefore that the Benelux countries were excluded from this arrangement which of course might be of a wider application than that stated in the Final Communiqué. Yet they would be as closely concerned as any of the powers mentioned if the case referred to were to materialize. It is, however, clear that the Benelux countries, in such an eventuality, could always make use of the organs of the Brussels Pact – the Consultative Council, for instance.[1]

The results of the Six Power Conference, as far as Benelux as a whole, and the Netherlands in particular were concerned, may be summarized as follows:

a) Benelux had obtained a certain degree of association with allied policy in Germany (Final Communiqué, I).

b) Benelux was to be fully associated with the preparation "of a more detailed agreement setting up the International Authority for the Ruhr", in which the three countries were to have one vote each (Final Communiqué, II and Annex).

c) With respect to non-discrimination against, and the protection of, foreign interests in Germany, it was agreed that the Benelux powers would be further associated in the study of these questions in an inter-governmental group, charged with submitting recommendations to the Governments concerned. The principle of non-discrimination was reaffirmed. (Final Communiqué, II, C).

d) As for the political organization of Germany, the principle of a federal state was maintained. (Final Communiqué, III, A).

e) Regarding the territorial and economic claims of the Netherlands upon Germany, it was decided to submit to the Governments concerned proposals for dealing with "certain minor provisional territorial adjustments in connection with the western frontiers of Germany". Economic claims were not mentioned. (Final Communiqué, IV).

Viewed as a whole, these results cannot have given grounds for great satisfaction; the Netherlands, in particular, had every

[1] That the Benelux countries could not be consulted in the same manner as the occupying countries is easily explainable; for this would have meant the creation of a kind of consultative pact which would have produced constitutional difficulties in the United States. See also Note on German problem, 14.

reason to be disappointed as far as the response to their claims was concerned. And yet, in one respect the Benelux countries may well have felt that they had achieved something of importance. At long last, a machinery was set up, viz. the various working groups and the Ruhr Authority, through which Benelux could defend its specific interests and voice its opinion about points of allied policy with respect to Germany. All this was no doubt a step in the right direction, a step for which the Benelux Governments had worked long and earnestly. And from this point of view, even the claims question had an encouraging aspect. For a long time the Netherlands Government had waited for a reaction from their Allies – in vain; now at least they knew that, however unsatisfactory the response, the question was being dealt with.

And so, on June 12, the Benelux Governments stated that they approved the Recommendations on Germany, the substance of which had been made public in the Final Communiqué of June 7, 1948.

In conclusion, a few words about the inter-governmental working groups which followed the Conference. These groups were charged with the elaboration of the London Resolutions which had meanwhile been approved by all Governments concerned.[1] There were three of them, dealing respectively with *a*) the corrections of the western German frontier, *b*) the protection of allied capital interests in Germany and *c*) the establishment of an International Authority for the Ruhr. In all these groups the Netherlands were represented and "important work could be accomplished".[2] In the first group no final results were achieved until 1949, but it was clear from the beginning that the Netherlands desiderata regarding technical frontier adjustments met with even less understanding and sympathy than in London. In fact, Britain in particular opposed all but the most insignificant modifications of the border.[3]

[1] The French National Assembly made reservations on a number of points. However, the London Resolutions had to be accepted or rejected in toto; accordingly the other powers refused to resume discussions on the controversial points. The reservations of the Assembly will be found in Appendix 11.

[2] Note on German problem, 4.

[3] Drees in Second Chamber (frontier rectifications), April 6, 1949, 1411; Mem. Repl., First Chamber, *idem*, April 14, 1949, 5. See also: 1949, Germany, below, p. 133.

The group dealing with the problem of the allied capital interests in Germany, produced a number of recommendations with which the Netherlands Government were in complete agreement.[1] The group recommended, inter alia, that facilities should be provided for the transfer of D.M. earnings of existing properties and investments and thought that the OEEC might be of assistance in this matter.

However, the United States Government were opposed to this; they felt that as long as they were obliged to support the German economy, other nations should not weaken it by transfer of earnings. To this argument, the other countries concerned replied by pointing out that they could hardly be expected to strengthen the German economy by making new investments in that country, as long as the question of the existing investments had not been settled satisfactorily. For the time being, then, no results were achieved; but in 1949 the Netherlands Government stressed once again that "confidence in this sphere (could) only be restored", if arrangements for the transfer of earnings of old investments were agreed to.[2]

So much for the Six Power meeting of 1948. Its true significance lies in the fact that it marked a turning-point in the post-war history of the German problem. Netherlands policy towards Germany, it will be remembered, was based on the principles of Potsdam and the assumption of Four Power agreement. By the end of 1947 these bases were no longer valid; and the new situation found its expression, first, in the very meeting of the six powers, second, in the London Resolutions. Thus, as far as Holland was concerned, the Conference served as an unmistakable reminder of what had already been clear enough at the end of 1947: in the new circumstances the old policy could no longer be followed; here, too, "reconsideration" was necessary.

Is there any evidence, as far as the year 1948 is concerned, that the Netherlands Government were aware of this? And can this be shown in the emergence of a new Netherlands policy towards Germany?

[1] Note on German problem, 20.
[2] Note on German problem, 20. See also, below, p. 283.

As regards the first question, it is true that in December 1948 the Government thought it right to give a word of warning on two points. For instance, speaking of German reparations, they said that, in their opinion, these should be carried out according to previously made plans, but it should be realized that in the *application of these plans, account must be taken of the ultimate Netherlands and Allied interests.*[1]

Again, referring to the Netherlands claims upon Germany, the Government stated that they would certainly maintain their demands; what had not been granted in London, was to be retabled at the Peace Conference; but they warned the States General that such claims had political aspects which could not be dissociated from the general international situation.[2]

Such statements, although none too clear, are nevertheless proof of the fact that the Government were aware of the inevitable consequences of the London Resolutions. All the same, it will be noted that they did not go so far as to drop their demands altogether; but this may have been due to the same reason as why their warnings were so carefully worded: the subject of the claims, at that time, could still evoke strong emotional reactions in the country.[3]

It cannot be said, however, that the London events led to a new Netherlands policy towards Germany – at least in 1948. The Government reiterated that the integration of Germany into European economic co-operation was one of their principal objectives and they stressed that, without such integration, the reconstruction of Europe was bound to fail.[4]

But this was nothing new: in 1947 already, and again during the Brussels Pact negotiations, Holland had urged the desirability of German economic co-operation and had even foreseen the inevitability of political co-operation with that country. It would not appear, therefore, that a new element had been added to the country's German policy, but this impression may be

[1] Mem. Repl., Sec. Chamber, Dec. 13, 1948, 19.

[2] Mem. Repl., Sec. Chamber, Dec. 13, 1948, 19.

[3] It was observed in the Second Chamber that, for many people, the question of the territorial claims was the beginning and the end of Holland's German policy (Sec. Chamber, Febr. 1, 1949, 1112).

[4] Mem. Repl., Sec. Chamber, Dec. 13, 1948, 17.

misleading. Though little was said in public, it would be rash to conclude that nothing was being done in the way of reorientation. In fact, the Government statements of a few months later, in 1949, were to show the contrary.

We must now resume our survey of the developments in Netherlands-German economic relations during 1948. The first trade agreement with the Bizone was concluded in July 1948. This was an important event for the following reasons. It has been pointed out above that the trade lists of 1947, drawn up in consultation with JEIA, did not mention the Netherlands exports of agrarian produce to Germany. In other words, the occupation authorities were not prepared to admit that these products were a normal item and an essential part of Holland's traditional exports to Germany. This was for the Netherlands a point of absolutely prime importance. As long as the allied authorities were not willing to concede this point, there was, in truth, little reason for Holland to press for further trade discussions.

The true significance of the 1948 Agreement is to be found in the fact that the Dutch point was at long last admitted. Account was taken of the fact that about half the products to be supplied from the Netherlands should emanate from the agrarian sector.[1] Inter alia, a quota of some 200.000 tons of vegetables was admitted to the commodity lists. The 1948 Agreement, then, meant, to a certain extent, a return to the normal pattern of traditional German-Netherlands trade relations. In other respects, however, no great changes were introduced. Trade relations remained strongly regulated; the quotas granted, moreover, were relatively small. Finally, at times it was found difficult to realize the quota allowed.

Consequently it was not long before new difficulties emerged. At the end of 1948, the pressure on the Netherlands currency reserves, in particular the dollar reserves, had become exceedingly strong.

For what had happened? In the first place, revenues from services rendered to Germany were considerably lower than originally estimated. Secondly, JEIA often refused import

[1] Note on German problem, 16/17.

licences for Netherlands goods, in spite of the fact that quotas for such products had been granted in the 1948 Agreement. Thirdly, the immensely successful monetary reform of June 20, 1948 in Western Germany led to a considerable shortening of German delivery terms for goods to be exported to Holland which, of course, resulted in a higher out-flow of Netherlands foreign currency.

There were two alternative policies to remedy this situation. The authorities could either reduce the volume of total trade, or they could increase the Netherlands export quota. Only the second alternative was acceptable to the Netherlands; hence the supplementary agreement of December 1948, according to which the Netherlands could export extra goods and services to Germany to an amount of $ 30.000.000; and the Bizone to Holland to an amount of only $ 17.000.000. It would, then, be utterly misleading to say that the trade agreement with the Bizone had solved all difficulties in the field of Netherlands-German trade relations. This was definitely not the case. On the other hand, it resulted in a "considerable extension of the exchange of goods and services".[1] Still more important was the fact that the agreement restored, *in principle*, the traditional position of the Netherlands vis-à-vis Germany.

The Netherlands Government also concluded commercial a-greements with the Russian Zone. "Trade with the Russian Zone showed quite satisfactory developments, despite the many difficulties which exist there as well".[2] The Netherlands authorities attached great importance to these trade relations with the Russian zone (and, for that matter, the satellite countries). In fact, here was one more reason why the Nether-lands Government regretted the division of Germany, with all its consequences – it formed a serious obstacle to a satisfactory development of Netherlands trade with the Russian Zone.[3]

And yet, the general situation left much to be desired. In the first place, the total volume of Netherlands-German trade in the

[1] Note on German problem, 16.
[2] *ibid.*, 17.
[3] Stikker in Sec. Chamber, Febr. 4, 1949, 1183.

period of July 1948 until July 1949 did not amount to more than some 25% of the pre-war volume![1] But there was more. What was the position with respect to transfer of proceeds on Netherlands investments in Germany and revenue from services rendered? As regards the first item, little need be added to what has been said above: transfer was not allowed.

As for revenue from services rendered, this brings us once again to the subject of Netherlands shipping on the Rhine and the relations of Netherlands ports with their German hinterland.

At the end of 1947 the position of Netherlands shipping on the Rhine was bad. After the abortive agreement of July 1947 and the equally futile discussions of October 1947, no new steps were taken until, with the advent of the Marshall Plan, it seemed that a new climate had been created, less favourable to autarchic tendencies which hitherto had formed an obstacle to any satisfactory solution of the problem in question. Accordingly, after consultations between the Netherlands and Belgian Governments, another series of talks took place at Frankfort, June 10 and 11, 1948. It was, however, not until September that certain results were achieved. These were laid down in a "Summary of conversations and agreements, reached between the Netherlands and Belgian representatives with JEIA, Frankfort, September 24, 1948".[2] The two main points were the following:

a) in the choice between German and Benelux ports, the currency argument will no longer play a part; *b*) the occupation authorities withdraw their objections to the distribution of transit traffic between the Netherlands and Belgian ports, as desired by the Netherlands and Belgium, and to the establishment of an organ entrusted with this task – the so called "Rhine Central Booking Office".[3]

Thus it seemed that, from the Benelux point of view, real progress had been made. There was, it is true, no formal agreement; it was rather a gentlemen's agreement [4]; but the Netherlands Government attached great importance to these arrangements.[5]

[1] Note on German problem, 17.
[2] Mem. Repl., Sec. Chamber, Dec. 13, 1948, 18.
[3] Note on German problem, 18/19.
[4] Mem. Repl., Sec. Chamber, Dec. 13, 1948, 18.
[5] Mem. Repl., Sec. Chamber, Dec. 13, 1948, 18.

But when, after complications which need not be mentioned, they began to take effect, the practical results, from the Netherlands point of view, were rather disappointing.[1]

For example, in the sector of food imports (which were financed completely by the occupation authorities), only 10% of the total volume was as yet directed via Benelux ports. The discrimination against Netherlands shipping in German internal traffic did not stop; on the contrary, it formed an obstacle which, in the words of the Netherlands Government, "was actually tantamount to a lock-out".[2] The special charges on the German railways, which in reality constituted a discrimination against the ports of the Low Countries also continued as before. It is clear, therefore, that in practice nothing much had changed.[3]

Considering the problem of Netherlands-German relations as a whole, it must be said that the Netherlands had no reason for optimism. The Trade Agreement of August 1948, it is true, was a step in the right direction; but after all, it was only the beginning of a beginning. The root of the trouble was that the Netherlands were everywhere confronted with what was, in fact, an autarchic policy in Germany – a policy which, in the opinion of the Netherlands Government, should be resolutely opposed. They continued to protest against this discrimination. These discriminating policies conflicted not only with Netherlands interests, but also with Western European interests. The responsible bodies in Germany were obviously unwilling or

[1] Note on German problem, 19.
[2] Note on German problem, 19.
[3] The following figures may be of interest.

Comparison between the traffic in the North West
German ports and transit traffic in the principal
Benelux Ports

	1938		1948	
	Mill. tons	% total traffic	Mill. tons	% total traffic
Benelux ports (transit)	35	51	5.3	26
N.W. German ports	33.5	49	15	74
	68.5	100	20.3	100

(Netherlands Memorandum on the Netherlands-German Economic Relations, October, 1949, 2; see Appendix 16. See also, Note on te German problem, 18).

unable to understand that the Netherlands, a country of great importance for the German economy, could not continue being a considerable consumer of German products unless they were given an opportunity of earning the foreign currency necessary for that purpose. Nor could the Netherlands Government understand how such policies could be reconciled with the avowed aim of the Allied powers to associate Germany in the widest possible measure with the economic life of Western Europe. The Netherlands Government supported such objectives and conceptions; but they felt that discriminatory policies had no place in them.[1]

[1] Note on German problem, *passim*; Stikker in Sec. Chamber, Febr. 4, 1949, 1184.

CHAPTER X

1949: GENERAL POLICY

THE NORTH ATLANTIC TREATY

In October 1948, as we have seen, the Consultative Council of the Brussels Pact had approved the principle of a defensive pact for the North Atlantic area; and the next step was the drafting of the actual treaty which started on December 10 in Washington. On the other hand, the consultations with Norway, Denmark, Iceland, Ireland and Portugal took place in the beginning of January 1949; while on January 14, it was announced in the United States that countries prepared to enter some form of defence arrangement with the United States would enjoy preferential treatment with respect to U.S. deliveries of strategic raw materials and war material. However, the countries consulted – with the exception of Norway – did not react immediately; the negotiations between the five Brussels Pact powers, the United States and Canada therefore proceeded as before; and thus, although some time before, the Brussels Pact nations had expressed the fear that these consultations might prove a source of undesirable delays, such delays were in fact avoided. On March 18 the agreed text of the treaty could be published; and on April 4, 1949 Denmark, Norway, Iceland, Portugal and Italy signed with the seven original powers the North Atlantic Treaty.[1]

The conclusion of the North Atlantic Treaty was an event of great importance, not only for the participating countries, but also in international affairs as a whole. And apart from its general aspects, the Treaty was no doubt of specific significance for the United States, inasmuch as it marked a turning-point in their traditional policy towards – in the words of George Washington – the "ordinary vicissitudes" of European politics. If,

[1] The text of the Treaty is given in Appendix 12. The speech of Mr. Stikker on that occasion will be found in Appendix 13.

however, we consider the Treaty purely from the point of view of Netherlands foreign policy, and particularly in the light of the developments of the period 1945–1949, it will be clear that, however great its importance for Holland's security, it cannot be regarded as a turning-point in Holland's foreign policy: it was rather the logical continuation of the reorientation which was decided upon, or at any rate brought about, at the time of the Brussels Pact in 1948. The Netherlands, as we have seen, had always desired this wider association which included the United States and Canada; the identity of fundamental interests between Western Europe and North America, which economically found its expression in ERP, made such an association possible, and indeed, necessary; the Atlantic Treaty served the same ends as the Brussels Pact.

As far as the Netherlands Government were concerned – and the great majority of the States General supported that view [1] – both treaties were due to the legitimate desire of the contracting powers to ensure their national security,[2] which seemed threatened by the political expansion of the Soviet Union.[3]

Both pacts would have been unnecessary if the security arrangements of the United Nations had not collapsed, if the principles of collective security and universal co-operation had been successful; but this was not the case: "The Treaty we are about to sign marks the end of an illusion: the hope that the United Nations would, by itself, ensure international peace. Regretfully, we were driven to the conclusion that the Charter, though essential, is not enough in the world as it is, to protect those vital principles for which we of the Western world who have gathered here, stand. Therefore we felt it our duty to make this Treaty. So far from merely marking the end of an illusion it most especially marks the birth of a new hope of enduring peace".[4]

[1] Of course, the Communist Party and their representatives in the States General opposed the Treaty. Their position in this question was quite similar to that of their colleagues abroad and their arguments, which are internationally known, need no further elaboration here.

[2] Expl. Mem., North Atlantic Treaty (hereafter referred to as NAT), May 19, 1949, 7; Mem. Repl., Sec. Chamber, NAT, July 8, 1949, 17; Sec. Chamber, NAT, July 19, 1949, 1707 ff.

[3] Prov. Rep., Sec. Chamber, NAT, July 5, 1949, 13; Mem. Repl., Sec. Chamber, NAT, July 8, 1949, 17.

[4] Stikker in his Washington speech of April 4, 1949, see Appendix 13.

Actually, the North Atlantic Treaty, no less than the Brussels Pact, was the fruit of the failure of the United Nations' universal system.

Thus, as far as Netherlands foreign policy was concerned, the principle of the Treaty was no innovation; and the country's adhesion was generally supported. We shall, therefore, confine our discussion to a few points which, as was shown in the States General debates, were of specific interest to the Netherlands or acquired special significance if NATO's later difficulties are borne in mind.

In the first place, it must be recorded once again, that the Indonesian complications exercised their usual and unfortunate effects. There was full agreement with the Government's contention that the existence of friendly relations between the signatory powers was essential to the Treaty's success. But, it was asked, did such friendly relations really exist between the Netherlands on the one hand and Great Britain, the United States and Canada on the other? Were embargoes on arms deliveries not a sign of unfriendly intentions and did they not show an unfriendly tendency to interference in what was, according to the official Netherlands point of view, a purely internal affair? [1] Were discriminatory policies in Germany compatible with friendly relations? [2]

We have met with the same point of view before in connexion with the Pact of Brussels; and there is no point in repeating it in detail. But it should be pointed out that there was a fairly general doubt as to the implications of Article 4 of the Treaty, precisely on account of Indonesia. Did this article imply, it was asked, that Holland was obliged to consult all parties to the Treaty with respect to the Indonesian problem? And what would be the position if one or more signatories of the Treaty convicted another signatory of endangering peace and security in its own territory? [3]

These were obviously grave questions and it was impressed upon the Government that they could not be disposed of by saying that the Treaty was so important to Holland's security;

---

[1] Prov. Rep., Sec. Chamber, NAT, July 5, 1949, 14; Sec. Chamber, NAT, July 15, 1949, 1683, 1691, 1699, 1700.

[2] First Chamber, NAT, Aug. 3, 1949, 770/771.

[3] Prov. Rep., Sec. Chamber, NAT, July 5, 1949, 15.

this was true, but it was equally true that Holland was no less important to the other powers, for what would be the Treaty's value if Holland, the delta of Europe's great rivers, that point of intersection of strategic lines, did not participate? [1]

Mr Stikker, for his part, reaffirmed the Government's view that the Indonesian affair should be considered as a purely internal question, nor could Article 4 by any means license the contracting powers to meddle in each others affairs. If, further-more, it really should come to this, it would indicate a state of affairs in which there would be neither room nor reason for a Treaty like the present one.[2] For the rest, the Government had already made plain, in February 1949, the character of the alternatives between which the country had to choose; since then nothing had happened which could justify a change of mind.[3]

But the embargo question had other aspects as well. It was generally agreed that the world situation required the re-armament of Western Europe; and, as we have seen, the Brussels Pact powers had done something in that direction, although there were, of necessity, limits to their possibilities in this field. In fact, it was precisely this state of affairs which afforded one of the strongest reasons for the conclusion of the North Atlantic Treaty. Now, in accordance with Article 3 of the Treaty, the United States were expected to deliver arms, munitions and raw materials to the European powers, "to maintain and develop their individual and collective capacity to resist armed attack". Thus, the question arose whether the Netherlands Government considered the British and American embargoes compatible with Article 3; and it was pointed out to them that several members of the United States Congress had made statements to the effect that in this field discrimination should be applied against the Netherlands on account of Holland's policy in

[1] Sec. Chamber, NAT, July 15, 1949, 1684, 1691. In the First Chamber (Aug. 3, 1949, 770) the Government were urged to see to it that Holland's position among the Treaty powers should never be a subordinate one, a position which, for one thing, would not be in accordance with its strategic importance. In that connexion the Government were warned against the danger of the United States using the Treaty principally as a means to ensure their own security, a point of view which might have disastrous consequences for the Netherlands. In other words: the Netherlands expected to see its territory not merely *used*, but also *defended* by the allied armies.

[2] Mem. Repl., Sec. Chamber, NAT, July 8, 1949, 19.

[3] See above, p. 88.

Indonesia, which apparently did not quite meet with these members' approval. What, in these circumstances, it was asked, could Holland expect in connexion with Article 3? [1]

In his reply, Mr Stikker said that these statements were objectionable and regrettable; and the Netherlands, supported by the other powers of the Brussels Pact, had insisted during the negotiations that a successful realization of the Treaty could only be based on the principle of equal treatment of all participating powers.[2] Not without reason had the Foreign Minister stressed these words in his Washington speech.[3] In this connexion, he referred to an exchange of letters between the United States Government and those of the Brussels Pact nations, of April 5 and 6, 1949, according to which it would appear that for the United States, too, "entire solidarity" and "common defence" were guiding and fundamental principles. For the rest, the Netherlands had repeatedly protested against these embargoes; but it was not Holland's policy to make the ratification of the Treaty dependent upon the repeal of these restricting measures.

So far, this was exactly the position taken up in connexion with the Pact of Brussels. But this time the Government went a good deal further. Mr Stikker pointed out that the North Atlantic Treaty demanded much more from the Netherlands than from other participating nations.

The country had heavy military and economic commitments in Indonesia. Were the Netherlands in a position to discharge their responsibilities in Indonesia AND, at the same time, those toward their partners in the Treaty? That was the point, a point, moreover, which was clearly connected with the embargo question and the policies of Britain and the United States. Nobody could as yet give a definite answer to this question; but Mr Stikker made it plain that, if in the future the Netherlands would have to choose between those two sets of responsibilities, the Government would feel bound to grant priority to their responsibilities towards the peoples of Indonesia.[4] It could

[1] Prov. Rep., Sec. Chamber, NAT, July 5, 1949, 14.
[2] Mem. Repl., Sec. Chamber, NAT, July 8, 1949, 18.
[3] See Appendix 13.
[4] Stikker in Sec. Chamber, NAT, July 19, 1949, 1710/1711. It might be asked whether the Netherlands Government at that juncture were really still in a position to choose between the alternatives suggested.

be readily admitted that this was a highly unsatisfactory situation; and he sincerely hoped that these alternatives would not have to be faced. But it was not the fault of the Netherlands Government that the possibility of such a choice could not be entirely discarded. It was in the power of other Parties to the North Atlantic Treaty to put the Netherlands in a position which would enable them to participate fully – as they desired – in the realization of the common objectives. If, however, measures were taken which prevented the recovery of the Netherlands (Germany!) or which made the maintenance of law and order in, and the development of, the overseas territories impossible, it was not Holland that should be blamed, but rather the Governments responsible for such political and economic measures. Such divergences between co-operating allies could not, in the long run, be tolerated. This had been made quite clear to the Governments concerned; as for the Netherlands, they could only hope that such interfering and discriminating measures would soon belong – with the situations which had given rise to them – to the past.[1]

As for Article 5 of the Treaty, it is a well known fact that the formal obligations under this Article are less stringent and far-reaching than was the case in the Pact of Brussels. The reasons for this state of affairs need not be discussed here.[2] Although they were well appreciated in the States General, there was a certain amount of regret that a more stringent formula had been impossible to obtain. It was even contended that Article 5 might have discriminatory effects if one of the Brussels Pact powers were attacked, for in that case the other Brussels Pact nations would be involved automatically, but the rest of the Atlantic powers would not.[3]

---

[1] Stikker in Sec. Chamber, NAT, July 19, 1949, 1711.

[2] The essential paragraph of Article 5 is: "The Parties agree that an armed attack against one or more of them in Europe or North America shall be considered an attack against them all; and consequently they agree that, if such an armed attack occurs, each of them, in exercise of the right of individual or collective self-defence recognized by Article 51 of the Charter of the United Nations, will assist the Party or Parties so attacked by taking forthwith, individually and in concert with the other Parties, *such action as it deems necessary*, including the use of armed force, to restore and maintain the security of the North Atlantic area ...". It should be borne in mind that in the United States only Congress has the right to declare war; an automatic military aid formula was consequently out of the question.

[3] Sec. Chamber, NAT, July 15, 1949, 1691.

But the Government took a less sombre view of these matters. Mr. Stikker compared the Brussels Pact, the North Atlantic Treaty and the United Nations system to a set of three concentric circles. The inner circle was of course the Brussels Pact, with its completely automatic aid formula; then followed the North Atlantic Treaty with admittedly weaker mutual obligations; and finally, the United Nations system in which the aid formula was still less stringent. "In other words, if the Netherlands were to fall victim to an armed attack, the Brussels Pact allies would be involved automatically; the other Atlantic allies would have to consider at once what assistance should be rendered; finally, the Security Council might decide to render support".[1] This system, it was stated, was not unsatisfactory; at any rate, the formula of Article 5 was the best that could be obtained in the circumstances.[2]

In connexion with the Treaty, the position of various countries was referred to in the States General – for example, Spain. In the opinion of the contracting powers, that country could not, for the time being, become a party to the Treaty.[3] It was, however, put to the Government that, if Portugal were accepted, there seemed very little reason for excluding Spain. But the Government, fully maintaining their position of December 1948 [4], did not accept this argument. For, after all, the Security Council had seen fit to take certain measures in the case of Spain; in the case of Portugal they had not.

With respect to the possible adhesion of Turkey and Greece to the Treaty, the Government were of the opinion that they should not assume obligations where Netherlands interests were not directly or indirectly involved. This point of view was generally supported; and there was, particularly as far as Turkey was concerned, some doubt whether that country and the Western European nations really shared a "common heritage and civilization." [5] As regards Western Germany itw as

[1] Stikker in Sec. Chamber, NAT, July 19, 1949, 1709 ("... en tenslotte zal eventueel de Veiligheidsraad tot hulpverlening besluiten").
[2] Mem. Repl., Sec. Chamber, NAT, July 8, 1949, 18.
[3] Mem. Repl., Sec. Chamber, NAT, July 8, 1949, 18.
[4] See above, p. 83.
[5] Expl. Mem., NAT, May 19, 1949, 9; Prov. Rep., Sec. Chamber, NAT, July 5, 1949, 15.

felt that its co-operation in a rearmament programme at that juncture was not acceptable.[1]

Finally, the Government assured the States General that the whole territory of the Netherlands in Europe was covered by the Treaty. The whole country would be defended; and everything would be done to maximize its defence.

Some of these points discussed in the States General are merely of historical interest; but this was not the case with the following question which, indeed, was to become far more topical later than it was in 1949. We refer, of course, to the problem of the extent, the range of the Treaty and the Organization.

In their statements in the States General the Government recalled that in the Pact of Brussels the social, cultural and economic aspects of the planned system of association were covered in a fairly thorough manner. This was, to a certain extent, not the case in the North Atlantic Treaty. None the less the Government felt that these aspects were of considerable importance. In fact, the military assistance of the United States to the European nations was pointless, if not firmly based on the already existing broad economic assistance programme. In other words, the North Atlantic Treaty was "a necessary complement to the broad economic co-ordination now proceeding under the European Recovery Program, but there is no formal connection between the Pact and the ERP since the latter includes countries which will not participate in the Pact".[2] The real connexion, however, was much more significant: without the communion of interests, as symbolized in ERP, there would have been no Atlantic Treaty.

The Netherlands Government felt that the Treaty and its Organization should not concentrate on the preparation of military defence only. They did not consider that for these other purposes it was necessary to create special organs – as had been the case in the Brussels Pact; but special and continuous attention should be paid to the social and economic aspects of the Treaty and the Organization. Nor did they desire

[1] Mem. Repl., Sec. Chamber, NAT, July 8, 1949, 18.
[2] Expl. Mem., NAT, May 19, 1949, 10; Stikker in Sec. Chamber, NAT, Aug. 3, 1949, 781, quoting the words of the State Department on March 19, 1949.

that the Council, referred to in Article 9 of the Treaty, should only devote its attention to incidental questions in connexion with the implementation of the Pact: the Council should rather co-ordinate the political and military policies of the participating powers.[1]

These Netherlands statements of 1949 are not without interest if the subsequent course of events is borne in mind; nor must we overlook the fact that during the debates of the States General even more far-reaching views were submitted to the Government. There was general agreement that the Treaty should not be regarded as a negative phenomenon. No doubt, taking a narrow view, it could be argued that the Treaty came into existence as the result of, and as a reaction to the Russian threat; but in so arguing the fact was forgotten that the concept of the Atlantic co-operation was older than was generally believed. It would be wrong to assume a strict and narrow relation between the Treaty and more or less momentary international conditions. In other words: it should be realized that we were confronted by two things which should be sharply distinguished: on the one hand, the international situation of 1948 and 1949 which no doubt demanded quick and efficient military co-operation; on the other hand, however, steadily developing conditions which required much more than purely negative military measures. What, then, should be done? Obviously this: with this Atlantic Treaty, such economic and social policies should be adopted as might be expected to make the concept of an Atlantic community a living and powerful reality, worthy of human faith and human defence; the values embodied in the Treaty and to be defended by it, should not be corrupted by opportunist measures as, for instance, the inclusion of Spain; they should be demonstrated to the world by positive deeds. In short, the North Atlantic Treaty Organization, instead of merely being a military expedient, should be positive in character and effect.[2]

With this formulation of a view which is, or rather should be, of contemporary interest, our discussion of the North Atlantic

[1] Expl. Mem., NAT, May 19, 1949, 10, 11.
[2] Sec. Chamber, NAT, July 15, 1949, 1686 ff.

Treaty comes to an end. The measures of 1949 to implement the Treaty need not be discussed here. In fact, the day of the Treaty's conclusion might well mark the natural end of our survey of developments in Holland's fundamental problem in foreign policy, for the Pact was really both the end and culminating point of developments which began in 1945 or, perhaps, even earlier with van Kleffens' speech of December 28, 1943. But these wider aspects can be more fittingly discussed in our concluding chapter.

THE COUNCIL OF EUROPE

The commission created by the Foreign Ministers of the Brussels Pact powers, it will be recalled, worked during November and December 1948 and January 1949 on its report, which was presented to, and studied by, the Consultative Council during its London meeting at the end of January 1949. The Council agreed that there should be established a European organization, to be called "The Council of Europe" and instructed the Permanent Commission of the Brussels Pact in London to prepare proposals on the basis of the Council's directives; finally, it was decided that some other states – Denmark, Norway, Italy, Sweden and Ireland – should be invited to take part in the preparatory negotiations. Representatives of these ten powers met in London and worked on the new organization's statute (March 28–April 14, 1949); and finally, on May 5, the ten Foreign Ministers signed the Statute of the Council of Europe.[1]

The vicissitudes of the Council of Europe are quite outside the scope of this work. Here, we are only concerned with the attitude and policy of the Netherlands Government towards the new organization. It will perhaps be remembered that in his statements of December 1948, Mr. Stikker gave no evidence of overwhelming enthusiasm for these new departures.[2]

---

[1] Expl. Mem., Statute of the Council of Europe, May 28, 1949, 14. The text of the Statute will be found in Appendix 14.
[2] See above, p. 84.

But when, barely two months later, the subject was again discussed in the States General, the Government appeared to have changed their mind – to a certain extent. To be sure, they were still in favour of a policy of slow, but certain progress, they still felt that needless duplication of international organizations should be avoided, they still could not envisage the establishment of a federal state, nor could they accept that the organization about to be established should be invested with sovereign rights. But they did welcome the establishment of the Council of Europe which they would like to regard as a forum where European public opinion might and should voice its beliefs and convictions.[1] Moreover, they stated that during the negotiations in the Permanent Commission (the debate took place just before the recommendations of the Commission were published) they had opposed British suggestions with respect to the composition of the Consultative Assembly, namely, that its members should be appointed by the national Governments and that delegations should vote en bloc according to their Governments' instructions. Such a procedure, Mr. Stikker declared, could not be reconciled with the idea of a European forum; the Consultative Assembly should advise the Governments and if the delegations would be nothing but their Governments' mouthpieces, the Governments might as well consult themselves and have done with it.[2] Accordingly the Netherlands representatives had sided with their French and Belgian colleagues, with the result that a compromise had been reached: each Government would decide the procedure to be followed in appointing the representatives of its country; and as far as Holland was concerned, the Government favoured the designation of those representatives by the States General, in consultation with the Government. In certain quarters this was strongly supported, for it is not difficult to understand why already at the very beginning of organizational developments, the vital question of the responsibility and the influence of the national parliaments became a point of discussion. The Government, it was said, should consider that what were called the "functionalist" and "federalist" approaches to the organization of Europe really referred to two aspects of one and

[1] Stikker in Sec. Chamber, Febr. 4, 1949, 1186.
[2] Stikker in Sec. Chamber, Febr. 4, 1949, 1187.

the same problem: the transfer of part of the national authority; two forms, both equally necessary.[1] They were not opposed to each other; and if the Second Chamber, in its Resolution of April 23, 1948, had strongly endorsed the functionalist principle, the time had now come, it was declared, to stress the concept of a federal assembly and the desirability of popular influence.[2] Accordingly, the following motion was tabled:

"The Chamber,
    in view of its Resolution of March 19, 1948 .... relative to a permanent association of States and that of April 23, 1948 .... relative to the establishment of a community under the rule of law of democratic States, federally joined;
    considering that the conception, referred to in the Resolution last mentioned, of specialized authorities in which, as far as possible and desirable, authority must be granted to supra-national organs, requires to be augmented;
believing that in international affairs, too, direct popular influence cannot be dispensed with;
    declares itself to be of the opinion that efforts should be made to combine the two conceptions just stated;
        on the one hand, that of specialized authorities subordinated to the Governments, in which, apart from governmental experts, room should be made for experts from various walks of life;
        on the other hand, that of a European Assembly, to be formed in consultation with the national parliaments;
    invites the Government to ensure, in elaborating the decision taken at London on January 28, 1949 to establish a Council of Europe, that in the forthcoming Consultative Council the principles of free discussion and free decision will be given full scope;
......................" [3].

It is to be noted that the Government did not object to this this motion, although Mr. Stikker was well aware – in spite of the revised text – of its real object: the establishment of a system

[1] Sec. Chamber, Febr. 1, 1949, 1121.
[2] For the Resolution of April 23, 1948 see above, p. 77; Sec. Chamber, Febr. 3, 1949, 1161.
[3] This was, strictly speaking, the motion's second version; the original text of the last three paragraphs gave a much clearer picture of what was behind it:
    "on the one hand, that of specialized authorities in which, apart from governmental experts, room should be made for experts from various walks of life;
    on the other hand, that of a European Assembly, in which international supervision and control on a parliamentary level will be made possible;
accepts the decision, taken at London – with the co-operation of the Government – on January 28, 1949 to form a Council of Europe, consisting of a consultative council and a committee of ministers, as an important beginning of the developments which in the opinion of the Chamber are desirable".
    (Sec. Chamber, Febr. 4, 1949, 1189 and Febr. 8, 1949, 1196).

of international, parliamentary supervision. What is more, the Minister declared that he, personally, would not oppose such supervision, though he was not yet quite clear as to what was to be supervised – the proceedings of the Ministerial Committee as such, or the policies of the individual Governments; while, of course, only time could tell whether or not such desiderata were realizable in practice. Still, the Government accepted the motion; and it was carried almost unanimously, only the communist Members rejecting it.[1]

In view of all this, it would no doubt be wrong to suggest that the Government had completely deserted their position of December 1948; but it must be conceded that by February 1949 a considerable change had taken place. Not only a considerable, but also a sudden change; Mr Stikker felt as much and spoke of "unexpectedly rapid developments"; at another point in the Debate he referred to the fact that the idea of a European Federation had found increasing favour "at the other side of the Atlantic Ocean" and although he readily admitted that Holland's policy should never be determined merely by Washington's wishes, yet the fact that co-operation with the United States in the present circumstances was a cornerstone, not only of the foreign policy of Holland, but also of Western Europe, and that the United States Government were now known to approve and support all action to fortify Europe's unity, should be an incentive, in his opinion, to further efforts directed towards a European Federation.[2] Significant words! They show us, not only the motive of the sudden evolution just described, but also to what extent developments in the main sphere of foreign policy govern and determine the course of events in sectors of lesser importance. Here, too, the Netherlands Government had obviously decided to adapt their policy to the new situation.

As a result, there was a significant change in the parliamentary discussion on this subject as compared with those of preceding years. Let us, for instance, consider the discussions on the Statute of the Council of Europe in the States General of June and July 1949.

After all that has been said in previous chapters about parlia-

[1] Sec. Chamber, Febr. 8, 1949, 1198.
[2] Sec. Chamber, Febr. 4, 1949, 1186/7.

mentary opinions on the subject of federalism and the closer association of States in Europe, it really seems unnecessary to dwell on the proceedings of 1949 in great detail. But the following points should be briefly mentioned. There was great satisfaction that at long last a European organization had been established, but if the Statute were tested against the two Resolutions of the Second Chamber of April 23, 1948 and February 8, 1949, it was evident that the new organization was little more than a very modest beginning which, moreover, had as yet nothing to do with federalism: there was no transfer of sovereignty.[1] There was the Ministerial Committee, but since there had to be unanimity in political affairs, there was no question, it was observed, of a common sovereignty, but rather of co-ordinated sovereignties; the principle of unanimity should either be weakened or done away with.[2]

Again, the Consultative Assembly was practically subordinated to the Ministerial Committee, so subordinated in fact, that it might be compared to a controlled parliament. How, in such circumstances, could it be a forum of European public opinion? The Assembly had no real power at all; it should at least be in a position to deploy some initiative, and as for its future – a European Parliament should remain the fundamental objective.[3] In that connexion it was clearly undesirable that the Assembly should have to share its secretariat with the Ministerial Committee.[4] The number of seats in the Assembly was too small to make it truly representative; and other nations should be admitted to the Council of Europe – Western Germany in particular, which could not be missed in this work.[5] Furthermore, a number of organs should be invested with authority; there should be a social-economic council which should work with the Strasbourg organization and be subordinate to it.[6]

---

[1] Prov. Rep., Sec. Chamber, Statute of Council of Europe June 21, 1949, 22; Prov. Rep., First Chamber, *idem*, July 20, 1; Sec. Chamber, *idem*, July 5, 1949, 1621.

[2] Prov. Rep., Sec. Chamber, *idem*, June 21, 1949, 22; Sec. Chamber, *idem*, July 5, 1949, 1627.

[3] Prov. Rep., Sec. Chamber, *idem*, June 21, 1949, 22; Prov. Rep., First Chamber, *idem*, July 20, 1949, 1; Sec. Chamber, *idem*, July 5, 1949, 1616.

[4] Prov. Rep., Sec. Chamber, *idem*, June 21, 1949, 22; Prov. Rep., First Chamber, *idem*, July 20, 1949, 2.

[5] Prov. Rep., Sec. Chamber, *idem*, June 21, 1949, 22; Sec. Chamber, *idem*, July 5, 1949, 1617, 1627.

[6] Prov. Rep., Sec. Chamber, *idem*, June 21, 1949, 22.

In short, many Members thought that the Statute did not go far enough. On the other hand, it was well realized that the Statute was the result of a compromise between no less than ten States, and that there were evident dangers in granting binding authority to supra-national organs as long as the nations united in them were not willing to accept the implications of such a state of affairs. In fact, no real federation was conceivable unless its member-states showed a strong measure of political homogeneity.[1] Even so, many still thought that the makers of the Statute had been too prudent – vide the position of the Assembly which, in the majority's opinion, was unsatisfactory.[2]

The Strasbourg organization, then, was anything but a federalist construction; but it might grow into one; and the Statute was in any case welcome proof of the growing co-operation and, indeed, association between the Western European states. The hope was expressed that the Council, by co-ordinating the common interests and beliefs of Western Europe, might contribute to Western Europe regaining its former position of authority and influence in the world.[3]

Obviously, these parliamentary opinions were not markedly different from those expressed in preceding years; but the Government view was.

To begin with, Mr. Stikker pointed out that in his view those who had criticized the Statute had overlooked some elements which, from the federalist point of view, were in no way negligible but it is noteworthy that he did not show any particular enthusiasm for the Statute's arrangements concerning the relations between the Ministerial Committee and the Consultative Assembly.[4] He agreed that the Assembly's powers were few, but stressing the possibilities of amending the Statute, he gave an assurance that the Netherlands Government were ready to consider and support, if this would prove desirable, proposals to increase these powers.[5] In the present circumstances, he felt,

[1] Prov. Rep., Sec. Chamber, *idem*, June 21, 1949, 23; Sec. Chamber, *idem*, July 5, 1949, 1617.

Prov. Rep., Sec. Chamber, *idem*, June 21, 1949, 22; Prov. Rep., First Chamber, *idem*, July 20, 1949, 1; there were, on the other hand, Members who thought that, for the time being, the Assembly should make do with what it had got.

[3] Sec. Chamber, *idem*, July 5, 1949, 1630.

[4] Mem. Repl., Sec. Chamber, *idem*, June 27, 1949, 25.

[5] Mem. Repl., First Chamber, *idem*, July 22, 1949, 3.

the Ministerial Committee should be co-operative, nor would he personally fail in this respect.[1] In principle he had no objections to an increase in the number of seats in the Consultative Assembly [2]; he was also prepared to support a functional division of the Secretariat, if experience would confirm its advisability.

It was his opinion, he said, that the possibilities of the Assembly as a European forum in the present circumstances had been underrated; but however that may be, it should always be borne in mind that the present Statute was the result of a compromise reached in international negotiations. The two Resolutions of the Second Chamber confirmed that in Holland there was widespread support for far-reaching proposals of federation; but this was not the case in some other countries. It might be doubted whether, on the subject of Europe's unity, the Norwegian, the Turk or the Italian thought alike; nor could we overlook the position of Great Britain in the British Commonwealth. In such circumstances the "maladie du compromis" was a familiar phenomenon; and although *the Netherlands Government had been prepared to go further,* the Statute as it was now submitted represented a maximum – it had been impossible to obtain more. He hoped that in time further developments in the direction of federation would prove possible and that the States General, by a judicious use of the rights granted to them, would contribute to this; in fact, he trusted that European co-operation would, in the not too distant future, develop into a real European Federation.[3]

This Government statement [4] was even more positive than that of February; and the difference with the pronouncements of preceding years is striking. One thing is particularly noteworthy: the States General – and perhaps others as well – were clearly told that, if the Statute was less "federalist" in character

[1] Mem. Repl., Sec. Chamber, *idem*, June 27, 1949, 26.

[2] Sec. Chamber, *idem*, July 6, 1949, 1637.

[3] Mem. Repl., Sec. Chamber, *idem*, June 27, 1949, 25; Sec. Chamber, *idem*, July 6, 1949, 1638.

[4] Stikker also declared that the Netherlands Government would support the entry of Turkey and Greece into the Council of Europe; and he hoped that Western Germany would be admitted as an Associate Member as soon as possible. In reply to what had been said about the Council's rôle in the rehabilitation of Western Europe and its place in the world, he observed that it was not impossible that such thoughts had in fact occurred to some founding members of the Council (Sec. Chamber, *idem*, July 6, 1949, 1637).

than had been hoped for in some quarters, the Netherlands Government could not be blamed for that; the fault lay elsewhere.

In August, the Strasbourg organization began its work. The first meeting of the Ministerial Committee took place on August 8; the first session of the Assembly began on the same day and ended on September 8. The principal events of that first session are well known; for our present purpose it is enough to recall that there was very soon a conflict of powers between the Ministerial Committee and the Assembly which began with the question of the Assembly's agenda. On this particular point the Assembly had some success; in November 1949 the Committee decided not to exercise its right of control and in May 1951, gave the Assembly the right to prepare its own agenda. But there were other aspects to this question as well. The Assembly was to attack the right of veto in the Ministerial Committee and was later to criticize the Ministers for their attitude towards the Assembly's recommendations. And this is the second point that may be noted. The Assembly might very well produce recommendations and did, in fact, produce a number of them during its first session; but the important thing was of course, what the Ministerial Committee were going to do with them. Many felt that the Ministers had virtually shelved them, and it was this situation which was the main topic of debate, when the Council of Europe was again discussed in the States General at the end of the year. Once again, the Netherlands Government had to state their position towards these new developments.

The Government were closely questioned on the attitude of the Ministerial Committee. Mr. Stikker had said that in his opinion the Assembly would be wise not to discuss purely technical subjects; that might be true, but it was equally true that international control on a parliamentary level was necessary. Many felt certain that the Assembly could do useful work in this field; the question was whether or not the Committee were of the same opinion. Were the Government in agreement with the Committee's attitude? There was, it was said, no reason to blame the Assembly; but some of the Committee's decisions did not augur well for their future relations with the Assembly; in fact, it was now a matter of doubt whether the Committee really wanted the Council of Europe to be a success. It was believed that the Committee's attitude was due to the influence of a few states; and it was suggested that the Benelux ministers, and for that matter, the ministers of all Continental powers, should resist such influences. In this connexion reference was made to the position of Great Britain which apparently wanted to have its cake and eat it.[1]

Mr. Stikker was not surprised at the criticisms of the Committee's attitude, nor was he himself completely satisfied with some of their decisions. But these criticisms should not be directed against him; not he alone had to decide on the Strasbourg recommendations, but a Committee of no less than twelve Foreign Ministers. That fact should be borne in mind; it should also be remembered that his colleagues were responsible to their national parliaments, whereas it could not yet be said that the Ministerial Committee as a whole were responsible to the Assembly.[2] Moreover, the Committee could not be expected to take immediate decisions on matters which the Assembly had debated thoroughly and for a long time; and if some of the Assembly's recommendations had been referred to inter-governmental bodies, that did not necessarily mean that they had been rejected.

What was, in his view, the Assembly's essential function in the present circumstances? It should discuss, and if possible, agree on a problem, an aspect of European policy, political, economic, social or otherwise. The members of the Assembly should then propagate such European conceptions and thoughts in their own parliaments and national circles – they might, for instance, in this manner contribute to the weakening of protectionist influences and thus enable the responsible Governments, supported by their parliaments, to pursue policies of economic integration and greater political unity.[3]

The Strasbourg organization was still in its infancy. Whether or not it had supra-national features was a controversial question

---

[1] Sec. Chamber, Nov. 22, 1949, 625, 626, 632; Prov. Rep., First Chamber, March 1, 1950, 4, 6/7.

[2] Stikker in Sec. Chamber, Nov. 23, 1949, 653, 663; Mem. Repl., First Chamber, April 14, 1950, 14.

[3] Sec. Chamber, Nov. 23, 1949, 653.

which he did not want to decide; but one thing was certain: as yet the Assembly was no European Parliament and the Committee of Ministers no international Government.[1] If we went too fast in that direction, the Strasbourg organization, as it now was might be the first victim: for the dangers were obvious. For that reason, too, a system of specialized differentiation in the Ministerial Committee, as had been suggested, as yet found no favour in the Government's eyes. Such were, in outline, some of the Government's views at the beginning, the middle and the end of 1949.

The essential points of the Government position were, at a somewhat later date, well summed up by Mr Stikker when he said that he, personally, was a federalist; that he was convinced that if Western civilization was to be saved, it was necessary to build a federated Western Europe, with an executive organ without the veto power and with a controlling body – the whole linked in some way or another with the Atlantic community. But these things could not yet be realized. The position of the various members of the Council of Europe was not alike; the federal conceptions were less developed in the Scandinavian countries than in the Latin ones; Great Britain had its Commonwealth; Holland too, had considerable interests overseas. All such factors could not be overlooked and the Netherlands Government were certainly not willing to accept a situation in which England would be, as it were, cut off from the Continent. In these circumstances our policy should be one of careful progress, concentrating ourselves on such points and formulae as were acceptable to all powers concerned.[2]

Thus, at the end of the year, Holland was participating actively in a number of alliances and international organizations, such as the North Atlantic Treaty Organization, the Pact of Brussels, the Council of Europe and the European Recovery Program and O.E.E.C. The majority of the Second Chamber were fully justified when they reflected upon the fundamental changes which had occurred in Netherlands foreign policy since 1945.[3]

[1] Sec. Chamber, Nov. 23, 1949, 654.
[2] Sec. Chamber, Oct. 18, 1950, 180 ff.
[3] Prov. Rep., Sec. Chamber, Oct. 27, 1949, 1.

The Government statements of November 1949 on the occasion of the annual debates on Foreign Affairs which – after all that has been said above – did not contain any new elements as far as the main issue was concerned, were in perfect harmony with this state of affairs which by now had even lost its novelty. To be sure, Mr Stikker stated during the debates that the United Nations remained of great importance; and the Government would continue to support it; but these statements seemed to be very much in the nature of perfunctory bows, for he gave the States General to understand, after having pointed out that the United Nations could not function as planned on account of the rupture between the great powers, that the world organization could still usefully serve as a meeting place for the Foreign Ministers of the great powers and as a cooling-off place for heated passions.[1] That was practically all; and the contrast with the Government statements of 1946, even of 1947, is illuminating.

The Foreign Minister was convinced that the difficulties between the great powers would be of long duration; at the moment the United Nations was incapable of solving them [2]; and although the Government would welcome all signs of improved relations with Russia – an essential pre-condition of an enduring peace – it was meanwhile their first duty "to put their own affairs in order": in other words, organization of the Atlantic community and European co-operation.[3]

[1] Sec. Chamber, Nov. 23, 1949, 651; First Chamber, April 25, 1950, 687.
[2] First Chamber, April 25, 1950, 687, 688.
[3] Mem. Repl., First Chamber, April 14, 1950, 13; First Chamber, April 25, 1950 688.

CHAPTER XI

1949: GERMANY

During the whole of 1949 the events set in motion by the Six
Power Conference of the previous year continued on their more
or less predestined course. Naturally there were complications;
in the elaboration of the London Resolutions some controversial
points arose for which no immediate solutions could be found.
Still, when in April 1949 the Foreign Ministers of the United
Kingdom, France and the United States, meeting in Washington,
reached agreement on the last of these outstanding difficulties,
the road was at long last free for further developments in Germany.

The Foreign Ministers discussed a) the Occupation Statute,
b) the German Constitution, c) the dismantling programme,
and d) the International Authority for the Ruhr. All these
questions were of the greatest possible interest to the Netherlands,
but Holland's influence on the course of events in these matters
was small. The Occupation Statute and the German Constitution
were questions for which the responsibility rested with the
occupying powers; but the Netherlands were given an opportunity to state their views. As regards the dismantling program, it
may be mentioned that the decisions of April 1949 granted a
great number of concessions to the Germans, whilst, with respect
to the Ruhr question, an Agreement regarding the establishment
of an International Authority was signed in London on April
28, 1949.

The meeting of the Foreign Ministers in Washington cleared
the way for great changes in Germany itself. It will be recalled
that the German Constituent Assembly, commonly known as
the Parliamentary Council, met for the first time on September
1, 1948. After many deliberations and controversies, both in
the Council itself and with the Military Governors, its labours

were concluded with the drafting of a Fundamental Law (Grund-gesetz) which, having been sanctioned by the Military Governors, became law on May 23, 1949. In the opinion of the Netherlands Government, it "brought about an apparently successful solution of the division of powers between the Federal Government and the Governments of the Laender, constituting the federation" [1]. After elections had taken place, Dr Adenauer became Federal Chancellor; and the Military Government was brought to an end. These events had their counterpart in the Russian Zone: in March 1948, a People's Council had been established; one year later a rather centralized constitution was adopted and on October 7, 1949 the establishment of the German Democratic Republic was announced, of which Mr Pieck became President.

Once again, the Council of Foreign Ministers met in Paris (May 23-June 20, 1949). This meeting, brought about by inter-national negotiations in connexion with the Berlin crisis, raised the hopes of all those who, at the end of 1947, had regretted the breakdown of the Four Power deliberations. But again the results of the Conference were disappointing. The proposals of the Soviet Union aimed at the re-establishment of the system of Four Power control under which a German Council of State was to function as a central economic and administrative body. More-over, the USSR was to be included in the control of the Ruhr. These proposals were not acceptable to the West. After all, the West had made considerable progress with the organization of democratic political institutions in Germany, and the Western powers felt that the best, indeed the only way, to bring German unification about was for the Russian Zone to be included in the system planned and elaborated during the Six Power Confer-ence and subsequent negotiations. But this was of course re-jected by the Russians; nor can this be very surprising if one bears in mind the implications involved. So there was, once again, a deadlock. It was, however, decided that further discussions were to take place regarding another meeting of the Foreign Ministers. More important, in the meantime quadripartite talks were agreed upon with the object of alleviating the consequences of the administrative separation of Germany and Berlin. Financial

[1] Note on German problem, 7.

and economic questions in particular were to be considered, with a view to removing some obstacles to the extension of trade and the development of financial and economic relations between the Western and Eastern Zones.[1]

Finally, the occupation authorities were to recommend the German economic authorities in the Eastern and Western Zones to foster closer inter-zonal links.[2]

Thus, the results of the Conference, as far as the fundamental issue was concerned, were no doubt negative; but in the words of the Netherlands Government, "it cannot be denied that the Conference has been of great value, because the broken contact has been restored" [3]. And certainly, with respect to the vexatious effects of the division of Germany on trade and traffic, it was permissible to cherish some slight hope of improvement.

Unfortunately, disappointment followed disappointment. The existing antithesis in Germany deepened; no improvement could be seen in inter-zonal relations; nor did the Ministers' representatives reach agreement about a new meeting of the Council of Foreign Ministers. So the year brought no change in the relations between the occupying powers; the parting of the ways of 1947 appeared to be permanent and definitive; and the subsequent developments, of course, contributed to making it more so.

The situation as regards the Western powers' relations with Western Germany, and in Western Germany itself, was quite different. Here developments were rapid and continuous.

After the elections of August 1949 and the formation of the Western German Government under Dr Adenauer, it soon appeared that further consultations between the Western powers were necessary. One reason in particular made such consultations desirable. The dismantling agreement of April 1949 embodied large and important concessions to the Germans, but it became quite clear during the elections of August 1949 that the Germans demanded still more and greater concessions in this field. Add to this that the Russians had meanwhile established an East German government and it will be understood that, in the given

[1] Note on German problem, 5/6.
[2] Note on German problem, 6.
[3] Note on German problem, 6.

pattern of things, the Western powers felt that something more had to be done.

Accordingly, further discussions took place in Paris on November 9 and 10, 1949. They were followed by talks between the Allied High Commission in Germany and the Federal Chancellor, which ultimately resulted in a statement of November 25, the so-called Petersberg Agreement.

Here we shall only briefly recall the main points of that statement. The Federal Government undertook to maintain the demilitarization of the Federal Republic and to co-operate closely with the Allied Security Board; to promote the principles of freedom, tolerance and humanity; to take measures against monopolies and cartelization; and finally, to apply for membership of the International Authority for the Ruhr. For their part, the Allies undertook to facilitate Germany's membership in several international organizations; they agreed to a gradual re-establishment of German consular and commercial representation abroad; the limitations imposed on German shipbuilding were abolished to a considerable extent; the dismantling of twenty-three factories was to be stopped, while finally, the Allies undertook to study the possibilities of ending the existing state of war with Germany.

The Petersberg agreement was no doubt one of considerable moment. For Germany it meant yet another step on the road to becoming an equal-ranking-state in the European community.

In the preceding pages we have, of course, mentioned only a few of the most important events in and around Germany. They were all of them of singular interest to the Netherlands and their relations with Germany; and for this reason alone they cannot be left out in any survey, however incomplete, of Netherlands foreign policy. But it is clear that from the point of view of the present work, they were of a general, as opposed to a specific, importance. There can be no doubt that the Netherlands Government, in a general sense, supported the policies just described, but as has been pointed out, they – or for that matter the Benelux as a whole – were not in a position to influence the fundamental course of events one way or another. The Government, generally speaking, were kept informed by the great powers; on one or two occasions they were offered the opportunity to state their views. The Benelux Ministers took part in the Paris discussions of November; Holland was a member of the International Authority for the Ruhr; thus it will be seen that the principle of consultation and even participation, established at the Six Power Conference, was maintained during 1949. But even so the real influence of the Netherlands in these matters – the general policy of the Western powers in the German question – was necessarily small.

In our context the specific objectives of the Netherlands regarding the territorial and economic claims and the economic relations with Germany are more important. But here, too, there were few possibilities for Netherlands policy. The Six Power Conference had already shown this; and it was confirmed by the final results in the question of the claims which must be discussed now.

In March 1949 a Protocol was signed by the representatives of the United States, the United Kingdom, France and the Benelux countries, according to which certain adjustments in the western boundaries of Germany were to be put into effect.[1] As far as the Netherlands were concerned, the rectifications eventually put into effect, formed only a fraction of the original territorial claims of 1946. In fact, the territory to be ceded did not amount to more than some 70 square kilometers, with 9 to 10.000 (German) inhabitants. Furthermore, they were of a purely technical character, being of advantage only in the field of:

     a) local communications
     b) improvement of local canal- and waterworks;
     c) improvement of customs arrangements.

When, in March/April 1949, the question of the adjustments was discussed in the States General, the Government rightly pointed out that the proposed changes had nothing whatever to do with compensation for war damages.[2] Nevertheless – and this turned

---

[1] See for "Six Power Communiqué regarding provisional rectifications of the western German Frontier" of March 26, 1949, Appendix 15.

[2] Mem. Repl., Sec. Chamber, frontier rectifications, April 1, 1949, 5.

out to be a vital point in the debates – the adjustments involved the annexation of some 70 square kilometers and, even more important, the addition of about 10.000 Germans to the Netherlands population. These changes might conveniently be called "adjustments", but in point of fact, what we had to deal with here, it was observed, was downright annexation, involving moreover, the transfer of Germans to the Netherlands. These annexations were said to be without *economic* value; and in these circumstances the Government were asked whether it was really in the national interest to accept modifications of this character.[1]

The Netherlands Government felt that they should be accepted. It was quite true that the final outcome of the 1946 claims was most disappointing; but that was due to international developments. It was certainly remarkable that in 1945 and 1946 the Netherlands claims had not been accepted because the Western powers, having protested against the Russian fait accompli on the eastern frontier of Germany, felt that they could hardly imitate the Russian example and protest at the same time. In 1948 Russia was considered no longer; but this time it was on account of Germany that the Western powers were not prepared to meet the Netherlands demands.[2]

In 1949 the same tendency prevailed – only more so; this was clear enough in view of the stream of concessions made by.the Western powers to Germany; and it was again adequately demonstrated when the British representative in the intergovernmental working group dealing with the frontier rectifications, while admitting that some of the Netherlands demands were reasonable enough, actually proposed that, if the Netherlands wanted such demands to be complied with, they should en revanche contribute to removing other anomalies by ceding parts of Netherlands territory to Germany! [3]

All this was no doubt particularly galling; but it did not follow that it would be right to refuse such adjustments as had been offered. The Government intended to reserve their rights; they were, they said, fully resolved to put forward their original

[1] Prov. Rep., Sec. Chamber, *idem*, March 31, 1949, 3; Sec. Chamber, *idem*, April 6, 1949, 1407; Prov. Rep., First Chamber, *idem*, April 14, 1949,1.
[2] Stikker in First Chamber, *idem*, April 21, 1949, 517.
[3] Drees in Sec. Chamber, *idem*, April 6, 1949, 1411.

claims at the peace conference with Germany[1]; and they considered that if the present rectifications, which were admittedly of no
economic importance, were refused, such a policy might harm
our later position at the peace conference with respect to claims
and adjustments of economic significance. Nor were the Government prepared to postpone the effectuation of these adjustments.
This would be most unpractical; it was of particular importance
that the adjustments should be carried out before the Western
German Government assumed their functions.[2] If it were suggested
that further negotiations with the Western German Government
might result in more satisfactory arrangements, it should be remembered that the various German Governments had always
refused to co-operate with Holland in these matters. Were the
present German Government, in the present circumstances,
likely to adopt a different attitude?[3]

It was therefore the Government's view that the present
adjustments should be effected, while they reserved their rights
for all such demands as had not been granted. On the whole the
States General agreed with this point of view, but there were
some Members who doubted the advantages of these corrections
compared with the possible, even probable harm they might do
to the economic relations between the two countries. In this
respect reference was made to the statements of German officials
and the German press. That these statements were not in accordance with the facts, that they represented the actual state
of affairs in a demonstrably false and misleading fashion,[4] was
not very surprising; nor could such a press campaign be a reason
for the Netherlands to change their policy. But all this indicated
the emergence of keen resentment in Germany which for many
reasons should be avoided. If the proposed rectifications – or
rather annexations – had been of economic significance to Holland, the situation would have been different. It was well
known that the Netherlands people, generally speaking, were
not in favour of annexation policies; and the Netherlands Govern-

[1] Mem. Repl., Sec. Chamber, *idem*, April 1, 1949, 6.
[2] Stikker in First Chamber, *idem*, April 21, 1949, 521.
[3] Mem. Repl., Sec. Chamber, April 1, 1949, 6; Stikker in First Chamber, *idem*,
April 21, 1949, 517.
[4] The Foreign Minister also stressed the somewhat dubious character of the
German reactions (First Chamber, *idem*, April 21, 1949, 519).

ment rightly stressed this reluctance in their 1946 Memorandum. Nevertheless, there had been war damage; and if the proposed annexations would have contributed to the economic recovery of the Netherlands, the undesirable effects of annexation policies, it was felt, should have been accepted as well. But the rectifications were stated to be without economic value – then why adopt a policy of annexation with all its possible disadvantages and none of its advantages?

But the Government did not accept this argument. They felt that the danger of permanent resentment in Germany should not be overrated; and in any case they did not consider that for this reason Holland should refuse or reject the adjustments proposed.

Other points of a similar nature were made during the debates; and it was clear that although the States General as a whole supported the Government position, they did not do so without some considerable misgivings.

On one point they made their position unmistakably clear. That two of the most important technical adjustments, in the Dollard – Eems region, had been rejected, was generally resented; and the following motion was adopted in the First Chamber:

"The Chamber,
  of the opinion that the questions of the Eems and the re-establishment and maintenance of the frontier in the Dollard, in which Netherlands interests of the greatest importance and urgency are involved, can be settled in such a manner as may – without harming German economic and private interests – satisfy all just Netherlands desiderata;
  regrets that so far in these problems, even in principle, little has been attained;
  requests the Government to continue their efforts in this field at once and with the greatest energy possible ...."

In the opinion of the Government this motion rightly indicated the policies to be pursued and it was for that reason welcomed by them.

So far our discussions have dealt only with the more immediate aspects of the rectifications problem. But there were other, perhaps even more important aspects of the question. It might, for instance, be asked whether territorial claims, so natural in 1945 and 1946, had not grown into something of an anachronism in the light of the situation of 1949. The attitude of the Western powers (with the exception of France!) indicated that this was, indeed, their opinion; but what was the position of Holland in this respect?

As for the Government, it is clear that at this juncture – the beginning of 1949 – they did not consider the international situation reason enough to give up either their original demands or the adjustments granted in 1949. Far from it; they accepted these adjustments; they would have accepted more of them, had the Western powers allowed them to do so. In other words, it does not appear that, for reasons of, let us say European, as opposed to purely Netherlands interests, Holland was ready to drop its 1946 demands lock, stock and barrel.

But in the States General a different view was heard. The argument was as follows.[1] It was contended that as regards Germany an altogether new type of policy was required. Policies justified and natural in 1945 and 1946 – years, when under the influence of war and occupation, a mentality of smashing and dominating Germany was triumphantly prevalent – could no longer be defended as efficient in the circumstances of 1949. They should be replaced, not by negative palliatives, but rather by a positive policy of consistent integration of Germany as an equal partner in the European community. And this not only for the sake of European reconstruction, but also because of European security; with such policies there was every reason to hope that problems which had proved insoluble in 1918 could be settled in a satisfactory manner.

That was the principle of the argument; and applying it to the question of the Netherlands claims in general and the present adjustments in particular, it was further observed that in 1946 it had been the Government's view that the economic recovery of the country was of primary importance; all the same, the annexation of some 1750 square kilometers with about 119.000 inhabitants had been demanded. Now it could be shown that both economic and territorial claims belonged to a way of thinking which in 1949 was out of place. As to the territorial claims, this should be clear without further explanation; but as far as the economic claims were concerned, the matter was not so simple. What kind of conception was behind them? Obviously the idea

[1] Sec. Chamber, *idem*, April 5, 1949, 1393 ff.

that the recovery of Holland's national economy could be effected within its national frontiers, without bothering too much about other national economies in Europe. But this, it was pointed out, was not true; Holland's national economy was irrevocably interwoven with the economic whole of Europe; it could not exist in an isolated position, not could it be re-established in isolation. Were this not so, then the claims upon Germany were rationally justified; but in that case all other claims upon Germany were right, with the ultimate result that the national German economy would be completely destroyed. What would, in such circumstances, become of European reconstruction?

The fundamental assumption, then, was wrong. The fact should be recognized that the economic recovery of the Netherlands could not be served by the weakening of Germany; and it should also be realized that from a purely Netherlands point of view, the existence of a democratic and economically strong Germany was much more important than the question whether Holland's eastern frontier lay 10 kilometers further to the East or not. Finally, the whole idea of annexations was wrong and irreconcilable with present day efforts to fortify Europe's unity.

Did it follow from all this that technical anomalies should not be removed? Of course not: adjustments of this character should be welcomed, but they should not go beyond this. And surely, it would have been better if these adjustments had been brought about by way of common agreement between Germany and Holland.

What of the future? The Government should not press for further economic or territorial concessions, with the exception of those really technical adjustments about which no agreement had yet been reached. But such adjustments should not be imposed upon Germany.

This must be the end of our discussion of the Netherlands claims upon Germany. It must be admitted that the final results, as compared with the original demands, were very meagre indeed. Once again, Netherlands policy had to give way to the irresistible facts and pressures of the international situation.

It must be noted that the Government did not immediately

react to the remarks, quoted above, about the wider aspects of Netherlands and Western policy towards Germany. It does not follow from this that they disagreed with what had been pointed out; although, of course, the simple fact that at that juncture they still maintained their claims in their original form tends to show that, if they agreed at all with the propositions put to them, they were not prepared to draw – at that moment – the same conclusions from them. But only a few months later the Government did state their views about the general aspects of the German problem and the policies to be pursued.[1]

These views are particularly noteworthy inasmuch as they show an unmistakable evolution in the Government's position since December 1948. Mr Stikker stated that two of the most important problems were those of security and the integration of Germany in the European co-operation. Of these two, the question of security was predominant for Western Europe and the Netherlands; and he went on as follows:

"As long as no definitive solution has been found for the German problem, as long as there is a dividing line in Germany and as long as no real proof has been furnished that the German people co-operate wholeheartedly in a democratic form of Government which will have a lasting character, the problem of security demands permanent vigilance.

There is, however, a close connection between the security problem and European co-operation. The inclusion of Germany, or at least of the part of Germany occupied by the Western Allies, is an inescapable requirement for a powerful Western Europe. Without the co-operation of Germany, there is practically no chance of complete recovery in Western Europe or of security in Western Europe. In the essential integration of Germany into Western Europe close contact will have to be maintained with the other states of Western Europe, also in order to prevent Germany from acquiring a position which would not be in keeping with Germany's real significance. Moreover, in this co-operation, Germany will have to show that it is inspired by a desire for fruitful collaboration on a democratic basis. The integration of Germany will, therefore, have to be effected in stages, closely linked with the development of the co-operation of the other Western European states. If it is effected on a sound basis, the inclusion of Germany in the cultural, social, economic and political co-operation between the other European states may in time lead to the removal of the danger of renewed German aggression ...."

In this statement special emphasis is placed on the importance of Germany's integration as a means to *security*; and this was a new element in the Government's position. It is clear that such

[1] Final Remarks, Note on German problem, 20.

views were in fundamental agreement with what had been advocated some time before in the States General. But did the Government also draw the same conclusions? The following quotation may serve by way of answer:

"The restoration of economic relations between the Netherlands and Germany may produce a considerable contribution towards the integration of Germany in European economic life. The Government is not blind to the fact that such a recovery may, owing to prevailing circumstances, help to a considerably greater degree than any form of reparations to make good the damage caused by the Germans in the war.

The appalling extent of this damage would undoubtedly provide good grounds for the Netherlands Government to demand a preferential position with respect to Germany in the economic field. It is the view of the Government that, at the present stage, a demand for such a preferential position would not contribute towards the co-operation with other nations for which it is striving ...." [1]

Such were the views of the Netherlands Government in July 1949. They had, it will be seen, progressed a good deal, but there were still signs that the "old mentality" had not disappeared completely. In December 1949, for instance, they still rejected the conception of a preliminary peace with the Western German Government on the grounds that such a step could only be interpreted as a clear move in the direction of a final division of Germany; this was inadvisable as long as there was a slight possibility of a solution of the German problem, in which both the Western allies and the Soviet Union would participate.[2] Such hesitations may well be regarded as being at variance, if not with the letter, at any rate with the spirit of the Government statement of July 1949. And it was precisely this element, not only in Netherlands, but also in Western policy, which was severely criticized in the States General in the spring of 1950.

On that occasion [3] it was generally contended that Germany should belong to Europe, or to be more exact, to Western Europe. To that extent there was perfect agreement with the Government. But the latter – and the Western powers as a whole – were warned that such an objective could only be

[1] Final Remarks, Note on German problem, 21.
[2] Mem. Repl., Sec. Chamber, Nov. 14, 1949, 12.
[3] Prov. Rep., Sec. Chamber, Note on German problem, March 30, 1950; Mem. Repl., Sec. Chamber, *idem*, April 24, 1950; Sec. Chamber, *idem*, May 3, 1950.

realized by following a policy of sincere and complete co-operation; a policy, on the other hand, which alternated between confidence and mistrust, of halfway measures, a policy, in short, of too little and too late, would not only fail, but might very well produce a second Rapallo in the end. It should be realized, moreover, that Germany's rearmament was inescapable. In these circumstances a clear cut choice should be made; the Western powers should adopt a consistent policy, which, loyally providing for Germany's complete integration as an equal-ranking power in the European co-operation, should at the same time neutralize the dangers which, it was readily admitted, were undeniably attached to Germany's re-establishment. Such a policy, it was added, should make use of *already existing federal and pre-federal organs in Europe and should provide for the federal organization of European defence, i.e. a European Army, with a European staff, placed under a European Authority and to be controlled by a European representative body.*

But for the time being, these ideas went a little too far to be quite acceptable to the Government. They pointed out, in the first place, that Germany could not, and moreover should not, be forced to re-militarize. In their opinion Western Europe should not now insist upon the integration of German manpower in the European defence, but should rather wait until such time as Germany herself were to show a manifest willingness to support and adopt such measures. Moreover, was it absolutely certain that Germany's re-militarization would increase Western Europe's security? Russian policy was no doubt motivated by imperialist considerations, but the fear factor, in particular fear of Germany, was not entirely absent. Might not the Soviet Union be driven to take ill-advised steps if Germany were re-militarized?

The Netherlands Government, then, were not without sympathy for the German point of view that as yet Germany should not assume co-responsibility for the defence of Germany and Western Europe.[1]

As regards the whole of the German problem, it could only be solved within the framework of co-operation. It was, consequently, the Government's policy to do everything possible to

[1] Sec. Chamber, *idem*, May 3, 1950, 1712.

strengthen European co-operation in all its various aspects – political, economic and military. And only if and when an integrated European defence had been created, would the time have come to discuss a possible German contribution to it; at such a time and in such circumstances, the Government believed, Germany herself would no doubt desire to take part in Europe's defence.

Such were, at the end of 1949 and the beginning of 1950, some of the Netherlands Government's views regarding the main aspects of the German problem. It will be observed that by the middle of 1949 the Netherlands views – as publicly expressed – were in fundamental agreement with the situation created by the rupture between the great powers and which had found its expression in the London Resolutions. Meanwhile, new developments were taking place and new problems were emerging, such as the European Defence Community, the preludes to which could already be heard in the debates just discussed; but all this belonged to the future.

In conclusion, a few remarks about the economic relations between Holland and Germany in 1949. A most important event was the conclusion of a new trade agreement in September 1949 which resulted in a considerable increase in the volume of trade between the two countries.

During the months prior to this agreement the position was not fundamentally different from that of preceding years. But in the summer of 1949 discussions were begun with the responsible bodies in Germany with a view to renewal of the trade agreement of August 1948. The climate in which these negotiations took place was somewhat different from that prevailing on similar occasions in the past. JEIA was shortly to be liquidated; the Petersberg Agreement was not yet in existence, but the influence of the Allies was already on the wane; more power was being delegated to the German authorities.

Up to now, as we have seen, trade movements between the two countries had been subjected to stringent regulations. All this was changed now. It was agreed that, as far as exports to Germany from the Netherlands or Netherlands overseas territories were concerned, all quantitative restrictions were, in principle, to be withdrawn, although an exception was made with respect to a limited number of products. On the other hand, both parties agreed, having regard to pre-war experiences, to maintain for the time being, restrictions with respect to Netherlands imports of German goods.[1]

This trade agreement was complemented by monetary agreements to the effect that the Netherlands undertook to spend in Germany all German currency, earned in German-Netherlands trade relations and that they would not demand payment in either gold or dollars in case the so-called swing was exceeded.[2] Considered as a whole, the new agreement was no doubt, from the Netherlands point of view, an important step forward. The volume of Netherlands exports to Germany increased by leaps and bounds, with the result that Germany, in September 1949, the sixth most important customer of the Netherlands, had climbed to the third position in October and to the first in December 1949.[3] The Netherlands claim upon Germany of course showed a similar development; in due course it was realized that Holland, too, should have to liberalize its imports to a certain extent. This problem was discussed during the negotiations of January and February 1950 – for the first time with representatives of the German Federal Government – which resulted in a Protocol, signed on March 16, 1950, according to which no change was made in the situation with respect to Netherlands exports to Germany; as regards German exports to Holland, it was agreed that existing quantitative restrictions for a great number of German products were to be abolished.

These developments were of some importance in other fields as well. The liberalization of Netherlands imports was, to a certain extent, also to Holland's advantage: the claim upon Germany should not be allowed to assume too large proportions. On the other hand, this time Holland was asked to make concessions; thus it became possible to relate this question to other

[1] Supplementary data, Note on German problem, April 24, 1950, 23.

[2] *ibid.*, 23.

[3] Supplementary data, Note on German problem, April 24, 1950, 23. Netherlands exports to Germany, which up to September 1949 had scarcely averaged Fl. 20 million per month, increased to some Fl. 30 million in October, to Fl. 75 million in November and some Fl. 100 million in December 1949.

problems where the situation was less satisfactory – the rôle of the Benelux ports and Netherlands shipping on the Rhine for instance. It will be recalled that the arrangements laid down in the "Summary" of September 1948 did not produce the results hoped for; in fact, in January and later on, JEIA issued certain directives and instructions which clearly aimed at the continuation of the situation as it existed before September 1948. During the whole of 1949 there was no fundamental change in this position. But at the end of the year Holland was in a position to demand at least some minor concessions. The negotiations of January and February 1950 resulted in a slightly improved situation, inasmuch as Netherlands craft were now allowed to participate in inner German traffic on the Rhine, whilst, as regards the share of the Benelux ports, the repeal of the system of centralized imports for some products resulted in greater activity in these ports.[1] Nevertheless the position remained extremely difficult; and, from the Netherlands point of view, entirely unsatisfactory. The discriminatory railway charges were still in full force; and there was no free shipping on the Rhine, as laid down in the Mannheim Charter.[2]

Nor could the situation in the sector of capital interests afford much reason for rejoicing. In fact, the opposite was true. In October 1949 the Netherlands Government submitted a Memorandum to the Governments of the United States, the United Kingdom and France which gave a résumé of their well known views on this subject.[3]

But the effects of the Netherlands démarche were once again disappointing. As far as the Recommendations of 1948 were concerned, the Netherlands Government had to contend with the fact that, although the Governments concerned had accepted them, neither the deblocking of allied assets in Germany, nor

[1] Supplementary data, Note on German problem, April 24, 1950, 24.

[2] In 1936 the then German Government had renounced the Mannheim Charter (Note of November 14, 1936), but in the opinion of the Netherlands Government the legal validity of this renunciation was very questionable (Note on German problem, 19). Moreover, Mr. Stikker considered that the Federal Government themselves, on the occasion of their return to the Central Commission for Rhine Shipping, had confirmed the undiminished validity of the Mannheim Charter and the relevant agreements and provisions (Sec. Chamber, Note on German problem, May 3, 1950, 1709).

[3] For the text of the "Memorandum on the Netherlands-German Economic Relations" of Oct. 1949, see Appendix 16.

the transfer of allied capital proceeds were implemented during 1949. As we know, the United States Government had particular objections to the transfer of capital proceeds. On these points no improvement had been achieved; nor could it be said that the effects of the deconcentration policies were always encouraging from the Netherlands point of view. In fact, these measures worked in more than one case to the detriment of Netherlands participation in the coal, iron and steel industries.[1]

Thus, considering the Netherlands-German economic relations as a whole, the position remained unsatisfactory. In the trade sector, it is true, progress had been made; but in the other sectors there continued to exist a state of affairs which, in the first place, was likely to deter foreign investors from making new investments in Germany [2] and in the second place, made a *fundamental* solution of the problem of the Netherlands-German balance of payments extraordinarily difficult.[3] In July 1949 the Netherlands Government, as we saw, had stated that they would not demand a preferential position with respect to Germany in the economic field. They felt themselves entitled, however, to demand:

".... that an end should be put at once to the factual discrimination against Netherlands interests compared with those of other Allies. It considers that the policy with regard to Germany should be such that no unnatural obstacles are placed in the way of the development of the economic relations between Germany and the countries with which it should co-operate. The Netherlanders are, therefore, of the opinion that they should not only resist discrimination, but they even think they may voice the hope that efforts should be made quickly and unswervingly towards promoting the economic co-operation which is so desirable ...... The direction of policy in Germany towards the economic co-operation ...... is of the utmost importance ...... because it will be necessary to prevent the resuscitation of conflicting economic interests with regard to Germany as we formerly knew them ......" [4].

[1] Supplementary data, Note on German problem, April 24, 1950, 25; Stikker in Sec. Chamber, *idem*, May 3, 1950, 1709.
[2] Supplementary data, Note on German problem, April 24, 1950, 25.
[3] *ibid.*, 23.
[4] Final Remarks, Note on German problem, 21.

CONCLUDING REMARKS

Before making such concluding remarks as befit a strictly factual account, let us first restate the main course of events during the years reviewed in the preceding pages. The salient points which emerge from the many statements quoted above may be summarized as follows.

As regards GENERAL POLICY, Holland clearly put its trust during the immediate post-war years in a policy of universal co-operation and collective security as embodied in the United Nations. In fact, during 1946 universal co-operation reigned supreme as the country's first objective in international relations. Even at the end of the fateful year 1947 the Government still stressed the importance of the United Nations in Netherlands policy; they maintained their negative attitude towards all ideas of Western European blocs or European Federalism; and they rejected overtures in connexion with the Dunkirk Treaty. But they did hint at future possibilities when they gave the States General to understand that in the case of a definite rupture between the great powers, reconsideration of the country's whole policy in Europe might become necessary. Yet, on the whole, their policy at that juncture was one of awaiting further clarification of the political situation in Europe and the world.

In 1948, the security of the Kingdom in Europe finally necessitated a reorientation in the country's foreign policy, the first stage of which took place in the form of the conclusion of the Pact of Brussels, later followed by the North Atlantic Treaty. The Pact of Brussels marked a most important turning-point; and henceforth the association with the Allies is stated to be the main preoccupation of the Government. We observed, however, that this was not followed – in 1948 – by a change in attitude

towards a Western European Bloc (still denounced when negotiations for the Brussels Pact were proceeding) or towards federalist conceptions, although the Second Chamber took a different
view of the question.

However, the year 1949 witnessed new developments in these
fields, too. Between December 1948 and February 1949 the
Netherlands Government rather suddenly altered their policy
towards the federalist objectives – a change which, admittedly
not unconnected with external influences, went far enough to
enable the Government to blame others for not pulling their
weight in the realization of federalist ideals. For the rest, Holland
continued to work in various alliances and international organizations; and the country looked to these alliances for its protection.

As regards GERMANY, we observed Holland's general position
vis-à-vis that country and how and why the Netherlands Government, basing their policy squarely on the assumption of four
power co-operation, formulated certain territorial and economic
claims. In following the history of these claims, it became
evident that the effects of the rupture between the great powers,
in particular that of Netherlands reorientation and participation
in the Brussels Pact and the North Atlantic Treaty, greatly
contributed to placing Holland, as far as its German policy was
concerned, in a somewhat ambiguous position; and the Six
Power Conference of 1948 finally showed how this ambiguity
had to be solved – not only in the question of the claims, but
also in the matter of reparations. Finally, the events of 1949
demonstrated how this state of affairs was slowly and gradually
taken into account and integrated in the official formulation
of the Government's German policy which, at the end of the
period under review, may be characterized in three words:
security through integration.

Such were the main points of the developments reviewed in the
preceding Chapters, one or two of which may be briefly commented upon.

A. It is perfectly clear that two distinct phases can be distinguished in the period 1945–1950: the first, in which Holland

relied on the United Nations system of collective security to protect its security; and the second, in which the country turned to a policy of alliances to attain the same end.

This being so, the question arises whether or not we can put a definite term to the first phase, the one – omitting the war years – between neutrality and alliance, which has been characterized in this study as a period of transition. Formally speaking, there is not the slightest difficulty about the problem: it ended on the day the Pact of Brussels was signed, March 17, 1948. But if we ask when exactly it was decided that the country's security could no longer be dependent on the system of the United Nations, the difficulties begin. The decision itself obviously rested on the conviction that four power co-operation – the essential condition for the United Nations' success and consequently, the basis of Netherlands policy – belonged definitely to the past. But at what point did the makers of Netherlands foreign policy become so convinced? Was it at the time of the abortive Four Power meeting of London in December 1947? Or was it earlier, at the time of the Russian refusal to participate in the Marshall Plan, i.e. of the abortive meeting between Bidault, Molotov and Bevin of June 1947?

The difficulty, of course, is that the type of sources which have been used in the present work are of relative use only when it comes to this sort of question.[1] For instance, on November 20, 1947, Baron van Boetzelaer stated, it will be remembered, that he thought it necessary to wait and see whether the near future would produce some measure of clarification of the political situation in Europe. This was, it will be observed, on the eve of the London meeting; and it may be assumed that in saying this he had this conference in mind. In December the London discussions ended in complete failure; this was immediately followed by Mr Bevin's speech and the negotiations for the Brussels Pact. Thus it would seem that as far as Netherlands policy was concerned, the London failure was something in the nature of a last straw and that *after* this failure the final decision was reached. If, however, we were to assume, as others do, that the final decision was already taken during, or soon after the

---

[1] Nor should it be too rashly assumed that departmental documents will always give the answer to such problems.

abortive Marshall meeting of June 1947, the Government position in the November debates of 1947 becomes somewhat difficult to explain, although it might be argued that it was not for the Netherlands Foreign Minister to state publicly, at the time when the great powers were meeting in London, that in the opinion of his Government, four power co-operation for all practical purposes belonged to the past.

It is obvious that statements in parliament, often contradictory – vide also the Government declarations of February 1948 – and very often made some time after decisions have been taken, cannot determine this question; and it is certainly quite possible that the events of June 1947 in Paris were, in fact, the immediate motivating factor. This problem, then, may be left to the future.

B. The developments related in preceding Chapters may well be regarded as confirmation of what was suggested in the Introductory Remarks, namely, that the effects of decisions in the main issue of foreign policy are apt to influence, sooner or later, the proceedings and possibilities in other, relatively less important sectors. The history of the Netherlands objectives in the German problem forms a case in point. At the beginning of 1948, Holland (and the other Benelux powers) fully exploited the opportunies provided by the Brussels Pact negotiations to obtain compliance with their demand to be consulted in the making of Western policy towards Germany. But from the moment that Holland entered the Six Power Conference in London, it must have been clear that the specific Netherlands demands stood practically no chance of being granted. For in the new situation *Germany's* favours were courted. Nor was the situation without its ironic aspects for if Holland, as a victim of German aggression, naturally insisted on compliance with its demands, it is clear on the other hand that that same Holland, having allied itself with the Western powers to ensure its security and being in perfect agreement with the broad objectives of Western policy in Europe and vis-à-vis Russia, could not fail to see that these demands were, au fond, incompatible with the requirements of Western policy in its contest with Moscow.

Yet, as we have seen, the Netherlands Government were

notably late in adapting their policy to these requirements of the international situation; they hesitated in so doing (and were severely criticized on that account); and when the process of adaptation finally did take place, it was only after a period of resistance against international pressure.

In the question of the Council of Europe and related matters, too, the Government's attitude cannot be dissociated from presumably effective sympathies and wishes elsewhere. The moral of all this seems to be that Governments had better gracefully accept the consequences of their fundamental decisions in foreign policy; for if they do not, they usually will be forced to accept them.

C. At the outset of this work, a speech made in 1943 by Foreign Minister van Kleffens was quoted, in which he presented a foreign policy programme for the Netherlands which some years later was, in fact, fully realized. Thus, it is not impossible that in the course of our discussions the impression was created – unconsciously so – that the developments of Netherlands foreign policy proceeded according to more or less previously determined lines – in short, according to a master plan. On the strength of Government statements in the States General it is not possible to say whether this, in fact, was so or not. But it does seem very unlikely. The hesitations in the Government's German policy, for one thing, would make such an assumption an improbable one. Above all, there is the curious fact that, if there was such a master plan, Mr Stikker was not aware of it. On August 3, 1949 he stated in the First Chamber, speaking on the North Atlantic Treaty, that he did not think anybody imagined in 1945 that such a treaty would be necessary in 1949. Whether or not this was so in 1945 may be left undecided here; but the fact that his predecessor proposed at the very end of 1943 a plan for a Western formation (including the United States and Canada) which, in principle, was very similar to the North Atlantic Treaty, had obviously been quite forgotten. And yet, it is not without interest to recall once again these quotations of van Kleffens' speech. He proposed, it will be remembered, a "formidable bloc in the West" in which Holland would be, it is true, dependent on the Western powers, but in which, conversely, these powers would have a need of the Netherlands.[1] "It would be difficult", he said on that occasion, "to think of a stronger position for our country". Stronger in terms of what? Of aggressive policies? Obviously not. This position Holland obtained in 1949, consequent on the decision of 1948 to take measures other than had been relied on hitherto in order to ensure the national safety. And it may be repeated once again that these decisions were taken because the country's security seemed threatened by the political expansion of the Soviet Union, because, in short, the global and continental balance of power was disturbed once again by the expansionist policies of a great power. In such a situation there was no room, as a guarantee of security, either for the crippled United Nations of which only the worst could be expected, or for neutrality of which the worst was already known. The North Atlantic Treaty gave the Netherlands a position which, in an unstable world, had already been regarded in 1943 as the strongest one possible – imperfect though it may be.

That it took nearly six years before the conception of 1943 was realized in the Treaty of 1949 is due to a great number of factors, many of which were entirely beyond the control of Netherlands policy. Still, the fact that van Kleffens' programme could, for a time, so completely recede into the background, might well be partially explained by the peculiar notions of the Netherlands people about the realities of the international community. And how did this people react to the fact that from now on Holland was caught up in the torrents of world politics? It was, after all, a tremendous change, not only for the Foreign Ministry, but even more for a people which had for a long time asked nothing better from the world than to be left alone.[2] [3]

[1] It may well be that, after all, the powers' need of the Netherlands turned out to be smaller than Mr. van Kleffens either expected or hoped for in 1943. But the strategic background of his speech was one in which neither atomic nor hydrogen weapons were, as yet, living realities.

[2] "There was but one policy for Holland: to be left in peace. Later on they called this a policy of neutrality" (Mr. Stikker, Sec. Chamber, February 4, 1949, 1179).

[3] The developments in the Netherlands Foreign Ministry's organization since 1945 are characteristic of the changes in Netherlands foreign policy after the war. Before 1940 the Foreign Ministry was a very small affair indeed, perhaps even then too small for its task of passive observation. On May 10, 1940 the whole strength of the Ministry

A full and complete answer to these questions would carry us too far; but the following quotations from one of Mr Stikker's statements in the States General may well serve both as a characterization and an explanation of the Netherlands people's attitude towards the developments related above:

".... the fact has to be faced that from now on Holland is in the middle of European politics. The consequences of these developments have been accepted: Benelux, Western European Union, Marshall Plan, and, in a little while, the Atlantic Pact and European Federalism – they are as many landmarks on this new road.

For it is a new and unknown road for the Netherlands people; and in following the new course, certain deficiencies of our people in international political training make themselves strongly felt. We have not yet fully understood all the consequences of the new state of affairs .... Our people formerly had no other ambitions than to develop the mother country and its overseas territories; political considerations have always remained foreign to them; consequently, they do not and they cannot sufficiently appreciate the important rôle which such considerations play in the foreign policy of other powers. Our people are convinced that, to have other nations support our views, it is necessary only to explain to them the rightfulness of the Netherlands cause .... The Netherlands people, in their insufficient political insight and experience, are apt to underrate the strength of the political considerations by which other nations are frequently guided. Our people, in international affairs, think chiefly in terms of justice and law, and not in terms of politics; and yet they shall have to take these political considerations into account, for if they do not, their picture of the international community will be necessarily false and irrealistic. The Netherlands Government during the years of the war in London had, it is true, more direct and intensive contacts with international political problems than ever before; it is equally true that during the occupation of Holland there emerged a significant and keen interest in the issues of foreign policy; but all this was insufficient to prepare the Netherlands people for the extraordinarily difficult position

did not amount to more than 81 officials in all. After the war this total increased sharply:
1946 : 188
1947 : 230
1948 : 267
1949 : 397
1950 : 422 (1)
The changes in the Ministry's organization were even more important. The new character of the country's foreign policy and the additional amount of work consequent on participation in so many international developments made a reorganization necessary. Before the war the Ministry was organized pre-dominantly along functional lines; after the war it was felt that an organization according to the regional principle was the proper one to deal with the new conditions. The reshaping of the Ministry started on January 1, 1950.

(1) *Organisatie en Reorganisatie van het Departement van Buitenlandse Zaken*, Government Printing Office, The Hague, 1950, pp. 49 en 228.

in which they were to find themselves after the war .... As regards the Foreign Ministry, they view these matters in a realistic light and they thoroughly appreciate the place of interest in the powers' policy; but whether the Netherlands people have a sufficient understanding of this state of affairs, must remain, in my opinion, a matter of legitimate doubt . . . ." [1]

[1] Sec. Chamber, February 4, 1949, 1179 ff.

A NOTE ON THE MARSHALL PLAN

The general features of what is commonly known as the Marshall Plan and the manner in which it was carried out, are so well known that it seems unnecessary really to say anything further about these aspects here. But what of Holland's place in all this? What, for instance, was the Plan's true significance for this country; and what was Holland's part in the developments set in motion by General Marshall's Harvard speech of June 5, 1947, culminating in the establishment of the Organization for European Economic Co-operation? The answer to these two questions may be summarized as follows.

The first thing to bear in mind is that war damage in the Netherlands was estimated at no less than Fl. 25.000 millions (in 1938 values) [1]. That was the position at the end of the war; the effects of such losses may easily be imagined [2] and the situation was further aggravated by the loss in foreign currency income consequent on the change in relations with Germany and the then Netherlands East Indies.

Immediately after the war the work of reconstruction was undertaken with great energy and determination; but this required immense sums in foreign currency; and even after the successful completion of the first phase of reconstruction, current production had still to be financed by liquidation of gold reserves and foreign assets.

This could not go on indefinitely; Netherlands gold reserves decreased from Fl. 1200 million in 1945 to Fl. 561 million in March 1948; holdings and balances abroad dropped by some Fl. 800 million, probably more, during the same period. By April 1948 the limit had been reached, if only in view of the obligations arising out of the foreign debt which, in April 1948, amounted to Fl. 2.360 million.

But further credits were not available; and so the only alternative was to stop, or at any rate considerably slow down, the work of reconstruction. Such was the position at the beginning of 1948; but at that crucial juncture the Marshall Plan began to take effect.

---

[1] See below, Appendix 5.

[2] Out of 2.200.000 houses, some 82.000 were completely destroyed, 40.700 severely, 386.000 lightly damaged. Almost 10% of fertile soil was inundated; 8.600 farms were completely destroyed, 6.000 heavily, 33.000 lightly damaged; 181 railroad bridges destroyed: 23 of the 26 most important ones were either destroyed or heavily damaged. 3000 vessels were sunk in Netherlands waters; port installations in Amsterdam, Flushing and Rotterdam were largely destroyed. The merchant navy was reduced from 1129 vessels in 1939 to 726 in 1945; only 499 locomotives were left out of 1042, some 6000 freight cars out of 30.000, 101 electric trains out of 299. (Netherlands Government, First Report on E.R.P., 1948, 23 ff.)

To say that Holland received about $ 1.000 million under the Marshall Plan would not convey very much in itself. Such totals acquire their real significance only if the alternative is considered: what would have happened if no assistance had been received at all? [1] If during 1948 the country had made use of all possible reserves. there would have still remained a foreign currency deficit of between fl. 1.000 and 1.500 million. To meet a deficit of this order, savings in government expenditure would have been of little use: they would not have yielded much more than Fl. 50 to 100 million in foreign currency.[2] Consequently, both consumption and investments would have had to be curtailed, each probably to the tune of Fl. 1.000 to Fl. 2.000 million.[3]

The effects of such cuts, particularly in the field of consumption, should not be underrated, for it should be borne in mind that the consumption levels of 1947 and 1948 contained very few luxury elements; and a cut of that order would have meant a real sacrifice in a situation which offered very little room for sacrifice in the first place. A cut in investments may have less direct consequences, but it affects the level of future production and hence, future prosperity. If investments had been curtailed, the loss in future production would probably have been not less than some Fl. 500 million annually.[4]

Thus, in the first place, the Marshall Plan made it unnecessary to carry out these measures; but it did more: it spared the nation the psychological blow which, in all probability, would have followed them. Surely, it would not have been surprising if uncertainty and despondency had replaced the slowly growing feeling of confidence in the country's future; and the political effects of such a change might have been serious. In short, as far as Holland was concerned, the Plan's true significance was both economic *and* political.

With General Marshall's Harvard speech of June 5, 1947 a period of intense international activity set in. Conference followed conference: first the abortive one between Bevin, Bidault and Molotov of June 27 at Paris, followed by the Sixteen Power meeting of July 12. On that occasion the powers created a Committee of European Co-operation which, under the chairmanship of Sir Oliver Franks, prepared the so-called Paris Report, presented to Secretary Marshall on September 22, 1947.

The Committee's task was by no means an easy one, for it had little to go upon; there was, of course, Marshall's speech, but little else. In what form would American assistance be given, for how long and how much? Furthermore, there were obvious complications in assessing European availabilities and requirements over a number of years. Should, for instance, long term problems be included as well as short term ones? Again, what of the German problem in this connexion? [5] Should it be

---

[1] J. Tinbergen: "The Significance of the Marshall Plan for the Netherlands Economy" in *Road to Recovery*, The Hague 1954, 23/25.

[2] First Report on ERP, 23.

[3] First Report on ERP, 33; J. Tinbergen, *op. cit.*, 23.

[4] J. Tinbergen, *op. cit.*, 23.

[5] The Committee invited the Commanders-in-Chief of the German Zones of Occupation to submit the same information as was expected from other participating countries. The Commanders of the Western Zones accepted this invitation. This was the final parting of the ways between Eastern and Western Europe as far as the

assumed that German productive capacity would be fully used? Such an assumption might well produce political difficulties. What should be assumed with respect to trade relations with Eastern Europe? Finally, was it feasible to forecast balance of payment developments over a certain number of years?

In due course, all these problems were satisfactorily solved, but what was Holland's point of view on all this?

The Netherlands Government had well understood the significance of Marshall's initiative; in fact, they had immediately contacted the British Government to discuss what should be done.[1] Prior to the Sixteen Power meeting of July 12, the Benelux countries had reached agreement on certain principles and objectives to be pursued in the Conference. At Paris the three countries worked together – Dr H. M. Hirschfeld represented Benelux as a whole in the Comité Exécutif – and their co-operation was not lost upon the other conferring powers.

The Benelux views may be summarized as follows.[2] They attached great weight to the development of inter-European trade relations on a multilateral basis. To achieve this, complete or at least partial convertibility of the currencies of the participating countries was necessary. They were, furthermore, of the opinion that the German problem should be dealt with. They felt that the volume of coal production in the Ruhr and of industrial production generally should be increased, and they demanded that deliveries from other countries should be paid either in goods or in convertible currency. Steps should be taken to further the development of German foreign trade within the framework of European multilateral trade relations. Finally, the economic policy of Germany should not be governed by purely German interests alone: it "must be fitted into the European economy so that it may contribute to a general improvement in the standard of living".

Finally, Benelux felt that attention should be given to a) the co-ordination of agricultural and industrial policy and production, b) the stabilization of monetary policy, c) the problems of East-West trade and d) the creation of such economic and financial conditions in Europe as might attract foreign private investors, particularly in the United States.

The ideas of the Benelux countries did not remain without results. It was due to their, and in particular to Holland's, insistence that an appendix on Germany was added to the Paris Report. The Benelux countries formed the sponsoring powers of a Study Group on the issue of Customs Unions. On the other hand, the Paris Report did not state any definite suggestions with regard to the form of co-operation between the European countries, without which the assistance programme could not be realized – although the Netherlands delegation in particular had wished for greater precision and clarity in the matter.

However, it soon became clear that the United States Government particularly desired the establishment of a multilateral organization in

European Recovery Program was concerned. (Expl. Mem., Convention for European Economic Co-operation, June 17, 1948, 1).

[1] H. M. Hirschfeld: "Conception and Origin of the Marshall Plan" in *Road to Recovery*, The Hague, 1954, p. 14.

[2] Hirschfeld, *op. cit.*, p. 13 ff.

Western Europe.[1] In these circumstances, the primary task for the European nations concerned was to reach agreement about the character of a multilateral convention and to decide upon the principles to be embodied in the statute of the new organization.[2]

Once again, the Benelux countries decided to adopt a common policy. During the negotiations prior to the Convention for European Economic Co-operation of April 16, 1948, Benelux advocated the following ideas. The new organization should be an open one, i.e. the door should not be closed to any country wishing to join at a later date. Also, the organization should be a "continuing" one. There were several countries which wanted the organization to be confined to those aspects of co-operation necessary for the realization of the Marshall Plan; accordingly they felt it should not exist any longer than the Marshall Plan itself. The Benelux powers rejected this conception, for they wanted European co-operation to go beyond the limited objectives of the Plan. Hence their insistence upon a continuing organization and their desire that this wider objective should find expression in the organization's statute.

Furthermore, Benelux considered that all participating powers should decide on all matters in mutual agreement. This point was to give rise to many and protracted negotiations and this was also the case with respect to Benelux' insistence upon a strong secretariat.

On the whole, these principles were accepted; but the Paris negotiations were not without their difficult moments. The French supported the position of Benelux with respect to a strong secretariat but the British did not; at the back of this was, of course, the issue of co-operation versus integration. The distribution of functions over the various countries was another question which produced some difficulties. In the end a Benelux Minister, P. H. Spaak, became first chairman of the Ministerial Council, later to be succeeded by the Netherlands Foreign Minister D. U. Stikker. Thus the Organization for European Economic Co-operation was founded; and after the establishment of the Economic Co-operation Administration in the United States, a beginning could be made with the realization of the European Recovery Program.[3]

In conclusion, a few words about the attitude of the States General towards these departures. Although the bilateral agreement between the United States and the Netherlands was not debated in the States Gene-

---

[1] The presentation of the Paris Report to Secretary Marshall was followed by a visit of a European Commission to Washington in October 1947. Once again, Mr. Hirschfeld represented the Netherlands; the chairman was Sir Oliver Franks. During these conversations various aspects of the Plan were discussed with the American authorities. It was made clear to the visitors that, so far as the issue of Western European co-operation was concerned, the Paris Report did not go far enough; the establishment of a multilateral organization in Western Europe was necessary. Thus, the Marshall Plan was to be realized both multilaterally and bilaterally. (Hirschfeld, *op. cit.*, p. 18).

[2] A small French-British commission was charged with preparing the ground; they visited various European capitals and arrived in the Hague in February 1948, where they conferred with a combined delegation of Holland, Belgium and Luxemburg.

[3] First head of the ECA mission to the Netherlands was Dr. Alan Valentine. Dr. Hirschfeld was appointed the Netherlands Government Commissioner for the European Recovery Program.

ral [1], the Marshall Plan was discussed both during the annual debates on foreign affairs of 1947 and during the debate on the Convention for European Economic Co-operation of April 1948. With the exception of the Communists, all parties welcomed the Plan, not only because they well realized the significance of American assistance to the Netherlands economy, but even more because they regarded the Plan as a sign of growing international economic solidarity. American assistance, it was considered, should be complementary to Europe's own efforts; Europe should make itself independent of foreign help; hence the general emphasis on the theme of European co-operation, of which the Marshall plan should be the beginning, but not the end. Once again the opinion was expressed that this co-operation should ultimately result in a federal system; supra-national agencies were spoken of. In short, the Marshall Plan was not seen merely as a temporary expedient, but rather as the beginning of, and a welcome impulse to, the wider and continuing co-operation and association of the nations of Europe. The Convention of April 1948 was welcomed for the same reasons. The Organization, it was said, should have authority; its membership should be as wide as possible: no state should be barred for ideological reasons; and its work, some Members affirmed, should be based on the principles of a directed economy and international planning, although others rejected such ideas equally firmly. On the whole it may be said that the policies of the Netherlands and, indeed, Benelux Governments in these matters were fully supported by the majority of the States General.[2]

[1] The "Economic Co-operation Agreement between the Governments of the Netherlands and the United States of America" of July 2, 1948, the text of which will be found in Appendix 17, was not a treaty in the formal sense of the word; in virtue of Article 60 (1948) of the Netherlands Constitution the States General were therefore merely informed of it, but they were not asked to approve it.

[2] See Foreign Affairs Debates of the States General, November 1947 and February 1948; and the debates on the Convention for European Economic Co-operation, July 1, 1948 (Second Chamber) and July 22, 1948 (First Chamber).

A NOTE ON BENELUX

During the first few years after the war much interest was aroused, particularly abroad, by the various forms of permanent and incidental co-operation between Belgium, the Netherlands and Luxemburg which, as a whole, became generally and popularly known by the name of "Benelux". As far as its economic aspects were concerned, this co-operation aimed at the formation of an Economic Union between the three countries; and it may be said to have started with the agreement of October 1943.[1] It is, however, a fact that progress in this field was slow and difficult during the period 1945–1950; why, then, this widespread interest and popularity?

To a certain extent this was probably due to the mood of the post-war years. Stimulating ideas were, one might say, in heavy demand; it was generally felt that intimate co-operation between the European nations was a vital necessity. Accordingly, the idea of an economic union between Holland, Belgium and Luxemburg was bound to find general favour inasmuch as it was in complete harmony with the demands of the time. Hence, a widespread enthusiasm for Benelux' actual and future achievements, often accompanied, it is true, by a complete lack of understanding of the numerous difficulties which are necessarily attached to all projects of economic integration.[2] But there were other reasons for the popularity of Benelux. If close co-operation in the *economic* field met with many difficulties, it was fortunately otherwise as regards *political* relations. The three countries worked together in the German problem and during the negotiations for the Pact of Brussels and the Marshall Plan. This political co-operation aroused interest and admiration; nevertheless, the fact that the primary economic objectives of Benelux had not yet been realized, did not escape the notice of some observers.

The political aspects of Benelux have been discussed elsewhere in this work; the purpose of this Note is merely to relate economic developments between 1944–1950.

It must not be supposed that the ideal of close political and economic co-operation between the three countries was of recent standing. In 1839, it is true, Holland and Belgium had dissolved their political ties; but there remained such a range of common interests that throughout the nineteenth century and the years before the Second World War repeated efforts were made to arrive at a system of more permanent economic co-oper-

[1] J. E. Meade, *Negotiations for Benelux: an Annotated Chronicle*, 1943–1956, Princeton, 1957, p. 2.

[2] H. M. Hirschfeld, ,,Benelux en de wijdere Europese samenwerking", *Internationale Spectator*, November 8, 1954, p. 647.

ation between the three countries. For various reasons no results were achieved; but it is clear that the developments of 1944 and later were based on long-standing tendencies.[1]

During the war years the Governments in exile worked intimately together; and in 1943 and 1944 they concluded two conventions which were closely inter-related. The first, the monetary agreement of October 1, 1943 was a bilateral payments agreement, although it was "something more than a purely technical arrangement to facilitate payments between one particular pair of countries .... In it the two governments agreed to consult closely in the future on economic and financial policies" [2]. The second agreement, of September 5, 1944, was of much greater importance. According to this Customs Convention, customs duties on trade between the contracting countries were to be abolished; as for imports from third countries, one common tariff of import duties was to be established. Finally, the Convention provided for the establishment of a number of Councils.[3]

Apparently, the first aim of the Convention was to establish a common tariff of import duties which is, of course, not the same thing as a Customs Union inasmuch as excise duties and other taxes were maintained on goods originating in the partner countries.[4]

[1] Benelux was widely supported in the States General. The economic co-operation between the three countries was warmly welcomed; and the speedy establishment of the Economic Union was generally desired. At times France was mentioned as a suitable partner in this economic co-operation which was not only regarded as most important for the three countries concerned, but also as an example to Europe. In fact, it was hoped that Benelux would prove to be the beginning of a European Customs Union. At all times the importance of economic co-operation between the three countries was keenly realized and it was felt that purely technical considerations should not impede further progress: the realization of Benelux demanded sacrifices from all parties.

Political co-operation between the three countries found no less support. In this field, too, Benelux was seen as the nucleus of a greater formation. Finally, the Chambers showed great interest in the cultural aspects of Benelux; and the Government were repeatedly asked not to overlook these obviously important aspects.

[2] Meade, *op. cit.*, 4. It should be borne in mind that Belgium and Luxemburg already formed an economic union since 1921.

[3] The text of the Customs Convention is given in Appendix 18.

[4] As regards the exact meaning of terms as Tariff Community, Customs Community, Customs Union and Economic Union, the following definitions, accepted by the countries participating in the Study Group for a European Customs Union in its session of November 10, 1947 may be of assistance:

a) Tariff Community: participating countries adopt a common tariff of import duties and substantially refrain from levying import duties on goods originating in any other member-state;

b) Customs Community: the above mentioned Tariff Community is carried further by the adoption of uniform Customs legislation and regulations;

c) Customs Union: comprises the Customs Community in which the excise duties and other consumption taxes including (if possible) those on the transfer of movable goods (turnover tax) have been unified;

d) Economic Union: of two or more sovereign States covers a definite economic territory:

1) wherein persons, goods and capital can move freely;

2) wherein the establishment and application of economic, financial and social policies are co-ordinated;

3) which acts in its relations to third countries as a single economic, financial and social entity, except in matters of purely national interest which cannot have repercussions on the partner countries.

This program might appear to be a very simple one, but all past experience with customs unions showed that the abolition of existing import duties, and the preparation of a new joint tariff were likely to require work of a most difficult and complicated character. Benelux was to prove no exception to the rule.

Besides, the convention was to go into effect immediately after the return of the signatory Governments to their respective countries and though, in September 1944, it was confidently expected that the liberation of all three countries would be only a matter of days or weeks, things turned out very differently as far as Holland was concerned. The complete liberation of the country did not take place until May 1945 and its economic position, unlike that of Belgium and Luxemburg, was found to be desperate. In these circumstances the implementation of the 1944 agreement had to be postponed.

However, at their meeting at The Hague on April 17 and 18, 1946, the three Governments examined the position afresh and they decided that the Customs Convention should take effect as soon as possible.[1] But in view of the change in economic conditions it was agreed to revise both the Customs Convention and the Tariff established in London. It was expected that the revised Tariff might come into effect on November 1, 1946 and that the tariff frontier between the Netherlands and the Belgian-Luxemburg Economic Union might be lifted a year later. It was also decided to request the various Councils to submit proposals on the unification of all customs duties and additional taxes levied by the three countries, to examine the possibilities of co-ordinating agricultural and industrial policies and finally, to decide upon the principles for a common policy to be pursued at the International Conference for Trade and Employment; and for co-ordination of commercial agreements to be concluded with third countries.

On the same occasion the Belgian Government agreed to grant several credits to the Netherlands in order to maintain the trade relations between the two countries at a certain level.

It soon became clear that in one respect the three Governments had been too optimistic: the revision of the common Tariff took a much longer time than originally expected. New joint lists were not completed until the beginning of 1947; they came into force on January 1, 1948. Thus the Tariff Community came into being, although in practice it was often wrongly called a Customs Union. At the same time, steady progress was made in the field of unification of excise duties and the like; towards the end of 1947 an agreement was reached on wines and on sparkling fermented drinks (other than beer), later followed by the protocol of December 16, 1948 and the Convention on the Unification of Excise Duties of February 18, 1950.

Meanwhile the various problems involved in the establishment of an Economic Union were carefully studied in all three countries. The advantages of such a Union were obvious, but so were the difficulties. Historical developments in Europe had given rise to a number of national economic structures, frequently designed to protect and promote purely national interests and consequently showing strongly opposing features.

---

[1] They also affirmed that the Customs Union should develop into a full Economic Union.

Any policy, therefore, aiming at greater economic unity was bound to fail, if not preceded by lengthy and complicated processes of adaptation. Long-standing differences of this character were not absent in the case of Holland, Belgium and Luxemburg. Furthermore, post-war economic conditions in Belgium and Luxemburg differed widely from those in Holland, which led naturally to different economic policies. The Netherlands Government embarked on a policy of controls; the Belgian Government did not; this situation was not particularly helpful as far as a speedy realization of the Economic Union was concerned.

Finally, the general economic position of Europe in the beginning of 1947 must not be overlooked. The increasing dollar shortage tended to jeopardize actual and potential results of all reconstruction efforts. In these circumstances, even the Tariff Community would have been of very little practical value; and further steps in the direction of an Economic Union would have been quite out of the question. Marshall's Harvard speech changed all that; it was Marshall's initiative which, in fact, made the ultimate realization of Benelux possible.[1] Such were some of the difficulties which had to be overcome.

In a series of meetings the three Governments prepared the ground for the gradual realization of their common objective. In January 1948 a list was agreed upon, showing industries, establishment or expansion of which would be subject to preliminary consultations between the three countries. At the Conference of Château d'Ardenne, June 1948, agreement was reached on the necessity of pursuing corresponding social, financial and economic policies in the entire Benelux area; for it was evident that the existing economic differences had to be bridged or reduced to normal proportions and that great new discrepancies should be avoided. Accordingly, the Presidents of the Councils of the Customs Convention were requested to study the various problems attached to 1) a return to free consumption; 2)a reduction of subsidies on production and consumption; 3) the co-ordination of investment programmes; 4) the unification of fiscal and social policies and 5) the maintenance of currency equilibrium. The Conference decided that if these problems were solved in a satisfactory manner, the Economic Union would come into force on January 1, 1950.

The Presidents' report was examined by the three Governments during their meeting at The Hague (March 1949). They agreed on the establishment of a Pre-Union, by way of transition to the full Economic Union. During the Pre-Union stage, which was to start on July 1, 1949, the three countries were gradually to abolish quantitative restrictions on intra-Benelux trade and other remaining barriers to the realization of the full Union. If the economic conditions prevailing at the time of the Hague meeting would remain the same and a global balance in the international payments of the two economies had been realized, "the three Governments will pass from the Pre-Union stage to that of the Economic Union proper on July 1, 1950". [2]

During the Pre-Union stage which did not begin until October 1, 1949 [3], further progress was made in abolishing intra-Benelux trade restrictions.

---

[1] Hirschfeld, *op. cit.*, p. 645.

[2] See for Protocol of the meeting at The Hague, Appendix 19.

[3] The Pre-Union Agreement was actually not signed until October 15, 1949, at the conclusion of the ministerial meeting in Luxemburg.

At the end of 1949 already two thirds of the total volume of trade between the three countries were free from restrictions, while import and export facilities were considerably extended in those sectors where total abolition of restrictions was not yet possible [1]. A number of liberating arrangements with respect to monetary and capital transactions were also agreed upon. Other measures were taken in the field of agricultural and fiscal policy.[2]

Thus it seemed that the full Economic Union might be realized in the not too distant future. However, these hopes were dashed by the economic consequences of the Korean conflict, while, at a somewhat later date, the question of industrial wage costs in the three countries caused further difficulties. But these problems and complications do not fall within the period under review.

---

[1] The Benelux countries were fully conscious of the importance of European co-operation for the success of their own experiment. Hence their interest in the abolition of quantitative restrictions in European trade relations; and their desire that Benelux should precede rather than follow the other OEEC partners in these efforts. (Hirschfeld, *op. cit.*, p. 648).

[2] The agricultural question has always been difficult because conditions and policies in the three countries differed widely. In May 1947, the agricultural ministers of the three countries reached agreement on a number of proposals which "marked the initiation of arrangements which frankly removed a very large amount of agricultural produce from the principles of the common market for the three countries – an important and basic exception to the free-trade principle within Benelux which has continued for many years". (Meade, *op. cit.*, pp. 19, 22 ff.).

SUGGESTIONS PRESENTED BY THE NETHERLANDS
GOVERNMENT CONCERNING THE PROPOSALS FOR
THE MAINTENANCE OF PEACE AND SECURITY AGREED
ON AT THE FOUR POWERS CONFERENCE OF DUMBARTON
OAKS, AS PUBLISHED ON OCTOBER 9, 1944

The tentative proposals for an international organisation for the maintenance of international peace and security, upon which the representatives
of the United States, the United Kingdom, the Soviet Union and China
have agreed during the conversations held this summer and autumn at
Dumbarton Oaks, have been made generally available (although they
are as yet in an incomplete state) for the purpose of study and discussion
by the peoples of all countries.[1]

The peoples which are united in the Kingdom of the Netherlands, and
particularly the people of the Netherlands in Europe, have at all times
taken a deep and active interest in every serious attempt to place international peace and security on a firmer basis. The present war has shown
that, for them, the maintenance of international peace and security may
well be a condition of survival. The proposals made and those still to be
made as a result of the Dumbarton Oaks Conversations will, therefore,
have their closest and most sympathetic attention.

Unfortunately, the conditions in which these peoples find themselves
at present, both in Europe and in Asia, are scarcely conducive to the
formation of a balanced and considered public opinion. In Asia, harsh
oppression by the Japanese stifles all genuine public debate. In that part
of the Netherlands in Europe which is still occupied by Germany, acute
starvation and unparalleled terror prevent the people from giving attention to anything beyond the question whether there will be food to-day
and to-morrow, and whether husband or son will not be caught by the
implacable enemy and sent to work in sub-human conditions on defence-
works directed against their own country. And in the liberated region,
where the Netherlands tradition of democratic institutions and a free
press are now bursting into fresh bloom after their suppression by the
Germans' leaden hand, destruction on every side, lack of communications,
and a deficient, though slowly improving food-situation bar the way to
serene and fruitful discussion.

In these circumstances, the voice of the Netherlands can for the time
being only make itself heard through the country's Government.

Hitherto, the Government have refrained from expressing an opinion
on the Dumbarton Oaks proposals. In the first place, because of the
announcement made on October 9, 1944, by the Governments whose
representatives drafted these proposals, stating their agreement that,

[1] See statement by Mr. Cordell Hull, Secretary of State of the United States of
America, dated October 9, 1944, coupled with the statement issued simultaneously on
the same day by the participating Governments.

after further study of these proposals, the necessary steps would be taken as soon as possible with a view to completing them; this announcement made it seem preferable to await results. In the second place, because of the great delicacy of this problem, on whose successful solution the future of a happier world so largely depends; preliminary studies seemed necessary. Thirdly, and chiefly, there was last autumn the possibility that the European part of the Kingdom would be set free in its entirety at an early date, so that public opinion could duly enlighten the Government as to the opinion and wishes of the nation, thereby giving greater authority to an expression of the Government's opinion.

Now that the proposals have not given rise to as much public discussion in all free countries as the Netherlands Government had hoped, and since the time of their completion and that of the liberation of the Netherlands seem uncertain, whilst some time has elapsed during which the Netherlands Government have given considerable study to this important matter, it is thought preferable to formulate, on some main points at least, a provisional opinion which, it is confidently anticipated, reflects that of many thoughtful people in the Netherlands. It is hoped that it may prove to be to some extent a contribution towards the attainment of international peace and security, perhaps the most important aspect of that freedom from fear which, proclaimed as our common goal by the President of the United States of America and incorporated as such in the Atlantic Charter, has been universally endorsed by the United Nations in their Declaration of January 1, 1942, as one of their primary objectives.

This is a problem which interests the smaller nations [1] no less vitally than the great powers. War may be extremely damaging to the latter; to the former it may mean well-nigh obliteration. If, then, these pages are found to contain words of a sceptical or critical nature, such words should not be taken in a deprecating or a negative sense, nor as an expression of doubt as to the sincerity of purpose of the proposals; nor do they imply preference for unlimited sovereignty, or for the return of the anarchic juxtaposition of states bound by no freely accepted code of common behaviour. The harrowing experiences of this war, and particularly the iniquities and bestialities of the German and Japanese occupation, have made the citizens of the Netherlands both sceptical and critical, and, on the other hand, anxious to obtain serious guarantees for the future. The reflections of the Netherlands Government will at no time be animated by a spirit of perfectionism, rejecting a sufficient minimum of good which is attainable for still more which is not. What the Netherlands Government seek is discussion in a sober, practical and constructive spirit, and they wish their remarks to be considered as offered in that spirit. Also, they wish to preface them by an expression of their gratitude to the great powers who took the initiative for the Dumbarton Oaks Conversations and to the statesmen who took part in them, for having produced a document which, although its original promoters have called it tentative, may well prove to be much more than a useful starting-point.

The plan has been authoritatively called "the keystone of the arch",

[1] The term "smaller nations (or powers)" is used in this memorandum to designate, in accordance with common practice, those states which, because of a deficiency in size, population, or industrial development, or in a combination of these elements, are not supposed to belong to the group of the great powers.

the arch which is to represent the organisation of the postwar international community. What are the pillars of that arch? The firm determination of the member-states to make the organisation a success? Or such regional groupings as are considered consistent with its purposes and principles? Or the system of voting which remains to be devised and inserted, and which will to a large extent be the critical element determining the scope of the organisation's possibilities? One thing is certain: a set of rules, however carefully devised and however perfect on paper, will never by itself suffice to maintain international peace and security. The best organisation is useless if the will of its members to wield it for the good of the world is lacking. Nothing but that determination can support the scheme and make it work as it should; without it, it will come crashing to the ground.

But it seems necessary that every citizen of the world should realise equally clearly that, whether there is such a scheme or not, nothing will help the world if the great powers are not in agreement, and they were certainly right in having this consideration constantly in their mind when working out the Dumbarton Oaks Plan. At the same time, it is confidently believed that the great powers will be the first to admit (1) that at all times they therefore are in duty bound, not only to themselves but to all other states, to come to an agreement on important matters of common concern, and (2) that, if they fail to reach an agreement, even the elaborate provisions of the Dumbarton Oaks Plan will be of no avail. Therefore, continuous, organised, and collective contact between the great powers as provided by the Plan is no doubt useful, and may well prove to be a most valuable complement of the services which their diplomatic representatives will continue to render in this respect. But whatever the means or agencies, it is the will to peace by agreement which matters, most especially on the part of the great powers.

In this connection, it is interesting to examine the question: from what side must we expect possible threats to the world's peace, threats calling for the application of the Dumbarton Oaks Plan?

It may be assumed that the future peace-settlement will contain provisions which, in the light of present technical knowledge, afford adequate guarantees that the great aggressor states (Germany; Italy; Japan) will henceforth be prevented from being a menace again. The training received by the younger generation in each of these three countries coupled, in the case of Germany and Japan at any rate, with a tendency towards organised violence and world hegemony, make it necessary for the United Nations, were it only for self-preservation, to leave nothing undone in this sense. But, whatever safeguards are devised in the peace-settlement, nobody can be certain that the progress of science or the varying play of international politics will not enable the aggressor states to indulge one day in fresh manifestations of their lust for power. If this should happen, an organisation like that planned at Dumbarton Oaks might well prove to be of the highest importance, although it must be said that, for this particular purpose, a special organisation whose aims would be limited to the restraint of the three aggressor states would probably be enough.

For whom, or rather against what contingencies, then, should such a general organisation be set up? It is to keep the smaller states in check, thereby preventing their possible quarrels from disturbing the peace of the world? The reply, no doubt, is that this purpose would not require such an organisation. In the course of this century, there have only been two wars of any importance between smaller states: the Balkan wars of 1912, and the Chaco-war between Bolivia and Paraguay; both were strictly local in character, and neither disturbed the general peace. Moreover, latest developments have shown that, in order to wage war with modern weapons, financial and industrial resources are now required which are beyond the means of most, if not all, smaller states. In their case, therefore, an organisation as outlined at Dumbarton Oaks seems hardly necessary.

There remain the five great peace-loving states, with all their actual or potential resources for using armed force on modern lines. So long as they are peace-loving and unwilling to have recourse to the use of armed force (and there is no indication that they will take any other course), an elaborate organisation for the maintenance of peace and security would not appear necessary. If, on the other hand, they should ever threaten (a remote possibility, no doubt) to resort to the use of unauthorised armed force, everything will depend on the voting arrangements and on the readiness of the war-minded great power to abide by the result of the voting. A plan such as the Dumbarton Oaks Plan may or may not be endowed with a generally acceptable voting-system, but it cannot provide the certainty that in all circumstances every member will abide by the outcome of the vote.

For all the uncertainties attaching to the Plan in this respect (uncertainties which can never be entirely removed by other or better machinery because they depend, not on machinery, but on the will to use it), the Netherlands Government nevertheless earnestly hope that it will be made possible for their country as for all other countries to participate in making a fresh experiment for the maintenance of international peace and security on the basis of the ultimate result of the Dumbarton Oaks conversations. So long as that result is not too imperfect, it will be infinitely better for all states, great and small, than no arrangement at all. But, apart from a number of points of secondary importance which can be dealt with at a later stage, there are two main questions which will certainly interest the people of the Netherlands to such an extent that the adhesion of the country to the Plan may well prove to be conditioned by the more or less satisfactory way in which they are solved. To these, attention may now be invited.

I

The first point which is of particular interest to the Netherlands, is the basis on which decisions of the organisation are to be reached, either by the General Assembly or by the Security Council. It is stated in chapter I of the draft that the purposes of the organisation should be, *inter alia*, to maintain international peace and security; and to that end to take effective collective measures for the prevention and removal of threats to the peace and the suppression of acts of aggression or other breaches of the peace, and to bring about by peaceful means the adjustment or settlement of international disputes which may lead to a breach of the peace. And in chapter II, containing the principles of the Plan, it is explained that all members of the organisation should undertake to settle their disputes by peaceful means in such a manner that international peace and security are not endangered, whilst they are to refrain in their international relations from the threat or use of force in any manner inconsistent with the purposes of the organisation. But there is no mention or indication anywhere in the proposals of the basis on which decisions are to be taken, except when a case is to be submitted to the international court of justice, when presumably international law is to be applied, or to arbitration which, according to the classic definition of the Hague conventions for the pacific settlement of international disputes (1899 and 1907), gives an adjudication on the basis of respect for law, a vague and not very satisfactory formula. With regard to all other cases (and they may well prove in practice to be the most crucial). there is no indication of any standard to be applied. It is only suggested that peace must not be endangered.

This proposal appears very unsatisfactory for the Netherlands, who attach the highest value to the recognition of some acceptable standard of conduct in international affairs. What guarantee does this proposal afford victims of international violence that their cause will be upheld? Is it not tantamount to putting a premium on pressure brought to bear by stronger on weaker states? Instead of an obligation for the Security Council to enforce the duty of memberstates, whether right or wrong, in no case to resort to violence, there would come into being an obligation for that Council to save the peace. Experience shows how easily this may come to be done by seeking solutions calculated to induce powers threatening to use violence to refrain from carrying out their threat; such solutions may well be at the expense of the threatened power, however innocent. The maintenance of international peace and security is a most desirable goal. But if, speaking *ex hypothesi*, a case arose of peace being bought at the price of what would be widely felt as injustice, that price might well seem unreasonable to many; such a settlement could not be expected to command respect and therefore 'to endure, and if another and better settlement were not found, the prestige of the Security Council and of the organisation generally, would suffer accordingly. In other words, it does not seem possible to leave everything to mere opportunism in matters such as considered here. A statement, duly embodied in the proposals where its absence is very striking, to the effect that some standard of justice will always be observed, would go a long way towards dissipating anxieties, and it appears difficult to see why, if the thing is self-evident, there could be any objection to making such a statement.

The question then is: how the standard to be observed should be formulated, and how appropriate measures can be devised to ensure its observation. With regard to the first point, a reference to international law would appear to be inadequate, not only because it would exclude relevant considerations of another nature, but also because it may be doubted whether international law, in spite of its being subject to change and evolution, may be relied upon at all times and in all circumstances to provide a completely satisfactory standard. Legitimacy as a standard would undoubtedly be too static where a notion is needed allowing for growth and development. The Netherlands Government do not claim to have found the ultimate solution, but they have asked themselves whether a reference to those feelings of right and wrong, those moral principles which live in every normal human heart, would not be enough. That certainly is not a rigid or static notion.

The question of ensuring the observation of such a standard would, of course, be no less important. It clearly could not be left to the Security Council to decide, for if that were done this Council would be allowed to sit in judgment on its own proposals. Nor could it, for practical reasons, be left to the Assembly, or to the arbitrary appreciation of individual member-states. At this stage, the Netherlands Government only suggest that a solution will have to be found for this problem to make the Dumbarton Oaks Plan more generally acceptable. At the same time, they offer as a solution the appointment of an independent body of eminent men from a suitable number of different countries, men known for their integrity and their experience in international affairs, who should be readily available to pronounce upon decisions of the Security Council whenever an appeal to that effect were addressed to them, either by the Council or by a party to the case in question. This body, it should be emphasized, should pronounce upon the matter solely from the point of view of whether the Council's decision is in keeping with the moral principles above referred to, and should render its decision within a set number of days so as to avoid all undue delay and any diminution of the Council's effective and speedy handling of a given case.

It has rightly been said that the Security Council should have as much freedom of action as possible, and that this is no time to lay down hard and fast rules. But in the manner just indicated there is no question of laying down hard and fast rules, and the Council would retain the unfettered liberty of taking any decision except a decision of the kind against which the Dumbarton Oaks Plan contains no guarantee, and which, in spite of its careful wording of principles and purposes, it does not rule out.

II

The second point calling for special attention concerns that very thorny question: the relationship between the great powers and the smaller states. This is not the place for an exhaustive examination of this difficult problem. A few remarks would, however, seem indicated.

There were before the war, roughly, 491 million Chinese, 166 million citizens of the Soviet Union, 135 million Americans, 48 million nationals of the United Kingdom and Northern Ireland, and 42 million Frenchmen. The smaller nations of Europe comprise together about 150 million, and those of Latin America (to give only these two examples) another 100 million – no inconsiderable numbers, absolutely as well as relatively, of human beings with a right to the pursuit of freedom from fear equal to that of the nationals of the great powers. This memorandum is presented with a deep sense of responsibility towards nearly eighty million people living under the flag of the Netherlands, of whom roughly nine are in Europe and seventy in Asia.

These millions of the smaller powers are entitled to an adequate voice in the councils of the organisation to be established. Their wish to live free from fear, the fact, already noted, that they are no menace to the general peace of the world, and the contribution so many of them have made to the common fund of human civilisation, give them an irrefutable claim in this respect. In order that smaller nations may have an adequate voice, the mere fact that they are to have six places on the Security Council in its proposed composition does not seem to suffice. Here again, much depends on the voting system which will be devised. If decisions, of whatever importance, were to be taken on the basis of a majority vote, the result would be that the vote of one single small power would be enough to give the great powers a majority. Is it not to be feared that, in the hard practice of international relations one such vote will always be available? It seems to the Netherlands Government that some safeguard will have to be found on this point, and a provision that the affirmative vote of at least three of the non-permanent members (one-half of their total membership) of the Security Council would be required, would go far to allay what would appear to be legitimate apprehensions on this point on the part of the smaller powers.

This point is of particular interest to a state like the Netherlands which, by reason of its population, situation and resources is in a position, once the country is restored both in Europe and in Asia, to make a substantial contribution to the success of the Plan. The Netherlands Government consider that states who, without belonging to the great power class, are in that position, should always be adequately represented on the Security Council; they think that due provision should be made for that purpose in an appropriate form.

The Dumbarton Oaks Plan proclaims that it is based on the sovereign equality of all peace-loving states. At the same time, and apart from any rules still to be made on the subject of voting, it sanctions a special and privileged position for the great powers. They alone are to be permanent members of the Security Council. The Military Staff Committee is to be composed exclusively of their representatives. All such special privileges and inequalities are at variance with the principle of the sovereign equality of all peaceloving states. And yet, however peremptory the objections which, from the democratic, legal, and theoretical point of view may be made against special advantages for the mighty, it is recognised that, in the present state of the international community, it is necessary for the smaller powers, if there is to be a chance of building a new organisation for the maintenance of peace and security, to give a special place to the great powers, in return for which they are entitled to ask that these great powers show in practice that they are conscious of the special duties and responsibilities these concessions place upon them. In any case, whilst it may be necessary to invest power with special rights, the question is how far this should be allowed to go. The smaller powers, who are invited in the Dumbarton Oaks Plan to perpetuate and legalise an existing *de-facto* position of inferiority, may be permitted to point out that, if exorbitant special rights were granted virtually placing the great powers above the law, this Plan would be of little avail for the rest of the world, inasmuch as a return of the world to anarchy would not be excluded.

This seems of special importance when the system of voting comes under discussion. It has been said that a great power should have the right to reserve its attitude even if all others are agreed on a certain line of conduct to be taken. It is not clear to the Netherlands Government whether this right would be intended to be reserved for great powers with regard to all decisions of the Security Council, of whatever kind, or only with regard to decisions involving coercion, in one or another of its numerous forms, of third parties. In respect of questions involving coercion of third parties (that is to say of a state to be coerced, whether a member

of the Security Council or not, other than the voting state), the Netherlands Government are inclined to believe that the international community is now sufficiently advanced to require every member of the
organisation to undertake, by the fact of joining it, to co-operate loyally
in applying any sanctions other than those consisting of the use of force,
if these sanctions are decreed by the organisation in accordance with the
rules of procedure. On the other hand, the Netherlands Government
consider that every nation, great or small, should be at liberty, in the
absence of stipulations to the contrary in special regional agreements, in
every separate case to determine whether or not it wishes to participate
in the application of armed force. It has rightly been said that no nation,
whatever its size, will ever allow itself to be committed by a Security
Council to a war in which that nation does not believe; however regrettable this may be, the fact cannot be overlooked. Care should be
taken not to repeat the mistake made in the Covenant of the League of
Nations, by virtue of which every member-state was pledged to apply,
if required, armed force against adversaries unknown in advance in the
company of unknown partners and in unknown circumstances. That
seems more than any state, great or small, can promise, and disappointment would surely follow upon disregard of this fact.

In respect of all questions, however, other than those concerning
the use of armed force, the Netherlands Government consider that
no state, great or small, should be granted the right of reserving its
attitude.

Whether, on the other hand, the right of free appreciation, in so far
as it is to be granted, should ever take the extreme form of a right of
veto (that is to say a right for individual powers to prevent the whole
organisation from acting when a substantial majority or perhaps even all
members but one or two deem action necessary, are agreed on the nature
of the action and are ready to participate) – that would appear to be
another matter. Here, too, the distinction between *any* decision of the
organisation, and the strictly limited category of decisions relating to
coercive action may be useful. It is clear that a veto with regard to *any*
action by the organisation would reduce its usefulness in respect of the
maintenance of peace to little if anything, for it would mean that any
power having the right of veto could prevent the discussion of any matter
raised, with the result that there would be no international forum left
before which the aggrieved state could legitimately plead its case; by
accepting a Plan containing such a right of veto, it would have signed
away its freedom to do so. The Netherlands Government therefore
believe that, if there is to be any question of a right of veto, it can only
be a right of veto with regard to measures of coercion, and they further
think that, if insisted on, it should be restricted to cases of coercion by
armed force. The Netherlands Government do not anticipate that any
of the smaller powers will claim such a right of veto.[1] As for the great
powers, the Netherlands Government only wish to observe with regard
to this point (a) that they cannot, of course, be blind to the fact that, if
unanimity between the great powers were required when it comes to the
application of armed force against third parties, this would in certain
cases be a substantial guarantee for the smaller powers, and (b) that the

[1] For the right of free appreciation, however, *vide supra*.

Netherlands Government have some difficulty in understanding why a great power should have a right of veto with regard to questions with which that great power is only remotely concerned.

It has also been said that a great power should have a right of veto not only when third parties are concerned, but also in a case to which that great power is itself a party. This is a very delicate subject, and far be it from the Netherlands Government to make any statement which would make agreement on an effective and workable plan more difficult. The following remarks are therefore offered in the hope that, without creating difficulties, they may at least make clear the provisional opinion of the Netherlands Government before any final action is taken in completing the drafting of the Plan.

The Netherlands Government believe that they understand the reasons and feelings which have led to the advancement of this claim, and they fully respect these motives. They also consider that it is the unassailable right of any country to state what conditions must be fulfilled if it is freely to enter into an association of nations. At the same time, the Netherlands Government think that they may state two things. The first is that, if the great powers were given the right of veto in cases to which they are a party, the Dumbarton Oaks Plan would only be useful for promoting the orderly settlement of international disputes between smaller states, and even this only on a limited scale because of the right of veto of the great powers. In cases of disputes between great powers, or between a great power and a smaller state, the Plan would afford no protection. Would this produce freedom from fear? – And in the second place, the Netherlands Government think that they may be permitted to say this: it is the good right of any great power to say that it will not enter into an association which gives authority to its members in certain circumstances to use force against that state. But it is difficult to see what advantage or attraction the Plan would have for the Netherlands if a right of veto were granted to great powers in their own cause.

It is quite true, of course, that coercion of a great power by armed force is an operation of very great magnitude. But in the opinion of the Netherlands Government this cannot justify an organisation for the maintenance of international peace and security, if it is to be worthy of that name, in desisting from the outset and *a priori*, from the use of force against a great power. Yet so great a limitation of the organisation's scope would result from a veto being given to great powers in their own cause. Is it not greatly to be preferred that coercion of a great power by armed force, should the case ever arise, be decided upon and carried out in an orderly manner by a recognised organ of the international community, rather than leave it once more to the hazardous interplay of combinations of the moment?

If this Government may express a hope, it is that the right of veto in a power's own cause be not insisted on by any state. This right can, so far as the Netherlands Government are aware, only be claimed on three grounds: that the powers concerned are genuinely peace-loving so that any decision against them would at all times be wrong and unjustified; that their good faith should not be doubted, with the same conclusion; or that they need a safeguard against possible conspiracies of others. With regard to the first argument, it may be asked why there should be any need to make a Security Plan if the possibility is to be ruled out that some time, perhaps only in the distant future, some member-state, great or small, may break international peace? Secondly, the question of good faith should, in the opinion of the Netherlands Government, play no part. This has nothing to do with good faith; a power may, and probably would, wish to veto in perfect good faith, convinced of the righteousness of its own cause, the use of force against itself. Moreover, if belief in attachment to peace and in good faith were demanded by the great powers on behalf of themselves, the smaller powers would be justified in asking what good reason there can be to suspect that they, the smaller powers, are less genuinely peace-loving, or that their good faith is doubtful or worse. What is there in their past record, as contrasted with that of the great powers, to justify the claim that, in respect of them, and of them only, the application of coercion should always be possible? – And finally, with regard to the third ground, is there any power, great or small, which need fear that it may become a victim, *as a result of its adhesion to the Dumbarton Oaks Plan,* of a conspiracy of others, so that reservation of a right of veto with regard to themselves is necessary for member-states? To the Netherlands Government it seems difficult, at any rate, to see in what measure such a contingency is, in point of fact, less likely to arise if a right of vetoing coercion is conceded to a power in its own cause, than if it is not conceded. It affords no real protection.

The points raised under this heading may be summarised as follows: –

(1) consent of one-half of the smaller states represented on the Security Council to be required for decisions being taken;

(2) due representation on the Security Council to be assured to states which, in order of importance, rank immediately after the great powers;

(3) with regard to voting:

(a) no veto to be given to any state except, if this were to be considered necessary, in questions of coercion by armed force of third parties, and then only to the great powers directly concerned;

(b) no right of free appreciation with regard to decisions duly arrived at to be given to any state, except in questions of coercion by armed force of third parties, and then to all states, great or small (except when expressly stipulated otherwise in special regional agreements), and whether these states are members of the Security Council or not.

A few provisional remarks remain to be made on special subjects.

1. The Plan does not exclude *regional arrangements or agencies* for dealing with such matters relating to the maintenance of international peace and security as are appropriate for regional action, provided such arrangements or agencies and their activities are consistent with the purposes and principles of the organisation. On the contrary, the Security Council is encouraged to use such arrangements or agencies. The Netherlands Government welcome this stipulation as stated. Nothing, in fact, would seem to them more dangerous for the peace of the world than regional groupings which, however good the intentions which gave rise to their formation, may at any time be set against each other or against any given state for want of proper and adequate co-ordination.

2. It has already been observed that the Plan as it stands provides no sufficient safeguards that the interests of the smaller powers will be duly taken into account in the *Military Staff Committee.* In order that these interests be duly safeguarded, it is not enough that the Committee should have the duty (as stated in the Plan) to invite any member of the organisation not permanently represented on the Committee to be associated with it when the efficient discharge of the Committee's responsibilities require that such a state should participate in its work. What is also necessary is that any member should have the right on its own initiative to lay before the Committee, either orally or in writing, questions properly belonging to the Committee's field of action, to have these questions discussed with the Committee in the form of an exchange of views, and to receive an answer in due course.

With regard to the actual planning of military operations, the Netherlands Government suppose that the Military Staff Committee could do that part of its work only to prepare campaigns against powers not represented on that body, that is to say against the vanquished enemy powers (if no special machinery were to be established to deal with them), or against the smaller powers, however unlikely it may be that these will ever break the peace of the world. For such plans must needs remain unknown to those against whom they are directed, and since the great powers are all represented on the Committee, they would be exactly informed with regard to any measures planned against any of them. In this respect, therefore, the usefulness of the Committee should not be over-estimated.

3. It will, no doubt, be understood if the Netherlands Government show a special interest in the proposed *International Court of Justice*. They welcome the proposals contained in the Plan for such a Court, in particular in so far as they envisage the continuation, after the necessary readjustments, of the existing Permanent Court of International Justice. Full opportunity should be given to all states to participate in the drafting of the Court's statute, and it is hoped that to that end such preparatory work as has already been done will be found useful.[1] Experience shows that every possible safeguard should be inserted in the statute to ensure as far as possible that the judges composing the Court not only are, but will also be recognised as being impartial and independent. Furthermore, it would seem desirable to the Netherlands Government in the interest of international justice that the Plan should contain an express stipulation to the effect that all member states (1) recognise the Court as having compulsory jurisdiction in justiciable disputes to which they are a party and for the solution of which the parties do not agree on another mode of settlement, and (2) recognise the Court's findings as binding.

4. The Netherlands Government warmly welcome the provisions of the draft concerning arrangements for international, economic and social co-operation. They consider that the *Economic and Social Council* to be created may be of great use for promoting a better understanding of international economic and social problems. They hope that this Council will be provided with a research department which would make available to the general public in all countries, on a strictly scientific basis, studies calculated to promote insight in those problems, which in the past have

---

[1] An informal committee consisting of experts from Belgium, Canada, Czechoslovakia, France, Great Britain and Northern Ireland, Greece, Luxemburg, the Netherlands, New Zealand, Norway and Poland, who happened to be available in London, has drafted a report on the future Court of International Justice.

so often, for lack of better knowledge, tended to cast heavy shadows on the relations between many countries.

These are the observations which, actuated by the sincere desire to make a contribution, however modest, to the success of the Dumbarton Oaks Plan, the Netherlands Government have to offer at the moment. At the same time, they wish to point out that their attitude must be one of reserve so long as the Plan is incomplete and in particular so long as the voting system to be inserted in the Proposals has not been fully worked out. Also, they can only repeat that the final decision concerning the attitude to be taken by the Netherlands Government rests with the Netherlands people, who will form their opinion through sober appraisal of the real merits of the completed Plan.

Januari, 1945

AMENDMENTS TO THE PROPOSALS FOR THE MAINTENANCE OF PEACE AND SECURITY AGREED ON AT THE FOUR POWERS CONFERENCE OF DUMBARTON OAKS SUPPLEMENTED AS A RESULT OF THE CONFERENCE OF YALTA, SUBMITTED BY

THE NETHERLANDS DELEGATION

TO THE SAN FRANCISCO CONFERENCE

In January 1945, the Netherlands Government have presented certain suggestions to the Governments of the United Nations and the Governments associated with them in the present war, concerning the Proposals for the maintenance of peace and security agreed on at the Four Powers Conference of Dumbarton Oaks as published on October 9, 1944. Having taken cognizance of the results of the Yalta Conference with regard to these Proposals and, of a number of observations made by various Governments and in the course of public discussion, the Netherlands Government have instructed their Delegation to submit the following amendments for consideration by the Conference. Whilst some of these amendments are of a largely technical nature, others concern matters of principle to which the Netherlands Government attach the greatest importance.

I

Chapter I (Purposes) and II (Principles)

Alternative Amendment

A (in case B is not accepted)

Insert in Chapter I sub 1 after the words "To maintain international peace and security":

"in conformity with the elementary principles of morality and justice and on the basis of due regard for international law ",

or

B (in case A is not accepted)

Insert in or add to the Chapter a statement setting forth the fundamental rights and duties of States.

Comment:

The Proposals state that one of the purposes of the Organisation should be: to maintain international peace and security. They do not state on which basis international peace and security should be maintained. The Netherlands Government consider the express indication of that basis as being indispensable. In the opinion of the Netherlands Government, this could be done by adopting either amendment *A* or *B*.

It is observed in this connection that the proposed voting procedure in the Security Council gives the permanent members of that Council special rights which tend to weaken the position of the other members of an Organisation based on the principle of the sovereign equality of all peace-loving states. The adoption of either of the amendments mentioned under *A* and *B* would afford these other members some reasonable compensation for and correction of this inequality.

As an example of a statement setting forth the fundamental rights and duties of states as mentioned sub *B*, the annex to this document reproduces "The principles for the International Law of the Future", formulated by a number of American and Canadian lawyers and published by the Carnegie Endowment for International Peace in its "International Conciliation" – Bulletin of April, 1944.

II

Chapter III (Membership)

Insert in paragraph I after the words "Membership of the Organisation should be open "to all peace-loving states"":

"which may be expected on account of their institutions and by their international behaviour faithfully to observe and carry out international commitments".

Comment:

The insertion of this rule, however important, would not appear to be necessary in so far as the States represented at the San Francisco Conference are concerned. The insertion would, however, seem to be useful in view of the admission into the Organisation at some future date of other States who, in order to qualify for admission, would thus be required to have given conclusive proof of their firm adherence to the rule "pacta sunt servanda".

III

Chapter V Section B
(Functions and Powers of the General Assembly)

Insert at the end of the first sentence of par. 3:
", and to raise the suspension of that member".

IV

Chapter V Section B
(Functions and Powers of the General Assembly)

Insert at the end of par. 5:
"A member of the Organisation which has not in due time paid its portion

of the expenses loses its right to vote in the Assembly and, if a member of the Security Council, forfeits its seat thereon''.

Comment:

A rule of this nature would tend to minimize the accumulation of arrears.

v

Chapter VI Section C (Voting)

Paragraph 3 to read:

"Decisions of the Security Council on all other matters should be made "by an affirmative vote including the concurrent votes of the permanent "members and of one half of, or – in cases in which the number of non- "permanent members entitled to vote is uneven – the majority of the "non-permanent members, provided that in decisions under Chapter 8, "Section A and under the second sentence of paragraph 1 of Chapter 8, "Section C, a party to a dispute should abstain from voting".

Comment:

It seems desirable, if the interests of the non-permanent members of the Security Council are to be duly safeguarded, to prevent that a decision of the Security Council can be taken by a majority consisting of the votes of the permanent members plus that of only two non-permanent members.

VI

Chapter VIII

(Arrangements for the Maintenance of International Peace and Security Including Prevention and Suppression of Aggression)

1. Section A (Pacific Settlement of Disputes and Determination of Threats to the Peace or acts of aggression)

Add two new paragraphs at the end of this Section, reading as follows:

8. "Should the Security Council deem that a failure to settle a dispute "in accordance with procedures indicated in paragraph 3 of Section A, "or in accordance with its recommendations made under paragraph 5 of "Section A, constitutes a threat to the maintenance of international peace "and security, it should determine the existence of such a threat".

9. "In general the Security Council should determine the existence "of any threat to the peace, breach of the peace or act of aggression".

2. Section B (Action with respect to the existence of Threats to the Peace or Acts of Aggression)

Paragraphs 1 and 2 to read as follows:

"1. Should the Security Council under paragraph 8 of Section A "determine the existence of a threat to the maintenance of international "peace and security, it should take any measures necessary for the "maintenance of international peace and security in accordance with the "purposes and principles of the Organisation".

"2. Should the Security Council in general, under paragraph 9 of Sec-
"tion A determine the existence of any threat to the peace, breach of the
"peace or act of aggression, it should decide upon the measures to be
"taken to maintain or restore peace and security".

3. In connection with sub *1* and *2* above, Section A should bear the
following title:
"Pacific Settlement of Disputes and Determination of Threats to the
"Peace or Acts of Aggression"; and Section B the title: "Action with
respect to Existence of Threats to the Peace or Acts of Aggression".

Comment:

> A distinction should be made, so far as voting is concerned, between
> the *quasi-judicial function* of the Security Council in promoting the
> pacific settlement of disputes and its *executive function* in taking
> action for the maintenance of peace and security. It would seem
> desirable to treat the function of the Security Council in determining
> the existence of any threat to the peace, breach of the peace or act
> of aggression, as part of its quasi-judicial function and to stipulate
> therefore that in such cases also, a party to a dispute should abstain
> from voting.

VII

Chapter VI Section D (Procedure)

Insert at the end of paragraph 5:
", and shall enjoy the same position with regard to discussion and voting
"as the other party to the dispute".

Comment:

> The adoption of this rule appears necessary if, as seems desirable,
> the position of parties to a dispute mentioned in this paragraph is
> to be equal.

VIII

Chapter VII

(An International Court of Justice)

Insert a new paragraph reading as follows:
"The Court shall give an advisory opinion of any legal question referred
"to it by the General Assembly or the Security Council".

Comment:

> If this Amendment is adopted the second sentence of paragraph 6
> of Section A of Chapter VIII should be deleted.

In connection with Chapter XII (Transitional Arrangements) the
Netherlands Delegation has been instructed to propose that an international commission be appointed by the General Assembly in its first
meeting to determine to what extent and in what manner rights and
duties of the League of Nations laid down in various international
conventions should be transferred to the new Organisation or otherwise
dealt with.

The Netherlands Government recommend that the provisions of the League of Nations Covenant with regard to the registration of Treaties as a condition for their validity be retained in the Charter of the new Organisation.

Annex

Principles for the International Law of the Future

Principle 1

Each State has a legal duty to carry out in full good faith its obligations under international law, and it may not involve limitations contained in its own constitution or laws as an excuse of a failure to perform this duty.

Principle 2

Each State has a legal duty to see that conditions prevailing within its own territory do not menace international peace and order, and to this end it must treat its own population in a way which will not violate the dictates of humanity and justice or shock the conscience of mankind.

Principle 3

Each State has a legal duty to refrain from intervention in the interna affairs of any other State.

Principle 4

Each State has a legal duty to prevent the organisation within its territory of activities calculated to foment civil strife in the territory of any other State.

Principle 5

Each State has a legal duty to cooperate with other States in establishing and maintaining agencies of the Community of States for dealing with matters of concern to the Community, and to collaborate in the work of such agencies.

Principle 6

Each State has a legal duty to employ pacific means and none but pacific means in seeking to settle its disputes with other States, and failing settlement by other pacific means to accept the settlement of its disputes by the competent agency of the Community of States.

Principle 7

Each State has a legal duty to refrain from any use of force and from any threat to use force in its relations with another State, except as authorized by the competent agency of the Community of States; but subject to immediate reference to and approval by the competent agency of the Community of States, a State may oppose by force an unauthorized use of force made against it by another State.

Principle 8

Each State has a legal duty to take, in cooperation with other States, such measures as may be prescribed by the competent agency of the Community of States for preventing or suppressing a use of force by any State in its relations with another State.

Principle 9

Each State has a legal duty to conform to the limitations prescribed by the competent agency of the Community of States and to submit to the supervision and control of such an agency, with respect to the size and type of its armaments.

Principle 10

Each State has a legal duty to refrain from entering into any agreement with another State, the performance of which would be inconsistent with the discharge of its duties under general international law.

Source: *Het Ontstaan der Verenigde Naties*, Government Printing Office, The Hague, 1950, pp. 152–169.

DECLARATION
REGARDING THE DEFEAT OF GERMANY AND THE ASSUMPTION OF SUPREME AUTHORITY WITH RESPECT TO GERMANY BY THE GOVERNMENTS OF THE UNITED KINGDOM, THE UNITED STATES, THE USSR, AND THE PROVISIONAL GOVERNMENT OF THE FRENCH REPUBLIC

5 *June* 1945.

The German armed forces on land, at sea and in the air have been completely defeated and have surrendered unconditionally and Germany, which bears responsibility for the war, is no longer capable of resisting the will of the victorious Powers. The unconditional surrender of Germany has thereby been effected, and Germany has become subject to such requirements as may now or hereafter be imposed upon her.

There is no central Government or authority in Germany capable of accepting responsibility for the maintenance of order, the administration of the country and compliance with the requirements of the victorious Powers.

It is in these circumstances necessary, without prejudice to any subsequent decisions that may be taken respecting Germany, to make provision for the cessation of any further hostilities on the part of the German armed forces, for the maintenance of order in Germany and for the administration of the country, and to announce the immediate requirements with which Germany must comply.

The Representatives of the Supreme Commands of the United Kingdom the United States of America, the Union of Soviet Socialist Republics and the French Republic, hereinafter called the 'Allied Representatives', acting by authority of their respective Governments and in the interests of the United Nations, accordingly make the following Declaration:

The Governments of the United Kingdom, the United States of America and the Union of Soviet Socialist Republics, and the Provisional Government of the French Republic, hereby assume supreme authority with respect to Germany, including all the powers possessed by the German Government, the High Command and any state, municipal, or local government or authority. The assumption, for the purpose stated above, of the said authority and powers does not effect the annexation of Germany.

The Governments of the United Kingdom, the United States of America and the Union of Soviet Socialist Republics, and the Provisional Government of the French Republic, will hereafter determine the boundaries of Germany or any part thereof and the status of Germany or of any area at present being part of German territory.

In virtue of the supreme authority and powers thus assumed by the four Governments, the Allied Representatives announce the following requirements arising from the complete defeat and unconditional surrender of Germany with which Germany must comply:

Article 1

Germany and all German military, naval and air authorities and all forces under German control shall immediately cease hostilities in all theatres of war against the forces of the United Nations on land, at sea and in the air.

Article 2

(a) All armed forces of Germany or under German control, wherever they may be situated, including land, air, anti-aircraft and naval forces, the SS, SA and Gestapo, and all other forces or auxiliary organisations equipped with weapons, shall be completely disarmed, handing over their weapons and equipment to local Allied Commanders or to officers designated by the Allied Representatives.

(b) The personnel of the formations and units of all the forces referred to in paragraph (a) above shall, at the discretion of the Commander-in-Chief of the Armed Forces of the Allied State concerned, be declared to be prisoners of war, pending further decisions, and shall be subject to such conditions and directions as may be prescribed by the respective Allied Representatives.

(c) All forces referred to in paragraph (a) above, wherever they may be, will remain in their present positions pending instruction from the Allied Representatives.

(d) Evacuation by the said forces of all territories outside the frontiers of Germany as they existed on the 31st December, 1937, will proceed according to instructions to be given by the Allied Representatives.

(e) Detachments of civil police to be armed with small arms only, for the maintenance of order and for guard duties, will be designated by the Allied Representatives.

Article 3

(a) All aircraft of any kind or nationality in Germany or German-occupied or controlled territories or waters, military, naval or civil, other than aircraft in the service of the Allies, will remain on the ground, on the water or aboard ships pending further instructions.

(b) All German or German-controlled aircraft in or over territories or waters not occupied or controlled by Germany will proceed to Germany or to such place or places as may be specified by the Allied Representatives.

Article 4

(a) All German or German-controlled naval vessels, surface and submarine, auxiliary naval craft, and merchant and other shipping, wherever such vessels may be at the time of this Declaration, and all other merchant ships of whatever nationality in German ports, will remain in or proceed immediately to ports and bases as specified by the Allied Representatives. The crews of such vessels will remain on board pending further instructions.

(b) All ships and vessels of the United Nations, whether or not title has been transferred as the result of prize court or other proceedings, which are at the disposal of Germany or under German control at the time of this Declaration, will proceed at the dates and to the ports or bases specified by the Allied Representatives.

Article 5

(*a*) All or any of the following articles in the possession of the German armed forces or under German control or at German disposal will be held intact and in good condition at the disposal of the Allied Representatives, for such purposes and at such times and places as they may prescribe:

(i) all arms, ammunition, explosives, military equipment, stores and supplies and other implements of war of all kinds and all other war material;

(ii) all naval vessels of all classes, both surface and submarine, auxiliary naval craft and all merchant shipping, whether afloat, under repair or construction, built or building;

(iii) all aircraft of all kinds, aviation and anti-aircraft equipment and devices;

(iv) all transportation and communications facilities and equipment by land, water or air;

(v) all military installations and establishments, including airfields, seaplane bases, ports and naval bases, storage depots, permanent and temporary land and coast fortifications, fortresses and other fortified areas, together with plans and drawings of all such fortifications, installations and establishments;

(vi) all factories, plants, shops, research institutions, laboratories, testing stations, technical data, patents, plans, drawings and inventions, designed or intended to produce or to facilitate the production or use of the articles, materials and facilities referred to in sub-paragraphs (i), (ii), (iii), (iv) and (v) above or otherwise to further the conduct of war.

(*b*) At the demand of the Allied Representatives the following will be furnished:—

(i) the labour, services and plant required for the maintenance or operation of any of the six categories mentioned in paragraph (a) above; and

(ii) any information or records that may be required by the Allied Representatives in connection with the same.

(*c*) At the demand of the Allied Representatives all facilities will be provided for the movement of Allied troops and agencies, their equipment and supplies, on the railways, roads and other land communications or by sea, river or air. All means of transportation will be maintained in good order and repair, and the labour, services and plant necessary therefore will be furnished.

Article 6

(*a*) The German authorities will release to the Allied Representatives, in accordance with the procedure to be laid down by them, all prisoners of war at present in their power, belonging to the forces of the United Nations, and will furnish full lists of these persons, indicating the places of their detention in Germany or territory occupied by Germany. Pending the release of such prisoners of war, the German authorities and people will protect them in their persons and property and provide them with adequate food, clothing, shelter, medical attention and money in accordance with their rank or official position.

(*b*) The German authorities and people will in like manner provide for and release all other nationals of the United Nations who are confined, interned or otherwise under restraint, and all other persons who may be confined, interned or otherwise under restraint for political reasons or as a result of any Nazi action, law or regulation which discriminates on the ground of race, colour, creed or political belief.

(c) The German authorities will, at the demand of the Allied Representatives, hand over control of places of detention to such officers as may be designated for the purpose by the Allied Representatives.

Article 7

The German authorities concerned will furnish to the Allied Representatives:

(a) full information regarding the forces referred to in Article 2 (a), and, in particular, will furnish forthwith all information which the Allied Representatives may require concerning the numbers, locations and dispositions of such forces, whether located inside or outside Germany;

(b) complete and detailed information concerning mines, minefields and other obstacles to movement by land, sea or air, and the safety lanes in connection therewith. All such safety lanes will be kept open and clearly marked; all mines, minefields and other dangerous obstacles will as far as possible be rendered safe, and all aids to navigation will be reinstated. Unarmed German military and civilian personnel with the necessary equipment will be made available and utilised for the above purposes and for the removal of mines, minefields and other obstacles as directed by the Allied Representatives.

Article 8

There shall be no destruction, removal, concealment, transfer or scuttling of, or damage to, any military, naval, air, shipping, port, industrial and other like property and facilities and all records and archives, wherever they may be situated, except as may be directed by the Allied Representatives.

Article 9

Pending the institution of control by the Allied Representatives over all means of communication, all radio and telecommunication installations and other forms of wire or wireless communications, whether ashore or afloat, under German control, will cease transmission except as directed by the Allied Representatives.

Article 10

The forces, ships, aircraft, military equipment, and other property in Germany or in German control or service or at German disposal, of any other country at war with any of the Allies, will be subject to the provisions of this Declaration and of any proclamations, orders, ordinances or instructions issued thereunder.

Article 11

(a) The principal Nazi leaders as specified by the Allied Representatives, and all persons from time to time named or designated by rank, office or employment by the Allied Representatives as being suspected of having committed, ordered or abetted war crimes or analogous offences, will be apprehended and surrendered to the Allied Representatives.

(*b*) The same will apply in the case of any national of any of the United Nations who is alleged to have committed an offence against his national law, and who may at any time be named or designated by rank, office or employment by the Allied Representatives.

(*c*) The German authorities and people will comply with any instructions given by the Allied Representatives for the apprehension and surrender of such persons.

Article 12

The Allied Representatives will station forces and civil agencies in any or all parts of Germany as they may determine.

Article 13

(*a*) In the exercise of the supreme authority with respect to Germany assumed by the Governments of the United Kingdom, the United States of America and the Union of Soviet Socialist Republics, and the Provisional Government of the French Republic, the four Allied Governments will take such steps, including the complete disarmament and demilitarisation of Germany, as they deem requisite for future peace and security.

(*b*) The Allied Representatives will impose on Germany additional political, administrative, economic, financial, military and other requirements arising from the complete defeat of Germany. The Allied Representatives, or persons or agencies duly designated to act on their authority, will issue proclamations, orders, ordinances and instructions for the purpose of laying down such additional requirements, and of giving effect to the other provisions of this Declaration. All German authorities and the German people shall carry out unconditionally the requirements of the Allied Representatives, and shall fully comply with all such proclamations, orders, ordinances and instructions.

Article 14

This Declaration enters into force and effect at the date and hour set forth below. In the event of failure on the part of the German authorities or people promptly and completely to fulfil their obligations hereby or hereafter imposed, the Allied Representatives will take whatever action may be deemed by them to be appropriate under the circumstances.

Article 15

This Declaration is drawn up in the English, Russian, French and German languages. The English, Russian and French are the only authentic texts.

Berlin, 5 June 1945.
16.40 Hours.

Signed by the Allied Representatives:
B. MONTGOMERY, F. M.
DWIGHT D. EISENHOWER
G. K. ZHUKOV
J. DE LATTRE DE TASSIGNY

STATEMENT BY THE GOVERNMENTS OF THE UNITED KINGDOM, THE UNITED
STATES, THE USSR, AND THE PROVISIONAL GOVERNMENT OF THE FRENCH
REPUBLIC ON ZONES OF OCCUPATION IN GERMANY

5 *June* 1945

Germany, within her frontiers as they were on 31st December, 1937, will,
for the purposes of occupation, be divided into four zones, one to be
allotted to each Power as follows:

an eastern zone to the Union of Soviet Socialist Republics;
a north-western zone to the United Kingdom;
a south-western zone to the United States of America;
a western zone to France.

The occupying forces in each zone will be under a Commander-in-
Chief designated by the responsible Power. Each of the four Powers may,
at its discretion, include among the forces assigned to occupation duties
under the command of its Commander-in-Chief, auxiliary contingents
from the forces of any other Allied Power which has actively participated
in military operations against Germany.

2. The area of 'Greater Berlin' will be occupied by forces of each of the
four Powers. An Inter-Allied Governing Authority (in Russian, Komen-
datura) consisting of four Commandants, appointed by their respective
Commanders-in-Chief, will be established to direct jointly its administration.

STATEMENT BY THE GOVERNMENTS OF THE UNITED KINGDOM, THE UNITED
STATES, THE USSR, AND THE PROVISIONAL GOVERNMENT OF THE FRENCH
REPUBLIC ON CONTROL MACHINERY IN GERMANY

5 *June* 1945

In the period when Germany is carrying out the basic requirements of
unconditional surrender, supreme authority in Germany will be exercised,
on instructions from their Governments, by the British, United States,
Soviet and French Commanders-in-Chief, each in his own zone of occupation, and also jointly, in matters affecting Germany as a whole. The
four Commanders-in-Chief will together constitute the Control Council.
Each Commander-in-Chief will be assisted by a Political Adviser.

2. The Control Council, whose decisions shall be unanimous, will ensure appropriate uniformity of action by the Commanders-in-Chief in
their respective zones of occupation and will reach agreed decisions on the
chief questions affecting Germany as a whole.

3. Under the Control Council there will be a permanent Co-ordinating
Committee composed of one representative of each of the four Commanders-in-Chief, and a Control Staff organised in the following Divisions
(which are subject to adjustment in the light of experience): —

Military; Naval; Air; Transport; Political; Economic; Finance; Reparation, Deliveries and Restitution; Internal Affairs and Communications;
Legal; Prisoners of War and Displaced Persons; Man-power.

There will be four heads of each Division, one designated by each Power. The staffs of the Divisions may include civilian as well as military personnel, and may also in special cases include nationals of other United Nations appointed in a personal capacity.

4. The functions of the Co-ordinating Committee and of the Control Staff will be to advise the Control Council, to carry out the Council's decisions and to transmit them to the appropriate German organs, and to supervise and control the day-to-day activities of the latter.

5. Liaison with the other United Nations Governments chiefly interested will be established through the appointment by such Governments of military missions (which may include civilian members) to the Control Council. These missions will have access through the appropriate channels to the organs of control.

6. United Nations organisations will, if admitted by the Control Council to operate in Germany, be subordinate to the Allied control machinery and answerable to it.

7. The administration of the 'Greater Berlin' area will be directed by an Inter-Allied Governing Authority, which will operate under the general direction of the Control Council, and will consist of four Commandants, each of whom will serve in rotation as Chief Commandant. They will be assisted by a technical staff which will supervise and control the activities of the local German organs.

8. The arrangements outlined above will operate during the period of occupation following German surrender, when Germany is carrying out the basic requirements of unconditional surrender. Arrangements for the subsequent period will be the subject of a separate agreement.

Source: <i>Documents on Germany under Occupation, 1945–1954</i>, Royal Institute of International Affairs, 1955, pp. 29–37.

PROTOCOL OF PROCEEDINGS OF THE BERLIN CONFERENCE, JULY 17–AUGUST 2, 1945. DEPARTMENT OF STATE PRESS RELEASE, MARCH 24, 1947

The Berlin conference of the three heads of government of the Union of Soviet Socialist Republics, the United States of America, and United Kingdom, which took place from July 17 to August 2, 1945, came to the following conclusions:

I. ESTABLISHMENT OF A COUNCIL OF FOREIGN MINISTERS

A. The conference reached the following agreement for the establishment of a Council of Foreign Ministers to do the necessary preparatory work for the peace settlements:

1

There shall be established a Council composed of the Foreign Ministers of the United Kingdom, the Union of Soviet Socialist Republics, China, France and the United States.

2

(I) The Council shall normally meet in London, which shall be the permanent seat of the joint secretariat which the Council will form. Each of the Foreign Ministers will be accompanied by a high-ranking deputy, duly authorized to carry on the work of the Council in the absence of his Foreign Minister, and by a small staff of technical advisers.

(II) The first meeting of the Council shall be held in London not later than September 1, 1945. Meetings may be held by common agreement in other capitals as may be agreed from time to time.

3

(I) As its immediate important task the Council shall be authorized to draw up, with a view to their submission to the United Nations, treaties of peace with Italy, Rumania, Bulgaria, Hungary and Finland, and to propose settlements of territorial questions outstanding on the termination of the war in Europe. The Council shall be utilized for the preparation of a peace settlement for Germany to be accepted by the Government of Germany when a Government adequate for the purpose is established.

(II) For the discharge of each of these tasks the Council will be composed of the members representing those states which were signatory to the terms of surrender imposed upon the enemy state concerned. For the purpose of the peace settlement for Italy, France shall be regarded as a signatory to the terms of surrender for Italy. Other members will be invited to participate when matters directly concerning them are under discussion.

(III) Other matters may from time to time be referred to the Council by agreement between the member Governments.

(I) Whenever the Council is considering a question of direct interest to a state not represented thereon, such state should be invited to send representatives to participate in the discussion and study of that question.

(II) The Council may adapt its procedure to the particular problems under consideration. In some cases it may hold its own preliminary discussions prior to the participation of other interested states. In other cases, the Council may convoke a formal conference of the state chiefly interested in seeking a solution of the particular problem.

B. It was agreed that the three Governments should each address an identical invitation to the Governments of China and France to adopt this text and to join in establishing the Council. The text of the approved invitation was as follows:

COUNCIL OF FOREIGN MINISTERS DRAFT FOR IDENTICAL INVITATION TO BE SENT SEPARATELY BY EACH OF THE THREE GOVERNMENTS TO THE GOVERNMENTS OF CHINA AND FRANCE

The Governments of the United Kingdom, the United States and the Union of Soviet Socialist Republics consider it necessary to begin without delay the essential preparatory work upon the peace settlements in Europe. To this end they are agreed that there should be established a Council of the Foreign Ministers of the five great powers to prepare treaties of peace with the European enemy states from submission to the United Nations. The Council would also be empowered to propose settlements of outstanding territorial questions in Europe and to consider such other matters as member Governments might agree to refer to it.

The text adopted by the Three Governments is as follows:

(Here insert final agreed text of the proposal)

"In agreement with the Governments of the United States, His Majesty's Government in the United Kingdom and Union of Soviet Socialist Republics, the United States Government, the United Kingdom and the Soviet Government extend a cordial invitation to the Government of China (France) to adopt the text quoted above and to join in setting up the Council. His Majesty's Government, the United States Government, the Soviet Government attach much importance to the participation of the Chinese Government (French Government) in the proposed arrangements and they hope to receive an early and favorable reply to this invitation."

C. It was understood that the establishment of the Council of Foreign Ministers for the specific purposes named in the text would be without prejudice to the agreement of the Crimea Conference that there should be periodical consultation between the Foreign Secretaries of the United States, the Union of Soviet Socialist Republics and the United Kingdom.

D. The conference also considered the position of the European Advisory Commission in the light of the agreement to establish the Council of Foreign Ministers. It was noted with satisfaction that the Commission had ably discharged its principal tasks by the recommendations that it had furnished for the terms of surrender for Germany, for the zones of occupation in Germany and Austria and for the inter-Allied control machinery in those countries. It was felt that further work of a detailed character for the coordination of Allied policy for the control of Germany and Austria would in future fall within the competence of the Control Council at Berlin and the Allied Commission at Vienna. Accordingly, it was agreed to recommend that the European Advisory Commission be dissolved.

II. THE PRINCIPLES TO GOVERN THE TREATMENT OF GERMANY IN THE INITIAL CONTROL

A. Political principles

1

In accordance with the agreement on control machinery in Germany, supreme authority in Germany is exercised, on instructions from their respective Governments, by the commanders in chief of the armed forces of the United States of America, the United Kingdom, the Union of Soviet Socialist Republics and the French Republic, each in his own zone of occupation, and also jointly, in matters affecting Germany as a whole, in their capacity as members of the Control Council.

2

So far as is practicable, there shall be uniformity of treatment of the German population throughout Germany.

3

The purposes of the occupation of Germany by which the Control Council shall be guided are:

(I) The complete disarmament and demilitarization of Germany and the elimination or control of all German industry that could be used for military production. To these ends:

(*a*) All German land, naval and air forces, the SS, SA, SD and Gestapo, with all their organizations, staffs and institutions, including the general staff, the officers' corps, reserve corps, military schools, war veterans organizations and all other military and semi-military organizations, together with all clubs and associations which serve to keep alive the military tradition in Germany, shall be completely and finally abolished in such manner as permanently to prevent the revival or reorganization of German militarism and nazism;

(*b*) All arms, ammunition and implements of war and all specialized facilities for their production shall be held at the disposal of the Allies or destroyed. The maintenance and production of all aircraft and all arms, ammunition and implements of war shall be prevented.

(II) To convince the German people that they have suffered a total military defeat and that they cannot escape responsibility for what they have brought upon themselves, since their own ruthless warfare and the fanatical Nazi resistance have destroyed German economy and made chaos and suffering inevitable.

(III) To destroy the National Socialist party and its affiliated and supervised organizations, to dissolve all Nazi institutions, to insure that they are not revived in any form and to prevent all Nazi and militarist activity or propaganda.

(IV) To prepare for the eventual reconstruction of German political life on a democratic basis and for eventual peaceful cooperation in international life by Germany.

4

All Nazi laws which provide the basis of the Hitler regime or established discriminations on grounds of race, creed or political opinion shall be abolished. No such discriminations, whether legal, administrative or otherwise, shall be tolerated.

5

War criminals and those who have participated in planning or carrying out Nazi enterprises involving or resulting in atrocities or war crimes shall be arrested and brought to judgment. Nazi leaders, influential Nazi supporters and high officials of Nazi organizations and institutions and any other persons dangerous to the occupation or its objectives shall be arrested and interned.

6

All members of the Nazi party who have been more than nominal participants in its activities and all other persons hostile to Allied purposes shall be removed from public and semi-public office and from positions of responsibility in important private undertakings. Such persons shall be replaced by persons who, by their political and moral qualities, are deemed capable of assisting in developing genuine democratic institutions in Germany.

7

German education shall be so controlled as completely to eliminate Nazi and militarist doctrines and to make possible the successful development of democratic ideas.

8

The judicial system will be reorganized in accordance with the principles of democracy, of justice under law and of equal rights for all citizens without distinction of race, nationality or religion.

9

The administration in Germany should be directed toward the decentralization of the political structure and the development of local responsibility. To this end:

(I) Local self-government shall be restored throughout Germany on democratic principles and in particular through elective councils as rapidly as is consistent with military security and the purposes of military occupation;

(II) All democratic political parties with rights of assembly and of public discussion shall be allowed and encouraged throughout Germany;

(III) Representative and elective principles shall be introduced into regional, provincial and state (Land) administration as rapidly as may be justified by the successful application of these principles in local self-government;

(IV) For the time being, no central German Government shall be established. Notwithstanding this, however, certain essential central German administrative departments, headed by state secretaries, shall be established, particularly in the fields of finance, transport, communications, foreign trade and industry. Such departments will act under the direction of the Control Council.

10

Subject to the necessity for maintaining military security, freedom of speech, press and religion shall be permitted, and religious institutions shall be respected. Subject likewise to the maintenance of military security the formation of free trade unions shall be permitted.

B. Economic Principles

11

In order to eliminate Germany's war potential, the production of arms, ammunition and implements of war as well as all types of aircraft and sea-going ships shall be prohibited and prevented. Production of metals, chemicals, machinery and other items that are directly necessary to a war economy shall be rigidly controlled and restricted to Germany's approved post-war peacetime needs to meet the objectives stated in Paragraph 15. Productive capacity not needed for permitted production shall be removed in accordance with the reparations plan recommended by the Allied Commission on reparations and approved by the Governments concerned, or if not removed, shall be destroyed.

12

At the earliest practicable date, the Germany economy shall be decentralized for the purpose of eliminating the present excessive concentration of economic power as exemplified in particular by cartels, syndicates, trusts and other monopolistic arrangements.

13

In organizing the German economy, primary emphasis shall be given to the development of agriculture and peaceful domestic industries.

14

During the period of occupation Germany shall be treated as a single economic unit. To this end, common policies shall be established in regard to:

(a) Mining and industrial production and its allocation;

(b) Agriculture, forestry and fishing;

(c) Wages, prices and rationing;
(d) Import and export programs for Germany as a whole;
(e) Currency and banking, central taxation and customs;
(f) Reparation and removal of industrial war potential;
(g) Transportation and communications.

In applying these policies, account shall be taken, where appropriate, of varying local conditions.

15

Allied controls shall be imposed upon the German economy, but only to the extent necessary:

(a) To carry out programs of industrial disarmament, demilitarization, of reparations and of approved exports and imports.

(b) To assure the production and maintenance of goods and services required to meet the needs of the occupying forces and displaced persons in Germany and essential to maintain in Germany average living standards not exceeding the average of the standards of living of European countries. (European countries means all European countries, excluding the United Kingdom and the Union of Soviet Socialist Republics.)

(c) To insure in the manner determined by the Central Council the equitable distribution of essential commodities between the several zones so as to produce a balanced economy throughout Germany and reduce the need for imports.

(d) To control German industry and all economic and financial international transactions, including exports and imports, with the aim of preventing Germany from developing a war potential and of achieving the other objectives named herein.

(e) To control all German public and private scientific bodies, research and experimental institutions, laboratories, etc., connected with economic activities.

16

In the imposition and maintenance of economic controls established by the Control Council, German administrative machinery shall be created and the German authorities shall be required to the fullest extent practicable to proclaim and assume administration of such controls. Thus it should be brought home to the German people that the responsibility for the administration of such controls and any breakdown in these controls will rest with themselves. Any German controls which may run counter to the objectives of occupation will be prohibited.

17

Measures shall be promptly taken:
(a) To effect essential repair of transport;
(b) To enlarge coal production;
(c) To maximize agricultural output; and
(d) To effect emergency repair of housing and essential utilities.

18

Appropriate steps shall be taken by the Control Council to exercise control and the power of disposition over German-owned external assets not already under the control of United Nations which have taken part in the war against Germany.

19

Payment of reparations should leave enough resources to enable the German people to subsist without external assistance. In working out the economic balance of Germany, the necessary means must be provided to pay for imports approved by the Control Council in Germany.

The proceeds of exports from current production and stocks shall be available in the first place for payment for such imports.

The above clause will not apply to the equipment and products referred to in Paragraphs 4 (*a*) and 4 (*b*) of the reparations agreement.

III. REPARATIONS FROM GERMANY

1

Reparation claims of the Union of Soviet Socialist Republics shall be met by removals from the zone of Germany occupied by the Union of Soviet Socialist Republics and from appropriate German external assets.

2

The Union of Soviet Socialist Republics undertakes to settle the reparation claims of Poland from its own share of reparations.

3

The reparation claims of the United States, the United Kingdom and other countries entitled to reparations shall be met from the Western zones and from appropriate German external assets.

4

In addition to the reparations to be taken by the Union of Soviet Socialist Republics from its own zone of occupation. the Union of Soviet Socialist Republics shall receive additionally from the Western zones:

(*a*) 15 percent of such usable and complete industrial capital equipment, in the first place from the metallurgical, chemical and machine manufacturing industries as is unnecessary for the German peace economy and should be removed from the Western zones of Germany, in exchange for an equivalent value of food, coal, potash, zinc, timber, clay products, petroleum products and such other commodities as may be agreed upon.

(*b*) 10 percent of such industrial capital equipment as is unnecessary for the German peace economy and should be removed from the Western zones, to be transferred to the Soviet Government on reparations account without payment or exchange of any kind in return. Removals of equipment as provided in (*a*) and (*b*) above shall be made simultaneously.

5

The amount of equipment to be removed from the Western zones on account of reparations must be determined within six months from now at the latest.

6

Removals of industrial capital equipment shall begin as soon as possible and shall be completed within two years from the determination specified in Paragraph 5. The delivery of products covered by 4 (a) above shall begin as soon as possible and shall be made by the Union of Soviet Socialist Republics in agreed installments within five years of the date hereof. The determination of the amount and character of the industrial capital equipment unnecessary for the German peace economy and therefore available for reparation shall be made by the Control Council under policies fixed by the Allied Commission on Reparations, with the participation of France, subject to the final approval of the zone commander in the zone from which the equipment is to be removed.

7

Prior to the fixing of the total amount of equipment subject to removal advance deliveries shall be made in respect to such equipment as will be determined to be eligible for delivery in accordance with the procedure set forth in the last sentence of Paragraph 6.

8

The Soviet Government renounces all claims in respect of reparations to shares of German enterprises which are located in the Western Zones of Germany as well as to German foreign assets in all countries except those specified in Paragraph 9 below.

9

The Governments of the United Kingdom and United States of America renounce all claims in respect of reparations to shares of German enterprises which are located in the Eastern zone of occupation in Germany, as well as to German foreign assets in Bulgaria, Finland, Hungary, Rumania and eastern Austria.

10

The Soviet Government makes no claims to gold captured by the Allied troops in Germany.

IV. DISPOSAL OF THE GERMAN NAVY AND MERCHANT MARINE

A. The following principles for the distribution of the German Navy were agreed:
1. The total strength of the German surface navy, excluding ships sunk and those taken over from Allied nations, but including ships under construction or repair, shall be divided equally among the Union of Soviet Socialist Republics, United Kingdom and United States of America.
2. Ships under construction or repair mean those ships whose construction or repair may be completed within three to six months, according to the type of ship. Whether such ships under construction or repair shall be complete or repaired shall be determined by the technical commission appointed by the three powers and referred to below, subject to the principle that their completion or repair must be achieved within

the time limits above provided, without any increase of skilled employment in the German shipyards and without permitting the reopening of any German shipbuilding or connected industries. Completion date means the date when a ship is able to go out on its first trip, or, under peacetime standards would refer to the customary date of delivery by shipyard to the government.

3. The larger part of the German submarine fleet shall be sunk. Not more than thirty submarines shall be preserved and divided equally between the Union of Soviet Socialist Republics, United Kingdom and United States of America for experimental and technical purposes.

4. All stocks of armament, ammunition and supplies of the German Navy appertaining to the vessels transferred pursuant to Paragraphs 1 and 3 hereof shall be handed over to the respective powers receiving such ships.

5. The three Governments agree to constitute a tripartite naval commission comprising two representatives for each Government, accompanied by the requisite staff, to submit agreed recommendations to the three Governments for the allocation of specific German warships and handle other detailed matters arising out of the agreement between the three Governments regarding the German fleet. The Commission will hold its first meeting not later than 15 August, 1945, in Berlin, which shall be its headquarters. Each delegation on the commission will have the right on the basis of reciprocity to inspect German warships wherever they may be located.

6. The three Governments agreed that transfers, including those of ships under construction and repair, shall be completed as soon as possible, but not later than 15 February 1946. The commission will submit fortnightly reports, including proposals for the progressive allocation of the vessels when agreed by the commission.

B. *The following principles for the distribution of the German merchant marine were agreed*:

1. The German merchant marine, surrendered to the three powers and wherever located, shall be divided equally among the Union of Soviet Socialist Republics, the United Kingdom and the United States of America. The actual transfers of the ships to the respective countries shall take place as soon as practicable after the end of the war against Japan. The United Kingdom and the United States will provide out of their shares of the surrendered German merchant ships appropriate amounts for other allied states whose merchant marines have suffered heavy losses in the common cause against Germany, except that the Soviet Union shall provide out of its share for Poland.

2. The allocation, manning and operation of these ships during the Japanese war period shall fall under the cognizance and authority of the combined shipping adjustment board and the United Maritime Authority.

3. While actual transfer of the ships shall be delayed until after the end of the war with Japan, a tripartite shipping commission shall inventory and value all available ships and recommend a specific distribution in accordance with Paragraph 1.

4. German inland and coastal ships determined to be necessary to the maintenance of the basic German peace economy by the Allied Control Council of Germany shall not be included in the shipping pool thus divided among the three powers.

5. The three Governments agree to constitute a tripartite merchant marine commission comprising two representatives for each Government, accompanied by the requisite staff, to submit agreed recommendations to the three Governments for the allocation of specific German merchant ships and to handle other detailed matters arising out of the agreement between the three Governments regarding the German merchant ships. The commission will hold its first meeting not later than September 1, 1945 in Berlin, which shall be its headquarters. Each delegation on the commission will have the right on the basis of reciprocity to inspect the German merchant ships wherever they may be located.

V. CITY OF KOENIGSBERG AND THE ADJACENT AREA

The conference examined a proposal by the Soviet Government to the effect that, pending the final determination of territorial questions at the peace settlement, the section of the western frontier of the Union of Soviet Socialist Republics which is adjacent to the Baltic Sea should pass from a point on the eastern shore of the Bay of Danzig to the east, north of Braunsberg-Goldap, to the meeting point of the frontiers of Lithuania, the Polish Republic and East Prussia.

The conference has agreed in principle to the proposal of the Soviet Government concerning the ultimate transfer to the Soviet Union of the City of Koenigsberg and the area adjacent to it as described above, subject to expert examination of the actual frontier.

The President of the United States and the British Prime Minister have declared that they will support the proposal of the conference at the forthcoming peace settlement.

VI. WAR CRIMINALS

The three Governments have taken note of the discussions which have been proceeding in recent weeks in London between British, United States, Soviet and French representatives with a view to reaching agreement on the methods of trial of these major war criminals whose crimes under the Moscow declaration of October, 1943, have no particular geographical localization. The three Governments reaffirm their intention to bring these criminals to swift and sure justice. They hope that the negotiations in London will result in speedy agreement being reached for this purpose, and they regard it as a matter of great importance that the trial of these major criminals should begin at the earliest possible date. The first list of defendants will be published before 1 September.

VII. AUSTRIA

The conference examined a proposal by the Soviet Government on the extension of the authority of the Austrian Provisional Government to all of Austria: The three Governments agreed that they were prepared to examine this question after the entry of the British and American forces into the City of Vienna.

It was agreed that reparations should not be exacted from Austria.

VIII. POLAND

A. Declaration.

We have taken note with pleasure of the agreement reached among representative Poles from Poland and abroad which has made possible the formation, in accordance with the decisions reached at the Crimea Conference, of a Polish Provisional Government of National Unity recognized by the three powers. The establishment by the British and United States Governments of diplomatic relations with the Polish Provisional Government of National Unity has resulted in the withdrawal of their recognition from the former Polish Government in London, which no longer exists.

The British and United States Governments have taken measures to protect the interest of the Polish Provisional Government of National Unity as the recognized Government of the Polish State in the property belonging to the Polish State located in their territories and under their control, whatever the form of this property may be. They have further taken measures to prevent alienation to third parties of such property. All proper facilities will be given to the Polish Provisional Government of National Unity for the exercise of the ordinary legal remedies for the recovery of any property belonging to the Polish State which may have been wrongfully alienated.

The three powers are anxious to assist the Polish Provisional Government of National Unity in facilitating the return to Poland as soon as practicable of all Poles abroad who wish to go, including members of the Polish armed forces and the merchant marine. They expect that those Poles who return home shall be accorded personal and property rights on the same basis as all Polish citizens.

The three powers note that the Polish Provisional Government of National Unity, in accordance with the decisions of the Crimea Conference, has agreed to the holding of free and unfettered elections as soon as possible on the basis of universal suffrage and secret ballot, in which all democratic and anti-Nazi parties shall have the right to take part and to put forward candidates, and that representatives of the Allied press shall enjoy full freedom to report to the world upon developments in Poland before and during the elections.

In conformity with the agreement on Poland reached at the Crimea Conference, the three heads of Government have sought the opinion of the Polish Provisional Government of National Unity in regard to the accession of territory in the north and west which Poland should receive. The President of the National Council of Poland and members of the Polish Provisional Government of National Unity have been received at the conference and have fully presented their views. The three heads of Government reaffirm their opinion that the final delimitation of the Western frontier of Poland should await the peace settlement.

The three heads of government agree that, pending the final determination of Poland's western frontier, the former German territories east of a line running from the Baltic Sea immediately west of Swinemuende, and thence along the Oder River to the confluence of the Western Niesse River and along the Western Niesse to the Czechoslovak frontier, including that portion of East Prussia not placed under the administration of the Union of Soviet Socialist Republics in accordance with the understanding reached at this conference and including the area of the former

Free City of Danzig, shall be under the administration of the Polish state and for such purposes should not be considered as part of the Soviet zone of occupation in Germany.

IX. CONCLUSION OF PEACE TREATIES AND ADMISSION TO THE UNITED NATIONS ORGANIZATION

The three Governments consider it desirable that the present anomalous position of Italy, Bulgaria, Finland, Hungary and Rumania should be terminated by the conclusion of peace treaties. They trust that the other interested Allied Governments will share these views.

For their part, the three Governments have included the preparation for a peace treaty for Italy as the first among the immediate important tasks to be undertaken by the new Council of Foreign Ministers. Italy was the first of the Axis powers to break with Germany, to whose defeat she has made a material contribution, and has now joined with the Allies in the struggle against Japan. Italy has freed herself from the Fascist regime and is making good progress toward re-establishment of a democratic government and institutions. The conclusion of such a peace treaty with a recognized and democratic Italian Government will make it possible for the three Governments to fulfil their desire to support an application from Italy for membership of the United Nations.

The three Governments have also charged the Council of Foreign Ministers with the task of preparing peace treaties for Bulgaria, Finland, Hungary and Rumania. The conclusion of peace treaties with recognized democratic governments in these states will also enable the three Governments to support applications from them for membership of the United Nations. The three Governments agree to examine each separately in the near future, in the light of the conditions then prevailing, the establishment of diplomatic relations with Finland, Rumania, Bulgaria and Hungary to the extent possible prior to the conclusion of peace treaties with those countries.

The three Governments have no doubt that in view of the changed conditions resulting from the termination of the war in Europe, representatives of the Allied press will enjoy full freedom to report to the world upon developments in Rumania, Bulgaria, Hungary and Finland.

As regards the admission of other states into the United Nations Organization, Article 4 of the Charter of the United Nations declares that:

"1. Membership in the United Nations is open to all other peace-loving states who accept the obligations contained in the present Charter and, in the judgment of the organization, are able and willing to carry out these obligations.

"2. The admission of any such state to membership in the United Nations will be effected by a decision of the General Assembly upon the recommendation of the Security Council."

The three Governments, so far as they are concerned, will support applications for membership from those states which have remained neutral during the war and which fulfil the qualifications set out above.

The three Governments feel bound, however, to make it clear that they, for their part, would not favor any application for membership put forward by the present Spanish Government, which, having been founded with the support of the Axis powers, does not, in view of its origins, its nature, its record and its close association with the aggressor states, possess the qualifications necessary to justify such membership.

X. TERRITORIAL TRUSTEESHIP

The conference examined a proposal by the Soviet Government on the question of trusteeship territories as defined in the decision of the Crimea Conference and in the Charter of the United Nations Organization.

After an exchange of views on this question, it was decided that the disposition of any former Italian colonial territories was one to be decided in connection with the preparation of a peace treaty for Italy and that the question of Italian colonial territory would be considered by the September Council of Ministers of Foreign Affairs.

XI. REVISED ALLIED CONTROL COMMISSION
PROCEDURE IN RUMANIA, BULGARIA AND HUNGARY

The three Governments took note that the Soviet representatives on the Allied Control Commissions in Rumania, Bulgaria and Hungary have communicated to their United Kingdom and United States colleagues proposals for improving the work of the Control Commissions, now that hostilities in Europe have ceased.

The three Governments agreed that the revision of the procedures of the Allied Control Commissions in these countries would now be undertaken, taking into account the interests and responsibilities of the three Governments which together presented the terms of armistice to the respective countries, and accepting as a basis, in respect of all three countries, the Soviet Government's proposals for Hungary as annexed hereto. (Annex I).

XII. ORDERLY TRANSFER OF GERMAN POPULATIONS

The three Governments, having considered the question in all its aspects, recognize that the transfer to Germany of German populations, or elements thereof, remaining in Poland, Czechoslovakia and Hungary will have to be undertaken. They agree that any transfers that take place should be effected in an orderly and humane manner.

Since the influx of a large number of Germans into Germany would increase the burden already resting on the occupying authorities, they consider that the Control Council in Germany should in the first instance examine the problem, with special regard to the question of the equitable distribution of these Germans among the several zones of occupation. They are accordingly instructing their respective representatives on the Control Council to report to their Governments as soon as possible the extent to which such persons have already entered Germany from Poland, Czechoslovakia and Hungary and to submit an estimate of the time and rate at which further transfers could be carried out, having regard to the present situation in Germany.

The Czechoslovak Government, the Polish Provisional Government and the Control Council in Hungary are at the same time being informed of the above and are being requested meanwhile to suspend further expulsions pending an examination by the Governments concerned of the report from their representatives on the Control Council.

XIII. OIL EQUIPMENT IN RUMANIA

The conference agreed to set up two bilateral commissions of experts, one to be composed of United Kingdom and Soviet members, and one to be composed of United States and Soviet members, to investigate the facts and examine the documents, as a basis for the settlement of questions arising from the removal of oil equipment in Rumania. It was further agreed that these experts shall begin their work within ten days, on the spot.

XIV. IRAN

It was agreed that Allied troops should be withdrawn immediately from Teheran and that further stages of the withdrawal of troops from Iran should be considered at the meeting of the Council of Foreign Ministers to be held in London in September, 1945.

XV. THE INTERNATIONAL ZONE OF TANGIER

A proposal by the Soviet Government was examined and the following decisions were reached:
Having examined the question of the Zone of Tangier, the three Governments have agreed that this zone, which includes the City of Tangier and the area adjacent to it, in view of its special strategic importance, shall remain international.
The question of Tangier will be discussed in the near future at a meeting in Paris of representatives of the Governments of the Union of Soviet Socialist Republics, the United States of America, the United Kingdom and France.

XVI. THE BLACK SEA STRAITS

The three Governments recognize that the convention concluded at Montreux should be revised as failing to meet present-day conditions.
It was agreed that as the next step the matter should be the subject of direct conversations between each of the three Governments and the Turkish Government.

XVII. INTERNATIONAL INLAND WATERWAYS

The conference considered a proposal of the United States delegation on this subject and agreed to refer it for consideration to the forthcoming meeting of the Council of Foreign Ministers in London.

XVIII. EUROPEAN INLAND TRANSPORT CONFERENCE

The British and United States delegations to the conference informed the Soviet delegation of the desire of the British and United States Governments to reconvene the European Inland Transport Conference and stated that they would welcome assurance that the Soviet Government would participate in the work of the reconvened conference. The Soviet Government agreed that it would participate in this conference.

XIX. DIRECTIVES TO MILITARY COMMANDERS ON ALLIED CONTROL COUNCIL FOR GERMANY

The three Governments agreed that each would send a directive to its representative on the Control Council for Germany informing him of all decisions of the conference affecting matters within the scope of his duties.

XX. USE OF ALLIED PROPERTY FOR SATELLITE REPARATIONS OR "WAR TROPHIES"

The proposal (Annex II) presented by the United States delegation was accepted in principle by the conference, but the drafting of an agreement on the matter was left to be worked out through diplomatic channels.

XXI. MILITARY TALKS

During the conference there were meetings between the Chiefs of Staff of the three Governments on military matters of common interest.

ANNEX I

Text of a letter transmitted on July 12 to the representatives of the United States and United Kingdom Governments on the Allied Control Commission in Hungary.

"In view of the changed situation in connection with the termination of the war against Germany, the Soviet Government finds it necessary to establish the following order of work for the Allied Control Commission in Hungary.

"1. During the period up to the conclusion of peace with Hungary the president (or vice president) of the ACC will regularly call conferences with the British and American representatives for the purpose of discussing the most important questions relating to the work of the ACC. The conferences will be called once in ten days, or more frequently in case of need.

"Directives of the ACC on questions of principle will be issued to the Hungarian authorities by the president of the Allied Control Commission after agreement on these directives with the English and American representatives.

"2. The British and American representatives in the ACC will take part in general conferences of heads of divisions and delegates of the ACC, convoked by the president of the ACC, which meetings will be regular in nature. The British and American representatives will also participate personally or through their representatives in appropriate instances in mixed commissions created by the president of the ACC for questions connected with the execution by the ACC of its functions.

"3. Free movement by the American and British representatives in the country will be permitted provided that the ACC is previously informed of the time and route of the journeys.

"4. All questions connected with permission for the entrance and exit of members of the staff of the British and American representatives in

Hungary will be decided on the spot by the president of the ACC within a time limit of not more than one week.

"5. The bringing in and sending out by plane of mail, cargoes and diplomatic couriers will be carried out by the British and American representatives on the ACC under arrangements and within time limits established by the ACC, or in special cases by previous coordination with the president of the ACC.

"I consider it necessary to add to the above that in all other points the existing statutes regarding the ACC in Hungary, which was confirmed on January 20, 1945, shall remain in force in the future."

ANNEX II

Use of Allied property for satellite reparations or "war trophies."

1. The burden or reparation and "war trophies" should not fall on Allied nationals.

2. Capital equipment. We object to the removal of such Allied property as reparations, "war trophies" or under any other guise. Loss would accrue to Allied nationals as a result of destruction of plants and the consequent loss of markets and trading connections. Seizure of Allied property makes impossible the fulfilment by the satellite of its obligation under the armistice to restore intact the rights and interests of the Allied nations and their nationals.

The United States looks to the other occupying powers for the return of any equipment already removed and the cessation of removals. Where such equipment will not or cannot be returned, the United States will demand of the satellite adequate, effective and prompt compensation to American nationals and that such compensation have priority equal to that of the reparations payment.

These principles apply to all property wholly or substantially owned by Allied nationals. In the event of removals of property in which the American as well as the entire Allied interest is less than substantial, the United States expects adequate, effective and prompt compensation.

3. Current production. While the United States does not oppose reparation out of current production of Allied investments, the satellite must provide immediate and adequate compensation to the Allied nationals including sufficient foreign exchange or products so that they can recover reasonable foreign currency expenditures and transfer a reasonable return on their investment. Such compensation must also have equal priority with reparations.

We deem it essential that the satellites not conclude treaties, agreements or arrangements which deny to Allied nationals access, on equal terms, to their trade, raw materials and industry; and appropriately modify any existing arrangements which may have that effect.

Source: *Documents on American Foreign Relations,* Vol. VIII, 1945–1946, Princeton University Press, pp. 925–938.

STATEMENT ISSUED BY THE NETHERLANDS GOVERNMENT
28th October, 1944

Several reports have been received from the Netherlands Resistance Movement showing that lately the Germans have wrought new extensive destruction and damage in that part of the country which is still under their occupation. A considerable part of this destruction and damage cannot reasonably be attributed to considerations of a military nature; it is manifestly wanton and malicious.

In the circumstances now prevailing it is deemed inadvisable to give specific instances, and for obvious reasons it is impossible to give a complete survey. This can only be done at a later stage.

To a lesser extent, the Germans have done the same, prior to their withdrawal, in the liberated part of the Netherlands. In respect of these areas, instances may now be given. Factories have been blown up or their equipment removed for no reason connected with operations; collieries have been extensively damaged; indiscriminate bombing with flying bombs has resulted in further damage.

A particularly harmful form of destruction and damage consists of flooding fertile regions with salt water, even in cases where fresh water was available. Other areas have been extensively flooded, either carelessly or without military necessity, with riverwater.

It goes without saying that the relief and reconstruction problem in the case of the Netherlands has thus become immeasurably more difficult. It may be said without exaggeration that it is now certain that, as a result of all the Germans have done, the recuperative power of the Netherlands with their very dense population will prove to be very gravely impaired, from the point of view of agriculture as well as from that of industry and commerce.

Coupled with the systematic looting on an unprecedented scale perpetrated by the occupying power, and with its exactions and spoliation in contravention of the Hague Convention of 1907 on landwarfare and of general international law and custom, this destruction and damage has now assumed truly enormous proportions.

It is impossible to expect, considering also the legitimate claims on Germany of other nations, that Germany will be able to make good the damage she has inflicted on the Netherlands by the transfer of economic assets from one side of the frontier to the other within a reasonable period. Experience gained at the end of the last war has shown the difficulties attending such transfer.

Considering further that it is in the general interest that Germany be made to realise once and for all that aggression does not pay, it is possible that the people of the Netherlands may reach the conclusion, in spite of their innate repugnance to all forms of armed conquest, that if in their case some substantial measure of reparation is to be made by the invader, a suitable part of adjoining Prussian territory should either be ceded to the Netherlands (provision being made for the absorption by Germany of the Prussian inhabitants), or brought into the Dominion and economic orbit of the Netherlands in some other manner, on a provisional or permanent basis.

It cannot be the task of the present Netherlands cabinet to commit the country, which cannot be properly consulted at the moment, to a definite policy in so important a matter on which a decision need not be taken at once. But the Netherlands Government consider it their duty to reserve the country's rights, in particular that of formulating its considered opinion and claims after its liberation, and to bring this to the knowledge of the Governments of the United Nations and of the public in general. In doing this, the Netherlands Government leave out of account the sorrow and suffering inflicted on the Netherlands people by the representatives of the people of Germany. The grief caused by their vindictive strangulation of the country's national life, by their mass-deportation of the nation's young manhood, by the starvation they have brought about, by their widespread killings and medieval torture, causing the death of thousands of good citizens, – this grief may cry for justice, but can never find adequate compensation in terms of material values.

Source: Proceedings of the States General, 1946–1947,
Annexes, Second Chamber, No 352.

MEMORANDUM OF THE NETHERLANDS GOVERNMENT CONTAINING THE CLAIMS OF THE NETHERLANDS TO REPARATIONS FROM GERMANY

Provisional Statement

INTRODUCTION

1. The Netherlands Ministry for Foreign Affairs has the honour, in compliance with an invitation sent by the Foreign Office to the Netherlands Ambassador to the Court of St. James, dated August 27th 1945 No. UE 3812/3812/77, to transmit a memorandum containing the claims of the Netherlands to reparation from Germany.

2. In submitting these data the Netherlands Government would like to make the following observations.

3. On more than one occasion, and lastly in a note addressed to the Governments of the United Kingdom of Great Britain and Northern Ireland, the United States of America, the Union of Socialist Soviet Republics and France, dated August 17th 1945, the Netherlands Government have made it known that in comparison with many other countries which suffered damage in this war the country's economy suffered exceptionally as a result of German aggression. For, although the position of the Netherlands until September 1944 was in many respects comparable to that of other occupied countries, after that date conditions deteriorated considerably. Consequently the Netherlands suffered more on account of the war than most, if not all, other occupied European countries.

4. The liberation of the three Southern provinces of the Netherlands and the gallant but abortive attempt to seize Arnhem, caused tremendous and widespread destruction. In the eight provinces which continued to be occupied by the Germans the enemy multiplied his predatory enterprises. The worst looting in Holland took place in this last phase of the war in Europe. The contiguity of the Netherlands and Germany which are not separated by an expanse of sea, made this easy. In some districts the country was stripped completely bare, a fact which in Western Europe is believed to be without precedent. In addition, more than eight percent of the agricultural area of the country was flooded, of which one half with sea water, with all the long-term damage to the soil resulting therefrom. Moreover, more than two percent of the total agricultural area was laid waste on account of the construction by the Germans of fortified zones, minefields and aerodromes, whilst another six percent have been rendered unfit for immediate use because of military operations. Considerable stretches of rich orchard country have been ruined for as long as it takes to grow fruit trees.

5. The case of the Netherlands is therefore exceptional and special.

6. The Netherlands Government are of the opinion that as an essential condition for the recovery of the country, and as a matter of plain justice, the people of the Netherlands have the undoubted right to the earliest possible restitution of all identifiable looted property taken from the country by the Germans, when such property is found outside the Netherlands, either in Germany or elsewhere. In the view of the Netherlands Government "looted property" includes all goods by their nature fit for restitution, which the enemy, his agents or his subjects, by favour of the occupation of the whole or of part of the Netherlands, have removed from the country's national patrimony as it existed before the occupation, either directly by acts of transfer or of dispossession, or indirectly by purchases or by transactions effected by means of payment which were created, imposed or extorted by the enemy due to the occupation. The Netherlands Government consider the restitution of looted property as a category per se which urgently demands special provisions.

It is a well established principle of law, that a person who discovers his property in the possession of another person, has the right to require its restitution, with priority over all creditors, and this, whether these creditors have an ordinary or a preferential claim. On page 1153 of the 7th edition of Thaller's "Traité élémentaire de droit commercial (1925)" this wellknown French jurist says (translated into English): "Every owner is armed with a jus in rem. The essential attribute of a jus in rem is its preferential character. Those who have a jus in rem are not subject to distribution on a pro rata basis. Their right takes precedence over all creditors."

The same principle prevails in Anglo-American law. According to paragraph 38 of the English Bankruptcy Act (1914) the right to claim restitution is denied the owner only in a few cases when the property in question has come into the possession of the creditor "by the consent and the permission of the true owner".[1]

For that reason J. W. Smith states in his "Compendium of Mercantile Law" (12th ed., p. 863): "The wrongful seizure of the goods by a wrongdoer would seem sufficient to take the goods out of the possession, order or disposition of the bankrupt".

The American Corpus Juris Secundum, the most modern compendium of United States law, recognizes a similar right of the owner [2] giving the same grounds as Thaller: "A reclamation proceeding in bankruptcy is in effect a proceeding in rem" (sub voce Bankruptcy, p. 940).

7. The damage done to the Netherlands by Germany far exceeds the removal by the Germans of property now to be restored in so far as it is still in existence and can be identified. In view thereof, the Netherlands Government furthermore insist on receiving a fair and equitable share of all German internal and external assets, to be used for reparation purposes, including usable industrial capital equipment, shares, or participations in enterprises, and all other German deliveries in kind, in gold, in foreign exchange, or in labour. All this with due regard to the exceptional position of the Netherlands as previously stated in this memorandum.

8. The Netherlands Government further recall that the Netherlands merchant navy has during five years of war taken an active part in the general allied war effort against Germany and Japan, and has given

---

[1] *Vide* Williams, Law and Practice in Bankruptcy, 13th ed. p. 276, sq.

[2] A claimant may maintain a petition in the bankruptcy court for the reclamation of identifiable property or its proceeds in the hands of the trustee in bankruptcy in which the petitioner claims an adverse interest or right of title (sub voce Bankruptcy, par. 264).

service second to none, suffering serious losses, which insofar as ships were concerned have been made good to an insignificant extent only. They therefore claim a fair and equitable share, both in regard to quantity and quality, of all vessels to be surrendered by Germany. This also applies to vessels destined for navigation on inland waterways, of, which thousands belonging to the Netherlands were seized by the Germans during the war and subsequently destroyed.

9. With regard to the claims of the Netherlands to reparation from Germany, the following should be taken into account.

10. All data contained in the following pages are of a provisional nature. The central part of the Netherlands was liberated as recently as May 1945, little more than five months ago. In this interval it has not yet been possible to establish the necessary machinery for a complete enquiry concerning war damage. This memorandum contains the estimates which are now available. They have been drawn up with great care, so that it may be expected that the final data – which will be presented later – will not differ appreciably from the present figures. All detailed data available will be produced on request.

11. Insofar as damage to and loss of property is concerned, this memorandum covers the period from May 10th 1940 to May 7th 1945. Damage of this nature incurred since May 7th 1945 has not been included. Although such subsequent damage was actually done to Netherlands property, e.g. as a result of the clearing of German fortifications, this has not been taken into account, as in the opinion of the Netherlands Government a final date had to be chosen, for which V.E. Day was considered the most appropriate.

With regard to damage resulting from loss of production, this memorandum includes damage of this nature incurred after May 7th 1945, in addition to that incurred during the above mentioned period.

12. The Netherlands Government feel that in the final reparation account the damage should not be calculated in values existing at the time when the damage was inflicted, but in values providing full compensation (replacement values) at the time when the reparation account will be finally established. In order to comply with the desire expressed by the Governments concerned, the replacement values of 1938 have been provisionally taken as a basis. It should be borne in mind, however, that had the damage inflicted been expressed in terms of the price level now pervailing in the Netherlands, all figures mentioned in this memorandum would have had to be raised by 75%.

13. In compliance with the indications given with regard to the presentation of data concerning reparation claims, all values contained in this memorandum are expressed both in terms of Netherlands guilders and in terms of 1938 U.S. dollars, according to the average rate of exchange during that year, when $ 1.— equalled Fl. 1.81 - 82.

14. Finally it should be made clear that in some paragraphs of this memorandum the Netherlands Government had to deviate from the required form of presentation on account of the insufficiency of data available.

EVALUATION OF DAMAGE CAUSED TO THE NETHERLANDS BY THE WAR
AGAINST GERMANY

For practical reasons reparation will have to be restricted to damage capable of being expressed in terms of money. It comprises four categories:

A. material loss of the national wealth of the Netherlands;
B. damage owing to loss of production during the years of war;
C. loss owing to forced transfer to Germany of part of the reduced production;
D. damage owing to loss of production suffered and still to be suffered after May 7th 1945.

These four categories are not so distinct from one another as this enumeration might suggest. On more than one point they are interrelated, which entails the danger of double counting. In the following statement care has been taken to avoid such double countings.

Section I

A. Material loss of the national wealth of the Netherlands

This loss has been caused by destruction by or in consequence of direct acts of war, requisitions and looting by the occupying power, by the omission of normal replacement and maintenance of capital-goods, as well as by other forms of diminution of wealth (i.e. depletion of stocks in industry, agriculture, horticulture and trade, diminution of live-stock and of durable consumer goods).

The loss on this account based on the price-level of 1938 is composed as follows:

a) direct damage owing to the war, the occupation and the evacuation . . . . *f* 5 390 million or $ 2 965 million
b) damage on account of looting . *f* 3 640 ,, or $ 2 002 ,,
c) arrears in normal replacement and maintenance of capital-goods, as well as other forms of diminution of wealth . . . . . *f* 2 395 ,, or $ 1 317 ,,

Total   *f* 11 425 million or $ 6 284 million.

This amount may be divided over the component parts of the national wealth as follows:

1. *Industry, Commerce, Banking and Insurance:* *f* 4 015 million or $ 2 208 million.
   a. *Industry:* *f* 2 200 million or $ 1 210 million,
   viz. damage to buildings and land . . . . *f* 200 million or $ 110 million
   damage to machinery and plant . . . . *f* 1000 ,, or $ 550 ,,
   damage to stocks . . . . . *f* 1000 ,, or $ 550 ,,

This damage includes an amount of *f* 400 million or $ 220 million caused by the bombardment of Rotterdam and of a number of towns in the Southern and Eastern part of the country, as well as by other acts of war, an amount of *f* 1 000 million or $ 550 million caused by requisitioning and looting by the occupying power of machinery, industrial plant and stocks of raw materials, semi-manufactured and manufactured goods and an amount of *f* 800 million or $ 440 million on account of the omission of normal replacement and maintenance of industrial and commercial assets and diminution of stocks.

b. Commerce: f 1800 million or $ 990 million,
viz. damage to shops, buildings,
    warehouses and plant . . . . *f*   400 million or $ 220 million
    damage to stocks . . . . . . *f* 1400   ,,   or $ 770   ,,

The above refers to war-damage to buildings, plant and loss of stocks to an amount of *f* 500 million or $ 275 million, loss owing to requisitioning of supplies to an amount of *f* 500 million or $ 275 million, as well as loss owing to the omission of normal replacement and maintenance of buildings and plant and diminution of supplies amounting to *f* 800 million or $ 440 million.

At the outbreak of war total stocks available in industry and trade amounted to about *f* 2 500 million or $ 1 350 million; at the end of the war these stocks had practically dwindled to nil. Considerable supplies of goods were lost by the bombardment of Rotterdam on May 14th 1940.

c. Banking and Insurance: f 15 million or $ 8 million.
This refers mainly to damage to buildings. The loss suffered by insurance companies is mentioned here pro memoria.

2. *Ocean shipping, Coastal shipping and Fisheries: f* 325 million or $ 179 million,
    viz. damage to ships . . . . *f* 300 million or $ 165 million
    damage to buildings . . . . *f* 25   ,,   or $ 14   ,,
About 50% of the Merchant Fleet was lost due to direct acts of war. The offices and plant on the wharves of the shipping companies also suffered considerable damage. Of the fishing fleet too, a considerable part was lost owing to acts of war.

3. *Harbours, harbour-works and port-installations: f* 300 million or $ 165 million.
Apart from bombardments this damage was mainly a result of the destruction and blowing up of the harbour-works and plant in Rotterdam. Amsterdam and along the larger rivers by the occupying power.

4. *Means of Transport: f* 680 million or $ 374 million,
    viz. damage to Railways . . . . . . *f* 300 million or $ 165   million
    damage to Tramways . . . . . *f* 30   ,,   or $ 16.5   ,,
    damage to Inland fleet . . . . *f* 100   ,,   or $ 55   ,,
    damage to Civil air fleet . . . . *f* 10   ,,   or $ 5.5   ,,
    damage to Road vehicles (lorries, *f* 240   ,,   or $ 132   ,,
    etc.) . . . .

Damage to these catagories amounting to *f* 240 million or $ 132 million was caused by direct acts of war. The rest, amounting to *f* 440 million or $ 242 million, refers almost entirely to loss due to requisitioning and looting by the occupying power. For instance nearly the entire rollingstock of the Railways was carried off, whilst a very great number of trams, omnibuses, lorries, motorcars and other means of transport by land or water were lost owing to looting.

5. *Roads, including bridges:* ƒ 100 million or $ 55 million.
The damage to bridges has, apart from direct acts of war, chiefly been due to destruction and blowing up by the occupying power. The damage to roads is stated under 7.

6. *Agriculture, horticulture and forestry:* ƒ 825 million or $ 454 million,
    viz. damage to buildings and territory ƒ 500 million or $ 275   million
        damage to machinery, implements
        and stocks . . . . ƒ 75   ,,   or $ 41.5 ,,
        damage to live-stock . . . . . . ƒ 250   ,,   or $ 137.5 ,,

Damage of this category amounting to ƒ 400 million or $ 220 million is due to direct acts of war, the construction of aerodromes and fortifications, evacuation, inundations (this includes an amount of ƒ 130 million or $ 71.5 million on account of the inundation of the Isle of Walcheren); ƒ 100 million or $ 55 million owing to requisitioning of supplies, agricultural implements and part of the live-stock, and ƒ 325 million or $ 179 million owing to the omission of normal maintenance of buildings and of agricultural implements and owing to decrease of supplies and live-stock.
In course of time data concerning the period during which the land in question has been or will be unproductive owing to acts of war, will be submitted.

7. *Public property:* ƒ 150 million or $ 82.5 million.
Owing to the fact that no detailed data concerning damage to public undertakings are yet available, this damage has been stated provisionally under damage to Industry (see above under 1). Damage to harbours, harbourworks, etc. in as much as these are public property, has been stated under 3. Further damage to public property refers to damage to aerodromes, buildings, schools, roads, waterways, sewerage, etc.

8. *Household articles and personal effects:* ƒ 1 200 million or $ 660 million.
The contents of a very great number of houses have been destroyed or heavily damaged as a result of acts of war. Damage on that account is estimated at ƒ 700 million or $ 385 million. Moreover, about 600 000 wireless sets and 1 000 000 bicycles were requisitioned by the Germans and the furniture of numerous Jews and other persons was confiscated. Damage on this account amounts to roughly ƒ 150 million or $ 82.5 million. Furthermore the loss owing to omission of the necessary maintenance and replacement of non-perishable consumer goods is estimated at ƒ 350 million or $ 193 million.

9. *Gold and foreign exchange, foreign investments and valuables:* ƒ 2 850 million or $ 1 567 million.
    a. Gold and foreign exchange: ƒ 1 210 million or $ 665 million.
This item refers to gold of the Netherlands Bank amounting to ƒ 292 million or $ 161 million, carried off by the occupying power, as well as to foreign banknotes amounting to ƒ 14 million or $ 7.7 million and to

silver, nickel and bronze coin seized to an amount of ƒ 4 million or $ 2.2 million. It should further be taken into account that the Netherlands National Wealth suffered a loss of about ƒ 900 million or $ 495 million in consequence of war-expenditure incurred by the Netherlands Government in London, in so far as this took the form of disposing of part of the Netherlands gold-reserve abroad, of Netherlands balances in foreign countries, as well as of commitments entered into in foreign countries.

b. Foreign investments: ƒ 1000 million or $ 550 million.

An amount of ƒ 500 million or $ 275 million refers to German and other foreign securities which the Germans obtained in this country by confiscating Jewish and other Dutch property, whilst damage amounting to ƒ 500 million or $ 275 million arose from loss of Netherlands investments in Central Europe in consequence of the war.

c. Valuables (carried off by the German occupying power): ƒ 640 million or $ 352 million,

viz. jewelry	ƒ 300	million or	$ 165	million
rough diamonds	ƒ 34.5	,, or	$ 19	,,
silver and gold objects	ƒ 5	,, or	$ 2.75	,,
platinum	ƒ 0.5	,, or	$ 0.275	,,
pictures	ƒ 200	,, or	$ 110	,,
objects of a scientific nature . .	ƒ 50	,, or	$ 27	,,
objects of an educational nature	ƒ 50	,, or	$ 27	,,

10. *Houses and buildings not otherwise included:* ƒ 970 million or $ 533.5 million.

   a. Houses: ƒ 820 million or $ 451 million.

100 000 houses have been entirely destroyed, 50 000 have been heavily damaged and 300 000 have been damaged by direct acts of war, by demolition in the coastal zone or as a result of evacuation. The damage on that account amounts to a total of ƒ 700 million or $ 385 million. The loss owing to the omission of maintenance and replacement is estimated at ƒ 120 million or $ 66 million.

   b. Churches, private nursing-homes, schools, buildings belonging to societies and associations, theatres, cinemas, etc.: ƒ 150 million or $ 82.5 million.

   This mainly refers to direct war-damage and damage due to demolitions in the coastal zone.

11. *Other material damage and loss.*

   Property pertaining to the liberal professions: ƒ 10 million or $ 5.5 million.

The table printed at the end of this memorandum gives a survey of the Netherlands National Wealth on September 1st 1939 and its decline owing to the war in conformity with the above enumeration, based on the values of 1938. Furthermore, it is pointed out that the damage referred to on page 208 under B, C, and D has been stated under Section III.

Section II

Budgetary expenditures allocatable to the war against Germany

The expenditure of the Netherlands Government on account of the conduct of the war against Germany amounts to ƒ 1 600 million or $ 880 million, viz. ƒ 700 million or $ 385 million on account of expenses of mobilization before May 10th 1940 and *f* 900 million or $ 495 million on account of war-expenditure of the Netherlands Government in London. In order to avoid this latter item being counted twice, it is recalled that this expenditure has already been included in Section I.

Section III

Man-years lost through the war against Germany

An exact statement of the number of man-years lost on account of the war-effort of the Netherlands against Germany owing to deportation of Netherlands subjects to Germany and to forced labour performed in behalf of the occupying power, cannot yet be submitted. This also applies to loss of life and to the number of sick and wounded. Data referring thereto will be supplied later.

Nevertheless a rough estimate may now be given of the damage incurred by these losses. In this connection reference is made to the categories of damage stated under B, C, and D on page 10, concerning which the following observations may now be made.

B. Damage owing to loss of production during the years of war

Instead of loss of production it is also possible to speak of a diminution of the national income. The various causes underlying the fact that the total national income during the period from May 10th 1940 to May 7th 1945 was lower than was normal before the war are discussed below.

An indication of the decline in production during the years from 1940 to 1944 is given by the following general index of the production of goods and services composed by the Central Bureau of Statistics at The Hague.

General index of agricultural and industrial production and of services rendered from 1938–1944.

1938 – 100	1941 – 91	1944 – 60.
1939 – 108	1942 – 80	
1940 – 99	1943 – 72	

On the basis of these index-numbers the Central Bureau of Statistics has calculated that the real national income, i.e. the national income expressed in terms of goods available for consumption and investment, has throughout the period of war been at least *f* 6 000 million or $ 3 300 million lower than it would have been if production could have been maintained at the level of 1938. The amount of *f* 6 000 million or $ 3 300 million has been based on the price level of 1938.

It should be remarked that the index-numbers used are mainly based on data concerning the extent of the production. The decline in quality of the production resulting from the consumption of substitutes and from poorer methods of production could not be taken into sufficient account. This is one of the reasons why the amount mentioned as *f* 6 000 million or $ 3 300 million may be considered as being rather low.

On the other hand it should be observed that it would not be right to add the total decline of the national income during the years of occupation as second loss to the amount of the loss of material wealth. This may best be shown by an examination of the causes to which loss of production during the years of war is to be attributed. These causes are the following:

1. The change in the international position of the Netherlands. Owing to the fact that Germany made war on the Netherlands, the supply of raw materials and auxiliary materials for industry and agriculture from overseas was stopped. The diminution of the national income which thus became inevitable, was further hastened and aggravated by the fact that Germany seized the greater part of the supplies. The direct loss caused by stocks being carried off, has been mentioned in Section I; the effect of this removal on the extent of the national income will be discussed below under 4. It may be stated here that the looting of raw materials etc. by the Germans can be no reason not to consider the change of the international position of the Netherlands due to the country's occupation as an independent cause of the decline of the national income. The reduction of the national income resulting from this cause should be fully charged to Germany's account.

2. The dislocation of Holland's economic policy becoming apparent from the fact that the historically-grown equilibrium of the country's industrial life has been upset and from the smaller "productiveness" of the government apparatus, etc. The diminution of the national income resulting from this cause, should be fully charged to Germany's account.

3. The working-power of the Netherlands nation as affected not only by murder, imprisonment or deportation to Germany of civilians, but also by civilians being bodily or mentally mutilated in the war or made victims of the insufficient food position, and by the death of members of the armed forces and of the merchant navy and of those fallen in the struggle put up by the resistance groups, etc. The diminution of the national income resulting from this cause should be fully charged to the account of Germany.

4. War-damage of a material nature. The loss of production caused during the war by damage of this kind should not be added in full to other forms of war-damage if double counting is to be avoided.

The capital goods employed in production derive their value from their total contribution to the ultimate product, i.e. to the national income. In the normal course of events there is on the one hand this contribution, whilst on the other hand the supply of capital goods is kept up to the mark by replacement and maintenance, charged against the national income.

During the occupation both these features had to be neglected. As neither replacement nor maintenance took place, loss of wealth was incurred; this loss of *f* 1 000 million or $ 550 million was entered under the heading of material damage. On the other hand, the omission of replacement and maintenance also meant that production for purposes of replacement and maintenance could not take place, so that the national income decreased to an amount equal to the loss already taken into account. This part of the total diminution of the national income should therefore not once again be counted as war-damage.

A similar reasoning holds good with regard to capital-goods lost owing to the use of force or in consequence of requisitioning in behalf of the enemy. Thus the whole contribution was lost which these capital-goods would have made to the national income during the occupation, and partly even for many years to come. The capitalized value of this contribution was included in Section I. The part of the total diminution of the national income resulting directly from the loss of this contribution may therefore not be counted once again as war damage. It may be calculated at the full value of the supplies of raw materials carried off or destroyed (*f* 900 million or $ 495 million) and at part of the value of the factory-buildings etc. destroyed and of the machinery etc. carried off (*f* 100 million or $ 55 million).

Ultimately, therefore, the amount of loss of production during the years of war which, in addition to the material war-damage, has to be charged to the account of Germany amounts to *f* 4 000 million or $ 2 200 million.

Of course it would also be possible to find this amount if all component items could be stated singly. This is only possible in a few exceptional cases. One of these is the wellknown railway-strike, which by order of the Netherlands Government in London set in on September 17th 1944. The loss incurred during the period of this strike is the equivalent of the amount normally required during such a period for purchasing coal etc., for paying wages and salaries, for the interest of the capital invested and for depreciation. This amount may be fixed at *f* 100 million or $ 55 million.

In order to give an idea of the importance of the loss of production involved it may finally be stated that the national income for 1938 is to be estimated at *f* 5 100 million or $ 2 800 million, not including the proceeds of investments in the Netherlands-Indies and in foreign countries.

C. Loss owing to forced transfer to Germany of part of the reduced production

The loss of production as calculated sub B is not the only form of loss suffered by the national income during the period of occupation. A considerable part of what was produced had to be put at the disposal of the occupying power or was exported to Germany and other countries, without a balance in the form of an equivalent payment in goods. This production in behalf of the occupying power is expressed on the money-side in the cost of the occupation and in the enormous increase of the balance of Reichsmark of the Netherlands Bank. The expenses on occupation-account are calculated, including the so-called "äussere Besatzungskosten", at a total of 9 500 million guilders or 5 225 million dollars, while the Reichsmarkclaim of the Netherlands Bank had ultimately risen to *f* 4 500 million or $ 2 475 million. This latter amount would be very considerably larger, if the expenses on occupation-account had not repeatedly been "recovered" by writing off from the Reichsmark account of the Netherlands Bank. The Netherlands Government had to refund to the Bank the amounts written off, so that consequently the amount of the cost of the occupation was correspondingly increased.

The total amount of the cost of occupation and of the Reichsmark-balance of the Netherlands Bank does not, however, exclusively consist of the countervalue of goods and services withdrawn from current production. The cost of occupation also includes amounts for the transfer of immovables and other property. As regards the claims of the Netherlands Bank, these did not only arise from the exportation of goods produced in the Netherlands, but also because Dutch, German, Hungarian and other securities, the property of Netherlands subjects, were compulsorily sold abroad in large numbers, and furthermore because labourers deported to Germany transferred wages to the Netherlands.

On the other hand, however, the cost of the occupation does not comprise all supplies and services in behalf of the German occupation, because all sorts of expenses were charged by order of the occupying power directly to the account of the Public Treasury. The expenses just referred to amount to a round sum of ƒ 250 million or $ 137 million. It should be emphatically stated in this connection that this amount does not refer to damage to property in consequence of the occupation. The said amount comprises items such as transport-services never paid for by the occupying power (e.g. the transport of German forces by the Netherlands Railways), unpaid rent of buildings seized by the occupying power, trading-losses and inevitable expenses resulting from measures of occupation. As was stated above, these items were charged directly to the account of the Public Treasure by order of the occupying power and have therefore not been entered under the heading "cost of occupation".

With the help of the available figures on the returns of production and exportation the Central Bureau of Statistics has calculated that Germany had to her disposal a net amount of ƒ 6 000 million of $ 3 300 million of the current production of goods and services throughout the entire period of occupation, which amount was therefore withdrawn from the Netherlands national income. This calculation is based on the prices of 1938.

D. Damage owing to loss of production suffered and still to be suffered after May 7th 1945

The chaotic condition, in which the country's economy has been left at the end of the war, is the reason that for some years to come we shall have to reckon with a greatly reduced real income. This is a result of damage done to the production-apparatus by the war and by the occupation and of damage inflicted to the productivity of labour by all kinds of psychic and physical factors. Detrimental consequences of imprisonment and forced employment in Germany, undernourishment, decline of the general state of public health, lack of workingclothes and footwear, insufficient housing, defective means of conveyance, bad equipment of factories and workshops, shortage of the most essential tools and auxiliary materials, are the principal causes of the now greatly decreased labour-productivity. Reconstruction will proceed but slowly, since it depends on how soon the most urgent shortages can be supplemented by imports from abroad and the most necessary repairs can be carried out.

Assuming that the labour-productivity at the end of the war amounted to 40% of the normal (the average of 1938), that from July 1st 1945 it increased regularly and that on account of this increase it will be 100% again at the close of 1947, one arrives at the conclusion that the loss owing to the decreased labour-productivity may be fixed at 85% of a normal net annual production. Taking the latter at approximately ƒ 5 500 million or $ 3 025 million, the loss for this item alone, based on the purchasing-power of the money of 1938, is ƒ 4 700 million or $ 2 585 million.

Just as with the loss sub B, some double counting has to be rectified. The amount involved is, however, not so considerable as in the case of the calculation of the loss of production during the years of occupation, since replacement and maintenance will be proceeding again and since no deduction is necessary for the large supplies of raw materials and auxiliary materials lost in the years of war. In connection with the fact that loss owing to the destruction of factories, etc. has already been entirely booked under Section I, in this case a deduction must take place. It seems right in view of the foregoing to fix the amount to be charged to Germany owing to loss of production suffered and still to be suffered after May 7th 1945, at ƒ 4 300 million or $ 2 364 million. In this case too, it should in theory be possible to calculate the total by adding up all items in which the future, loss of production is concretely expressed. In practice, however, this is only possible in a few exceptional cases.

Section IV

Cost of German occupation

The cost of German occupation amounts to a total of ƒ 9 500 million or $ 5 224 million,

viz. Reichskreditkassenscheine . . . . ƒ   135 million or $ 74 million
Expenses of German Forces [1] . . ƒ 7 030   ,,   or $ 3 866   ,,
Expenses of German Civil Administration . . . . ƒ   225   ,,   or $ 124   ,,
Compulsory Contributions to the cost of Germany's war against Russia . . . . ƒ 2 110   ,,   or $ 1 160   ,,

Total ƒ 9 500 million or $ 5 224 million

GERMAN INTERESTS IN THE NETHERLANDS IMMEDIATELY BEFORE THE WAR

The data to be supplied with regard to German interests in the Netherlands immediately before the war, cannot yet be furnished, as these interests are to a large extent concentrated in the central part of the Netherlands, which was only liberated by the Allies in May 1945, so that the time has been too short to collect sufficient information. However, it may be noted that a separate institution has been created for the registration and the administration of German interests. As soon as more detailed data are obtained, they will be made available, together with a survey of the way in which these interests are administered. Nevertheless, it can now already be stated that before the war the value of these interests was estimated at ƒ 1 000 million of $ 550 million. Considerable war-damage to these interests will, however, have to be taken into account. In this connection it should be observed that against these pre-war German interests in the Netherlands there exists the item of the not inconsiderable Netherlands interests in Germany, which before the war were estimated at ƒ 1 500 million of $ 825 million; here too, however, a considerable war-damage will have to be taken into account, a war-damage which has only partly been entered under the heading: Foreign investments, included in Section I.

SUMMARY

In view of the above the total amount which the Netherlands Government have decided to claim from Germany as reparation for war-damage

[1] These do not include the cost of occupation charged directly to the Public Treasury by order of the occupying power. On page 215 the amount of these expenses, not including the damage to goods mentioned in Section I, is calculated at ƒ 250 million or $ 137 million.

suffered, can, expressed in the money-value of 1938, be fixed as follows:

A. Material loss of the national
   wealth of the Netherlands . . . *f* 11 425 million or $ 6 284 million
B. Damage owing to loss of pro-
   duction during the years of war *f* 4 000   ,,   or $ 2 200   ,,
C. Loss owing to forced transfer to
   Germany of part of the reduced
   production . . . . *f* 6 000   ,,   or $ 3 300   ,,
D. Damage owing to loss of pro-
   duction suffered and still to be
   suffered after May 7th 1945 . . *f* 4 300   ,,   or $ 2 364   ,,
                                     _____
                                    f 25 725 million or $ 14 148 million.

THE NATIONAL WEALTH OF THE NETHERLANDS ON SEPTEMBER 1ST 1939
AND ITS DECLINE IN CONSEQUENCE OF THE WAR

(All data have been based on the pricelevel of 1938)

	Property on September 1st 1939 in millions	Decline owing to the war in millions
a. Agriculture and horticulture	*f* 3 800 or $ 2 090	*f* 825 or $ 454
b. Industry	*f* 5 000 or $ 2 750	*f* 2 200 or $ 1 210
c. Commerce	*f* 2 500 or $ 1 375	*f* 1 800 or $ 990
d. Credits and Banking	*f* 300 or $ 165	*f* 15 or $ 8
e. Traffic	*f* 1 500 or $ 825	*f* 1 005 or $ 553
f. Public property (incl. harbours and bridges, excl. utilities)	*f* 2 800 or $ 1 540	*f* 550 or $ 303
g. Churches, private nursing-homes, buildings belonging to private institutions, theatres, cinemas	*f* 500 or $ 275	*f* 150 or $ 82,5
h. Liberal professions (inventories)	*f* 50 or $ 27	*f* 10 or $ 5,5
i. Houses	*f* 5 000 or $ 2 750	*f* 820 or $ 451
j. Furniture	*f* 5 000 or $ 2 750	*f* 1 200 or $ 660
k. Gold-stock and foreign exchange	*f* 1 500 or $ 825	*f* 1 210 or $ 665
l. Investments in the Neth. Indies and abroad	*f* 7 000 or $ 3 850	*f* 1 000 or $ 550 [2]
m. Valuables	1	*f* 640 or $ 352
Total national wealth:	*f* 34 950 or $ 19 222	Total damage: *f* 11 425 or $ 6 284

[1] Sufficient information is not available, but will be supplied at an early date.

[2] The amount of *f* 1 000 million entered as loss on foreign investments only covers the loss on investments in the Central-European countries and the loss owing to confiscation of foreign securities belonging to Jewish and other Netherlands subjects. The loss on investments in the Netherlands Indies is therefore *not* included in this figure of *f* 1 000 million.

As has already been observed in the beginning of this memorandum, this amount will in course of time have to be expressed in terms of the price-level prevailing at the time of the final settlement of the reparation account. At the present price-level (175% of that of December 31st 1938) the total damage incurred would not amount to ƒ 25 725 million of $ 14 148 million ($ 1.— = ƒ 1.81 – 82, rate of exchange 1938) but to approximately ƒ 45 000 million or approximately $ 16 850 million, taking into account the present exchange rate of the guilder (i.e. 1 $ = ƒ 2.67).

Source: This Memorandum was published under the same title
               in 1945 by order of the Netherlands Government.

MEMORANDUM

The Royal Netherlands Government deem it opportune to formulate their point of view with regard to the demarcation of the future Netherlands-German frontier, and related problems.

In this connection Her Majesty's Government refer to their statement [1] of October 28th, 1944, which was brought to the notice of the Governments of the Allied Nations. In this statement Her Majesty's Government pointed out, inter alia, that a complex of measures taken by the occupying power had created a situation in the Netherlands of so serious a nature as to jeopardize the country's future recovery. On this ground the Netherlands Government reserved the right to put forward their point of view and to formulate their demands after the liberation of the Netherlands.

In the period elapsed since, it has been possible to survey the total amount of the losses suffered by the national economy. It has been proved that, if the Netherlands are to recover some measure of their national prosperity, the provision of certain compensations on the part of Germany will be indispensable. At the same time it will be necessary to envisage the safeguarding of the Netherlands economic system against discriminative German measures, such as have been taken in the past to the detriment of the Netherlands.

Her Majesty's Government have examined the question in what manner the incontestable claim to reparations on the part of Germany, to which the Netherlands are entitled, can be brought into effect, with due consideration of the claims of other Allied Nations. It has become clear thas the damage inflicted on the national economy has reached such proportions, that adequate compensation in the form of an allocation of German territory will not be practicable, in view of the extent of the annexations that would be involved. The Netherlands Government therefore are of opinion that the solution of the problem should mainly be approached on different lines. In this Her Majesty's Government have also been led by the consideration that the people of the Netherlands are traditionally opposed to annexation; besides, the Netherlands Government are unwilling to urge a solution which might harbour the seeds of future conflict, and of German irredentism, which in its turn might develop into a danger to peace and security in Europe.

Her Majesty's Government are therefore prepared to limit their territorial claims to certain frontier rectifications and to seek indemnification for the losses and damages sustained, in the economic sphere

[1] See above, Appendix 4.

primarily. It is their considered opinion that thus, while making a material contribution to peace and security and the amity of the European nations, the prerequisites for the recovery of the national economy will also be created. The Netherlands Government are fully aware that in this way no complete indemnification for the direct damages and losses inflicted by the enemy can be realized; and though they are no less aware that thus heavy burdens will be imposed upon the Dutch people, Her Majesty's Government are prepared to shoulder the responsibility of these burdens, provided always that the conditions, indispensable to the country's economic recovery, be established.

It should be remarked at this stage that with the questions and wishes to be mentioned hereafter the problem of the economic relations between the Netherlands and Germany is far from having been exhaustively dealt with. When the German question in its general aspect will be discussed in detail, several other problems will have to be raised by the Netherlands Government.

But the points discussed so far are of such paramount importance for the Netherlands that their satisfactory solution must of necessity be considered a vital factor in the economic recovery of the country.

The wishes of the Netherlands Government in the economic sphere are set forth in Annex 1. They can be distinguished in desiderata of a general economic character and demands of a more specified nature.

1. As a first specific demand the Netherlands are desirous to obtain for a period, in the first instance, of forty to fifty years, a number of German mining concessions mainly on the left bank of the Rhine, situated by preference between the eastern border of the province of Limburg and the Rhine.

The use to be made of these concessions shall be left to the decision of the Netherlands. The arrangement is to comprise concessions whether in actual exploitation or not, as well as any tracts or fields for which as yet no concession has been issued.

The Netherlands Government desire to stress the direct and vital economic importance to the Netherlands of obtaining these concessions (a number of mines considered in this connection has been specified in Annex 1). With respect to coal the Netherlands would thereby be enabled to balance the coal import and to broaden the basis of the coal position which is indispensable for the further industrialization of the country in connection also with the steadily growing population.

With respect to potassium some wishes have been formulated in Annex I.

2. The three following demands are of a general economic character:

Measures will have to be effected with regard to the charges of German rail, road and water transport as well as the port and storage charges, so as to prevent in future an unfair bias in their competition against the Netherlands ports. In all probability this will only be practicable by the establishment of interallied control on these tariffs generally for a period further to be decided. The Netherlands will have to be actively concerned in the machinery to be created for such control.

3. As a logical complement of the above Germany should be prohibited to construct new canals, tending to divert Rhine traffic into other than its natural channels.

4. The Netherlands deem it essential that the German monetary policy be conducted in a manner that will leave their vital interests unaffected. The memory is still vivid of the discriminatory character of German foreign currency regulations in the decade preceding the war, and of the strenuous effort called for on the part of the Netherlands to safeguard their interests, notwithstanding the country's strong economic position at that time.

Not only the traffic of goods but especially services rendered, amongst which the Rhine traffic deserves separate mention, were seriously impaired by the restrictive currency policy as practised by Germany.

Her Majesty's Government are fully aware of the fact that for a considerable time to come there will be no question of free monetary traffic between the Netherlands and Germany, but they consider their desire justified, in the interests of the Netherlands economy, that in case the natural route of German export or import passes Netherlands harbours the services rendered are to be paid for effectively. This demand applies likewise to the Netherlands transit commerce.

These economic demands cannot but be considered reasonable in view of the financial and economic chaos wrought by the war in the Netherlands. The Netherlands Government trust therefore that these demands will meet with the ready reception which, in the Government's opinion, they fully deserve.

It has already been set forth above that the Netherlands Government are opposed in principle to territorial expansion through annexation. In seeking restoration Her Majesty's Government have therefore laid the main stress on economic demands; apart from this however they feel compelled to make their wishes known as regards a certain number of rectifications of the Netherlands-German border. In formulating these territorial claims Her Majesty's Government deem it advisable to practise the greatest restraint.

The tortuousness of the Netherlands-German borderline has repeatedly caused difficulties in the past. These unsatisfactory conditions should now be settled. From the appended maps it may be seen how the frontier line will, in the opinion of Her Majesty's Government, have to run in future. An explanatory commentary may be found in Annex II.

In laying down their view on the frontier rectification the Netherlands Government have been guided by the following considerations:

1. shortening of the frontier line;
2. improvement of local communications;
3. local improvement of canal- and waterworks;
4. improvements from the social and economic point of view;
5. redress of local anomalies.

One of the results of the rectifications as indicated will be that the frontier line between the Netherlands and Germany will be reduced from 525 kilometers to 340 kilometers, this reduction to be effected by the cession of no more than 1750 square kilometers to the Netherlands.

As regards the German population domiciled in the territory to be ceded, Her Majesty's Government aim at incorporating as few German subjects as possible in the Netherlands body politic.

This principle finds, for instance, its practical application in the region to the east of Dinxperlo and Nijmegen, where the Netherlands Govern-

ment demand a smaller rectification than would appear logically indicated, in view of the dense population in this area.

According to statistical data of 1939 approximately 119.000 people
live in the territory to be ceded.

This population is for the greater part German. However, apart from
Netherlanders, non-German aliens are found among the population,
especially near South Limburg.

In the view of the Netherlands Government the autochthonous population in the aforesaid areas, which can prove to have resided there
before May 10th, 1940, should be allowed to stay. In this connection it
should be remarked that the "human rights" are fully guaranteed by the
Netherlands constitution.

Only those persons whose attitude during the National-Socialist regime precludes their incorporation in the Netherlands body politic, as well
as recognized warcriminals, shall be expelled.

As has been set forth above Her Majesty's Government consider the
compliance with their economic demands of primary importance to the
economic restoration of the Netherlands; they therefore restrict their
territorial demands to frontier rectifications.

However, Her Majesty's Government wish to emphasize that the two
matters are closely interrelated; therefore should their economic demands
– in particular those concerning mining concessions – not meet with the
expected approval, the Netherlands Government expressly reserve their
right to put forward more far reaching territorial claims. Her Majesty's
Government confidently expect that the reasonableness of their demands
will be recognized; they trust that the people of the Netherlands will
thus be enabled to rebuild their position in world economy.

Annex I

ECONOMIC DESIDERATA

The damage caused by enemy agression and occupation has assumed
such proportions that very special provisions for the restoration of the
prosperity of the densely populated Netherlands are deemed essential.
The desiderata which the Netherlands Government wish to put forward
in this connection can be broadly outlined as follows:

In the future certain measures should be taken to make Netherlands
economy less dependent upon its hinterland. For that purpose a more
intensified industrialization of the Netherlands will be a prerequisite,
demanding a broader coal basis. Furthermore a guaranteed supply of
potassium fertilizer will be necessary for agricultural purposes.

It is furthermore evident that restoration of trade and traffic with
Germany will always remain an indispensable factor for the country's
return to prosperity. With a view to allow full scope to the natural
advantages of the Netherlands with regard to the hinterland, well defined
and lasting guarantees will have to be obtained. It is the view of Her
Majesty's Government that these general desiderata may be realized in
the following way:

1. Mining

As to coal-mining it will be necessary for certain German mining concessions on the left bank of the Rhine, situated by preference between the

eastern border of the province of Limburg and the Rhine, to be handed over to the Netherlands. However, in two instances concessions on the right bank of the Rhine will have to be made over to the Netherlands, owing to the fact that the coal-layers, situated on the left bank, are worked from the right bank.

This arrangement will have to comprise concessions, whether in actual exploitation or not, as well as tracts and fields for which concessions have not yet been issued. The use which will be made of these concessions will have to be determined exclusively by the Netherlands. The concessions referred to are specified on List A, affixed to this Annex.

The production of the mines covered by this arrangement will be regarded in all respects as the produce of Netherlands soil. Should for example part of this production be made available for any part of Germany, this will have to be regarded as export from the Netherlands. If the production of these mines proves satisfactory, certain kinds of coal may become available for the world-market. Consequently the Netherlands may then be in a position to export coal from these districts.

However, the fact that this German coal will be at the disposal of the Netherlands economy may also lead to coal, mined on Netherlands territory, becoming available for the world market.

It is deemed essential that these mines be worked within the Netherlands economic system. The marketing of this coal should be exclusively a Netherlands concern and the financial transactions contingent thereon will have to take place within the Netherlands monetary system. This means that, when exporting coal from these mines, the Netherlands will be allowed to stipulate in which currency the export will be effectuated.

The current expenses of exploitation in Germany, that have to be settled in cash, e.g. the miners' wages, will be paid in marks. Should the receipts in Germany not be sufficient to cover these cash payments, the necessary German currency might be furnished by the Netherlands. This currency might be obtained by selling Netherlands foodstuffs to the mining population. It is evident that these plans need to be further elaborated; for instance the Netherlands Government wish to draw attention to transport-problems, labour-problems, the supplying of the mines with goods required for the exploitation, etc.

One point, however, calls for immediate attention. In all probability it will be necessary to invest fresh capital in these mines, so as to promote an efficient exploitation. In so far as this capital is invested by the Netherlands, it should be regarded as preferential with respect not only to established shareholders, but to existing creditors as well. Such an arrangement would be required pending a settlement with regard to the German owners. Whatever this settlement may be, the Netherlands capital investment should have priority.

Furthermore the Netherlands Government deem it advisable to set forth at this stage their point of view with respect to the duration of these arrangements. A period of 40 to 50 years is contemplated. If a normal economy will have been re-established in Germany at that time, a definite settlement will then have to be made. At this definite settlement the Netherlands capital investments created in the meantime will have to be fully recognized. In case normal economic conditions should not be re-established in Germany at that time, the possibility must be left open for extending the above-mentioned period.

As far as the unexploited mines are concerned, a settlement allowing for the transfer of the concessions to Netherlands concerns for an indefinite period will be necessary. On that basis alone can initiative for new exploitation be expected.

These are the main points of the settlement envisaged by the Netherlands Government; detailed considerations which might arise from a further study of this matter may be submitted at a later date. The Netherlands Government, however, wish to stress once more that a settlement of this nature is imperative, this being the only way to broaden the Netherlands coal-basis, as a necessary condition for the further industrialization of the country. It may be added that the growing population also requires a larger coal supply.

Finally the broadening of the coal-basis is also of the greatest importance for strengthening the Netherlands export position with a view to promoting the country's reconstruction.

With regard to potassium the Netherlands Government wish to observe the following. It is known that unexploited layers of potassium exist in the neighbourhood of Wesel and Xanten.

In so far as these concessions are German-held, Her Majesty's Government wish to lay claim to these concessions, specified on list B.

Arrangements, similar to those proposed above with regard to coal-mines, will have to be applied in this instance.

2. The unfair competition of the German seaports

Ever since German imperialism became a danger to the world, and particularly after the first world war, the Netherlands seaports suffered from unfair competition by the German ports of Hamburg. Bremen and Emden.

Characteristic of this competition were the special rates on the German railways in favour of the German seaports mentioned. Likewise the rates on the German canals were discriminative. Finally special port charges and transshipment charges also favoured the German North Sea ports to the detriment of Netherlands interests. This unfair competition should be eliminated from now on. The elaboration of measures to this effect will require careful consideration.

Meanwhile the Netherlands Government wish to set forth the following main points.

A general formula should be laid down by treaty, preventing the German Government from taking artificial measures favouring transport between the German interior and the German seaports to the detriment of transport via the Netherlands ports. The same principle should apply to transit-traffic through Germany. This subject being of too complex a nature to be defined in a general formula, a number of special provisions will have to be inserted in the afore-said treaty. For instance the railways shall charge no other than normal rates for transport to and from the German seaports. To ensure correct application of such a provision it will be indispensable for a given period to exercise close supervision over German railway rates in general. The port-charges and the trans-shipment-charges will have to be placed under similar supervision.

The Netherlands will have to take their due share in the machinery to be created for this purpose.

Furthermore a guarantee will be required that German authorities will not in any way subsidize German canal traffic.

Finally, similar safeguards will be necessary to prevent German road traffic from causing unfair competition to the Netherlands seaports, particularly in the matter of piece-goods transport.

The Netherlands Government desire to lay great stress on these wishes because the measures taken by former German Governments in this respect have proved to be most injurious to Netherlands economy. There is all the more reason for the Netherlands Government to underline the importance of guarantees to this effect, as the possibility is not excluded that Bremen and Hamburg may lose part of their natural hinterland.

Any attempt on the part of Germany to attract traffic to Bremen and Hamburg by artificial means should be prevented.

There is no need for Germany to consider herself unduly restrained by the proposed measures. Before the war already objections were raised, particularly in the Ruhr area and the Rhineland, against measures from Berlin, tending to interfere with the natural flow of traffic.

As to the traffic on the waterways to the Ruhr area, particular vigilance will be required to prevent the Germans from evading the above-mentioned provision by favouring traffic on the Dortmund-Eems canal, and thus once more to introduce unfair competition.

3. The German canal system

As a logical complement to the demands made in par. 2 the Netherlands Government wish to bring forward some desires regarding the German canal system. Her Majesty's Government are of opinion that Germany should be prohibited to construct new canals which might deflect traffic from the Rhine into other than its normal channels, whilst furthermore the existing canals of this nature should not be widened or deepened. The Netherlands Government particularly have in view the Dortmund–Ems canal and the Mittelland canal. These canals were at the time constructed to the detriment of Netherlands traffic. It will therefore have to be stipulated that these canals shall not be further developed for discriminatory purposes. Nor should the construction of the projected Hansa canal from Osnabrück to Hamburg be allowed to be proceeded with.

4. The Monetary System of Germany

The Netherlands Government deem it essential that the German monetary policy be conducted in a manner that will leave Netherlands vital interests unaffected. Since exchange control was established in Germany in 1931, their monetary policy was increasingly applied in order to discriminate against the Netherlands seaports, Netherlands transport, traffic and trade.

Consequently the natural advantages accruing from the Netherlands geographical position, and their place in international trade were greatly impaired. Owing to the economic strength of the Netherlands at that time it was possible to counteract by way of negotiations many of the harmful consequences of the German economic policy. As a result of the war the economic position of the Netherlands has been considerably weakened. As various reasons make it necessary to maintain German exchange control for an indefinite period – since this will offer the most effective means to control the economic intercourse between occupied Germany and the outside world – it is all the more necessary for the Netherlands

Government to demand that this complex of measures shall not be applied to the detriment of the Netherlands economy.

On account of their experience, the Netherlands Government are convinced that the German authorities, whatever their position may be, will always endeavour to abuse exchange-regulations to the detriment of non-German interests. It is only reasonable that the Netherlands demand that the foreign exchange policy of Germany be so conducted that these vital Netherlands interests will be fully safeguarded. For this reason the obligation should be imposed on Germany that, in the re-construction of her economic life, Netherlands interests be duly considered.

The Netherlands demands in this respect may be formulated as follows:

Foreign exchange, obtained by German exports shall have to be made available in such a manner that, in case the natural route of German export or import passes Netherlands ports, all services connected there-with be paid for effectively. The payment for these services will enable the Netherlands to reconstruct their economy, more particularly that of their seaports. This implies that the Netherlands may provide a market for German industrial products. The services in question concern Rhine traffic and other transport services, port charges, transshipment and storage charges, freight charges, commissions, profit margins, etc. It should be emphasized that the Netherlands are not only interested in transport services as such; the Netherlands transit-trade will also have to be duly considered.

This means that, if the Netherlands buy goods in the world market destined for Germany, or if they sell German products in the world-market a Netherlands firm, established in the Netherlands, should be given the same opportunities as a firm established in Germany. This demand is of paramount importance for the safeguarding of the international trade position of the Netherlands.

The economic advantages thus to be obtained, may be summarized as follows.

The position of the Netherlands as a centre of international trade and transit has been secured by the energy and ability of the people and the geographical position of the country. Before the war this position was challenged, during the war utterly destroyed by Germany. Now this position will have to be re-established. Therefore a guarantee is required that Germany shall no longer have the opportunity of endangering the prosperity of the Netherlands. This may be seen as an advantage, an advantage however, based on claims of justice and fairness.

LIST A

A. *Mines in production*

1. Walsum (right bank of the Rhine), inclusive concession Neu-Eversael (left bank of the Rhine).
2. Diergardt-Mevissen (left and right bank of the Rhine).
3. Rhein-Preussen (inclusive Rheinland).
4. Friedrich Heinrich (inclusive Humbold 1 and 2, Norddeutschland and Camp V).
5. Niederrheinische Bergwerke A.G. (inclusive Grossherzog von Baden, Ernst Moritz Arndt, Süddeutschland, Heinrich and Vluyn II).
6. Sophia Jacoba (inclusive Erkelenz).

B. *Concessions (undeveloped) not mentioned in A*
  7. Rossenray.
  8. Rheinberg.
  9. Alfred.
 10. Niederrhein (inclusive Bönninghart and Veen).
 11. Walther.
 12. "Deutscher Fiscus" (north of Kevelaar).
 13. Coallayers of Rombacher Hütte near Erkelenz.

LIST B

German Potassium Concessions near Wesel and Xanten
  1. Gewerkschaft Rheinberg.
  2. Rossenray and Neu-Eversael.
  3. Zeche Friedrich Heinrich.
  4. Gewerkschaft Friedrich Thyssen.

Annex II

As has already been set forth on page 221 of the preceding note, the Netherlands Government in defining their policy with regard to frontier rectifications, were guided by the following considerations;
  1. shortening of the frontier line;
  2. improvement of local communications;
  3. local improvement of canal- and waterworks;
  4. improvements from the social and economic point of view;
  5. redress of local anomalies.
By far the most important of the latter is the demarcation of the frontier in the Dollard and the mouth of the river Eems. In spite of repeated endeavours undertaken in the past by Her Majesty's Government it has never been possible to come to a satisfactory solution of this problem with Germany. For that reason, and also in view of the existing plans to reclaim the Dollard, – preliminary works of this nature already being in progress in that region –, incorporation of this area into the Kingdom seems indicated.
As a result of the reclaiming of the Dollard a new regulated channel will have to be maintained in the mouth of the Eems, a further consequence of which will be that the area east of "Hond" and "Paap", including the estuary known as "Oostfriesche Gaatje", will eventually become suitable for reclaiming purposes. For technical reasons connected with this "impoldering" the sea-dike from Emden to Pilsum via Knock should become Netherlands territory, the town of Emden and surroundings, however, remaining German.
In view of this "impoldering" and the projected diversion of the Eems-channel, it appears logical that the isle of Borkum, which furthermore controls the mouth of this river, should become a part of the Netherlands.
The remaining local anomalies along the Netherlands-German border, 24 in all, are not of sufficient importance to be specifically mentioned. For the greater part they consist of dwellings transsected by the borderline traffic impediments and conditions favouring contraband.
Her Majesty's Government deem it also advisable to include the peat-moor of Boertange, situated to the east of the southern part of the province of Groningen and the province of Drenthe, in the territory of the

Kingsdom. This region which is sparsely populated has always been economically neglected by Germany. The projected border rectification is considered necessary in view of a number of problems connected with waterworks and drainage. Moreover six local anomalies will thus be eliminated. Finally it may be noted that the Boertange marsh is already partially Netherlands owned, whereas the peat is cut almost exclusively by Netherlands labour.

By straightening the curve in the boundary line near Bentheim, an improvement of the waterways-system in the border-region and of the watersupply of the canals in south-east Drenthe and Westerwolde will become possible. This will also allow flood-control measures to be taken preventing inundations as have repeatedly occurred in the past. This region is likewise thinly inhabitated. This frontier rectification is one of the few that entail some economic advantages owing to the fact that oil is found in that area.

With a view to incorporate as few Germans as possible in the Netherlands, the town of Nordhorn with its c. 24 000 inhabitants, will remain German.

As a result of the minor rectification near Glanerbrug the cottonmills "Eilermark" and "Deutschland", in which Netherlands capital is invested for 100 per cent and 75 per cent respectively, will come within the Netherlands border.

A considerable shortening of the borderline is achieved by the rectification near Vreden. No economic importance is to be attached to this area, whilst the number of German nationals involved is insignificant.

The rectifications in the neighbourhood of Dinxperlo and those east of Nijmegen have given rise to many and various considerations. The needs for traffic-improvement by themselves would demand a borderline more eastwardly situated than the one projected at present.

A solution of the traffic problem, satisfactory on all points, would only have been possible however by adding to the territory of the Kingdom an area inhabited by approximately 115 000 people. The latter consideration has convinced the Netherlands Government of the desirability to restrict their demands to a minor rectification, which at least offers the advantage of a shortened frontier and removes the most pressing deficiencies in the waterways-system. The economic significance of this region should not be rated highly, the "Reichswald" being for the greater part destroyed.

In the province of Limburg, from Tegelen to Vaals, the frontier follows an excessively sinuous line; moreover the Netherlands territory to the north-east of Sittard is no broader than a few kilometers.

The Netherlands Government therefore deem it imperative that the present unsatisfactory situation be conclusively remedied. As shown by the map the projected borderline will shorten the present frontier to a considerable extent; moreover several minor improvements in the drainage system will be rendered possible by this rectification. Finally nine local anomalies will be eliminated.

The economic importance of this rectification should not be overestimated. Although a number of mining concessions and coallayers will be brought within the Netherlands border, only one colliery is situated in this area. The difficulties experienced, in the field of mining technology on account of the sinuous borderline of southern Limburg, are only partially being met by this rectification. It may be added, that owing to their location several coallayers are at present unexploitable (Melanie, Nordstern, Hillenswehr) whilst the existing borderline is detrimental to the mine called "Domaniale".

It should be mentioned that the country's import requirements in the future will amount to approximately $7\frac{1}{2}$ million tons annually. The Netherlands Government are however opposed in principle to cover these requirements by obtaining a further number of collieries by way of a more extensive border rectification than contemplated at present.

The manner in which the Netherlands Government hope to be enabled to cope with this shortage has been extensively set forth in Annex I.

It may finally be repeated that the proposed frontier rectifications will reduce the borderline from 525 kilometers to 340 kilometers whilst no more than 1750 square kilometers will be incorporated within the territory of the Kingdom.

According to statistical data of 1939 approximately 119 000 persons are living in that area. The problem pertaining to this German population has already been set forth in the preceding note.

Source: Proceedings of the States General, 1946–1947,
Annexes, Second Chamber, No 352.

MEMORANDUM OF THE NETHERLANDS GOVERNMENT ON ALLIED POLICY WITH REGARD TO GERMANY

GENERAL OBSERVATIONS

1. The principal object that the Netherlands have in view with regard to the German problem is the creation of adequate guarantees to ensure peace and security, and the creation of the prerequisites for the recovery of the national economy and the recovery of the prosperity of Germany in so far as this is essential to European and world prosperity.

2. Before concluding a peace treaty with Germany it will be imperative first to establish a common policy to be pursued in all zones of occupation. It is deemed essential that the states neighbouring on Germany participate actively in defining this policy. This applies in particular to the Netherlands, as the security and welfare of the Kingdom are in a high degree dependent on the prosperity of Germany and the foundations on which the latter is based.

3. As the entire territory of Germany is occupied, there is the risk that the governments of the German "Länder" and any other central agencies to be created, will be considered by the German people only to exist by the grace of the armies of occupation. In order to bring about a state of affairs in which risk is eliminated and also to keep the cost of occupation as low as possible, it should be attempted eventually to restrict military occupation to a number of strategic areas and points, such as ports, air-fields, traffic centres and, if necessary, industrial centres. This will enable the military boundaries of the zones of occupation to be abolished though it may remain necessary to maintain administrative zones of responsibility of the various occupying authorities. The armies of occupation might then be gradually converted to a police force on a military footing, subordinate to the highest civil occupying authorities.

4. Peaceful relations with Germany will only become possible if a minimum of economic and social security is assured to the German population. Though it is obvious that the present difficulties in Germany are in the first and foremost place due to their former rulers, there is the growing danger, unless things improve, of the responsibility being shifted, however unjustly on the Allied authorities.

For that reason it is necessary that in the first place the responsibility for the *provisioning* of Germany should be put in a central German organization, initially under close Allied supervision. The German people must come to see where the responsibility lies in this respect. Any applications for supplies from outside Germany to cover deficiences must be proposed and motivated by Germans, whereupon Allied experts shall decide whether these applications are reasonable. Policy on this point should be made public as soon as possible.

5. The denazification policy in Germany must be closely supervised by the Allies. On the one hand this is essential to future political security, but on the other, care must be taken to avoid denazification becoming a perpetual recurring point of discord among the Germans, which might slow down the return to political tranquility and economic efficiency. Denazification in German hands is a dangerous thing: objective fairness can scarcely exist among the Germans who deal with these matters, considering that before and during the war the majority of the German people were willing followers of the regime. In one case they will be too lenient and in another too severe, all of which tends to slow down recovery.

Unlike denazification the trying of war criminals is a purely Allied concern which needs no further elucidation.

6. The re-establishment of freedom of expression among Germans during the period of occupation is not only to be desired, but also necessary. Not only that it is essential to the restoration of sound principles of justice, but it is also necessary for the eradication of the element of fear. But, on the other hand, the Germans must be taught to respect the interests of the Allies. On this account certain restrictions will have to be imposed, to which the Germans must adhere in references to the Allies in their press or other public utterances. If this is not done, public discussion of the Allied conceptions of the future of Germany will lead to much unpleasantness. Naturally, the German people must later on be allowed to express an opinion on the peace treaty proposals once the Allies have agreed on them, but before that stage restrictions should be imposed in the interests of the Allies.

7. In order to be able to appreciate correctly the future of Germany it is imperative that on the part of the Allies steps are taken to collect as soon as possible data allowing a clear insight in the structure of the German population. This requires in the first place an accurate, be it provisional, German census. With regard to the present German pyramid in population and the birth and mortality rates, a forecast will have to be made of the expected development of the German population figures in the coming decades.

8. It is deemed desirable to institute at the earliest date an investigation into the existing sources of German prosperity, i.e. the deposits of raw materials and the possibilities of their production as well as into the productive capacity of existing German plants. The results of this investigation should be published. A census of German plants should likewise be considered.

I. PREPARATION OF THE PEACE TREATY WITH GERMANY

It stands to reason that it will be in the interests of peace and security to project a statute for Germany that will be durable and proof against the fluctuations of international politics.

To this end such a statute should in the opinion of the Netherlands Government be based on the following principles.

A. Politically, care will have to be taken to guard against a resuscitation of Prusso-German nationalism and German lust of world conquest. To realize this aim there will have to be binding agreements between the Allies and also the promotion and development of political relations and a mentality inside Germany calculated to further a peace-loving policy.

The necessity of binding agreements between the Allies is again referred to more extensively below (vide sub III). With respect to the future political relations in Germany the following may be observed.

The declaration of Potsdam contained the following statement on this point: "The administration of affairs in Germany should be directed towards the decentralization of the political structure and the development of local responsibility".

The Netherlands Government hold that this pre-eminently democratic principle could well be used for guidance in the future political organization of Germany.

Application of this principle will mean that Germany will be built up on a federal basis. To ensure the independence of the constituent parts of the future Germany, both in their own interests and in those of the Allies, the more preferable form of government would be a confederation of states rather than a federal state. A political organization of this kind would be no novelty to Germany, as the German League (1815–1866) was a confederacy.

The political development in Germany since the Potsdam conference already tends to move in this direction. In all the zones of occupation German "Länder" have come into being with populations varying from somewhat over one million to about twelve million. In this connection the question arises whether it might not appear desirable to modify in certain cases the provisional boundaries, making due allowance not only for political, but also for ethnographical, historical, geographic, economic and social factors. Considering that it will be in the interest of the entire world that the German "Länder" be regarded by their populations as a natural state of affairs, the Netherlands Government feel justified in recommending the further study of this question.

It would not be surprising if the conception of a new German confederacy should meet with opposition in Germany itself. As both recent and more remote experience has shown that what the Germans consider to be to their advantage turns out to be, in the political sphere, to the disadvantage of their neighbours, it would seem advisable to appreciate German objections of this kind in the light of that experience. In view of the German urge towards centralized administration it will further be imperative to complete the organization of the "Länder" and to have that organization firmly established in the "Länder" themselves by constitutional laws before central German ruling bodies are formed, notably where bodies vested with political authority are concerned. In this connection it may be stressed that in order to ensure in the future decentralization of Germany in the spirit of the Potsdam agreement it would be advisable to grant the eventual German Government only derived powers delegated by the "Länder", whilst it also seems advisable to include regulations in the constitutions of those "Länder" under which certain powers cannot be delegated to the Central Government.

B. Economically, care will have to be taken to guard against renewed German economic aggression in the future.

This will also require binding agreements between the Allies, and the promotion of an economic development in Germany which shall restrain the pursuance of an aggressive economic policy.

Here, the Netherlands Government wish only to draw attention to the necessity of creating guarantees, lest the following clause in the Potsdam agreement be reduced to a dead letter.

> "At the earliest practicable date, the German economy shall be decentralized for the purpose of eliminating the present excessive concentration of economic power as exemplified in particular by cartels, syndicates, trusts and other monopolistic arrangements".

Past experience with German governments has shown that, more than any other system of government these tend to behave in a monopolistic and dictatorial way. If the existing plans for socialization of the coalmines and heavy industries in Germany are realized – and the Netherlands Government wish to emphasize that in principle they are not opposed to socialization of branches of production suited to this purpose – care will have to be taken to ensure that socialization in Germany does not mean nationalization; in other words, that a new weapon is not forged, indirectly, for economic aggression, which would create instead of trusts, cartels and syndicates a supermonopolist, the *German* State. Naturally, if a federal Germany is formed, these monopolies will at least be spread over a number of "Länder". However, it seems doubtful whether this decentralization alone constitutes a sufficient safeguard. The danger is by no means imaginary that important industries in the various German "Länder" will be nationalized in an identical way, and that thus, behind the screen of decentralization, an unparalleled monopolistic organization is in fact set up.

In view of the foregoing considerations the Netherlands Government feel bound to stress that the problems of the decentralization of the large German concerns, increased foreign influence on them and the control – national and international – of those industries, will have to be thoroughly studied before any decisions on these points are taken.

The Netherlands are convinced that a certain measure of German recovery is essential to the continued recovery of her neighbours, and that certain difficulties can be removed only as German recovery progresses.

It is this consideration, the correctness of which is undisputable, which the Netherlands Government had in mind in determining their attitude towards the German problem. On the one hand the economic recovery of German is a pre-requisite for the economic recovery of Europe and for a healthy world economy. On the other, the economic recovery of Germany implies the increase of Germany's war potential.

In the opinion of the Netherlands Government, the problem raised by these conflicting interests can only be solved if, parallel to a reasonable degree of recovery of German economy, the decentralization of the political structure and the deconcentration of economic *power* in Germany is aimed at. If the deconcentration of economic power is carried through consistently, there can, in the opinion of the Netherlands Government, be no objection to granting the federal agencies those powers that are required to ensure the economic unity of Germany. This point is dealt with more fully below (vide sub III, par. 7, 8, 9, 10, 13, 14, 21, 24).

At Potsdam is was stated: "It is the intention of the Allies that the German people be given the opportunity to prepare for the eventual reconstruction of their life on a democratic and peaceful basis".

The coming years will have to prove whether the German people are prepared to contribute materially to the attainment of that end. It is the opinion of the Netherlands Government that the German people – in the first place in their own interests – could do this no better than by spontaneously helping in finding the ways and means to prove that the German people no longer hesitate when placed before the alternative of guns or butter, and at last have learned the lesson that aggression does not pay. The sooner their own efforts are steadily directed to that end, the sooner will they be trusted by their neighbours and the sooner will it be possible for them to take their place among the free and peaceful people of the world.

C. The Rhine-land and the Ruhr

On several occasions in recent years the Netherlands Government have pointed out that the future status of Germany is of the greatestimportance to the Kingdom. What applies to Germany as a whole, applies in particular to Western Germany, especially to the Rhine-land and the Ruhr.

In determining their attitude in regard to these territories the Netherlands Government are again led by considerations both of security and economy. It is now a generally accepted thesis that as regards the economic arsenal constituted by the Ruhr, special measures of security are required. However, difference of opinion exists as to how these measures should be applied in practice. In view of the geographical position of the Netherlands on the one hand and, on the other, the economic relations with the Rhine-land and Ruhr, it is important to the Kingdom that a solution to the problem be found that offers adequate guarantees, so that no greater damage be done to world economy in general and to European and Netherlands interests in particular, than required for reasons of security.

The degree in which special security measures will be necessary regarding the Rhine-land and the Ruhr, will in the first place depend on the statute to be projected for Germany. If consistent political decentralization of Germany, and deconcentration of economic power in Germany, as advocated above sub A and B, is accompanied by effective demilitarization and disarmament of Germany as a whole – which point will be dealt with more fully below – it stands to reason that there would be no necessity to conceive for the Rhine-land and the Ruhr measures differing *completely* from this general project. It would then be sufficient:

1. to create in these regions a separate régime for the *industries* there established;

2. to impose stricter sanctions if the régime is infringed by German authorities;

3. to ensure the application of the régime for a long period. In this connection a period is suggested of at least equal duration as that envisaged for the treaty concerning the disarmament and demilitarization of Germany (vide sub III);

4. to maintain an Allied occupation at a certain number of strategic points for a longer period than in the rest of Germany. The Allied Powers primarily responsible for the prevention of German aggression in Western Europe should supply troops for this occupation.

Such a solution would in the opinion of the Netherlands Government ensure adequate security and at the same time allow a healthy economic, financial, agrarian and transport policy to be carried out.

If a régime as referred to sub 1 above were placed under the supervision of an international body to be instituted for that purpose, the Netherlands Government are of the opinion that – in view of the special relations existing between the Kingdom and these regions, especially the Ruhr – they should be given adequate representation on this body.

In this connection the Netherlands Government wish to point out that in the Netherlands are available a large number of experts familiar with the problem concerned, possessing a thorough knowledge of the population and the industries established in these areas, and who would therefore be able to render important services to the international control agencies.

That the Rhine-Ruhr problem – important as it is – is only a part of the German problem in its entirety, is selfevident.

In the opinion of the Netherlands Government it would be the logical procedure to project a draft statute for Germany as a whole, and in that light to ascertain what special measures would be found to be required for the Rhine-land and the Ruhr. The *final* settlement of the two problems will have to be made simultaneously, as each of them is inextricably tied up with the security problem.

Another approach to the problem may be first to seek a tentative solution to the Rhine-Ruhr question and then to fit it into the framework of a general arrangement regarding Germany; it is obvious however that the future German borders should be defined first as otherwise any discussion of the German problem will of necessity remain sterile.

Should the latter approach facilitate the reaching of agreement the Netherlands Government see no objection to it, though they would prefer the former solution, as being more logical.

D. The Saar Territory

The settlement of the future status of the Saar, with regard to which the French Government have certain disiderata, constitutes territorially and economically a part of the Western German problem. Consequently, the Netherlands Government deem it desirable that a decision on the Saar territory should be taken together with the decision regarding the desiderata formulated by the other Western neighbouring countries with respect to Germany. In this connection the Netherlands Government refer to their Memorandum of 5th November 1946.

With due consideration of the above it may be added so as to avoid misunderstanding, that the Netherlands Government appreciate in principle the French desiderata concerning the Saar.

II. ECONOMIC AND FINANCIAL ASPECTS OF THE GERMAN PROBLEM

1. The damage suffered by the Netherlands will have to be met partly by reparation payments, but as these cannot lead to a solution of the difficulties in which the Netherlands find themselves in consequence of German aggression, additional measures are called for. This view had already found expression in the reservations made by the Netherlands with regard to possible annexation. Since the Netherlands are now prepared to limit themselves to frontier adjustments, the economic concession set forth by the Netherlands in the Memorandum of 5th November 1946 must be considered essential. These concessions will largely lose their character as such once harmonious economic co-operation in Europe will have been achieved and the prosperity resulting therefrom in a peaceful and democratic Germany will be developed in complete accord with the natural interests of the Netherlands.

2. It is therefore a matter of consideration whether the outline for a general economic co-operation in Europe, including Germany, should, not be concomitant with the conclusion of the peace treaty with Germany. Any arrangements relating to the structure of German industry and the extent of German production, import and export, will then have to be fitted into the framework of this European co-operation.

3. The cost of occupation will have to be reduced as much as possible; the whole of it will have to be borne by the German people. The Allied powers who advanced this cost of occupation may be expected not to obtain restitution by measures in Germany detrimental to the established interests of the Allied neighbouring states. Furthermore, the other Allied nations will have to be consulted in order to reduce the difficulties of administration experienced by the occupying powers, equably and according to capacity. In this connection it is only fair to expect that the plight of the countries formerly occupied by Germany be taken into consideration, especially with regard to the measure of their suffering from German terrorism and vandalism.

4. The cost of the reconstruction of Germany, will have to be borne by the German people. In view of the experience gained after the first world war it seems advisable that in principle no long term loans shall be granted by other countries to German governmental bodies. This conclusion and its consequences will have to be accepted even though it might retard the reconstruction of Germany.

5. Reparations in the form of dismantling and removal of industrial installations will have to be applied with caution. In principle they should be limited to factories exclusively engaged in the production of war materials, in so far as these are not listed for complete demolition. Removal of other factories should be restricted to exceptional cases, and then only in so far as the employment of German labour is not materially reduced and no unemployment results that cannot be adjusted in some other way.

6. Reparations from current production are in principle necessary. They cannot, however, be effected so long as a certain minimum standard of provisioning, further to be detailed, has not been reached in Germany. Besides this, it will be necessary to apply in principle also another standard, namely that the reparations will have to be placed on the ordinary service of the German Government budget.

A consideration of the reparations in this light allows of no illusions about their extent. Reparations in the form of export of goods will intrinsically impede the consumption of foreign goods on the German market, unless once again large loans would be granted to Germany. If in spite of all previous experience the solution would be sought in the latter direction, then a crisis may once again be expected in course of time. In view of the desolate position of German economy, the problem of reparations should be approached as realistically as possible.

7. To prevent German aggression in future, a durable disarmament of Germany is essential. For this purpose, however, there is no need to prohibit in Germany all those industries that may be used directly or indirectly for warlike purposes.

A war of aggression can only be carried out with lasting success if a certain harmony of all arms exists. If this is prevented from the outset, the conditions aimed at would in principle have been realized. But, since Germany began a war of aggression while such a harmony did not in all respects exist. it will be necessary to take more far reaching measures. The manufacture of armaments of all kinds should be prohibited in so far as these are not required for arming the police forces. In drawing up those paragraphs of the peace treaty that deal with disarmament, account will have to be taken of the problems of atomic energy, self-propelled weapons, armour and connected items. Furthermore, supervision will have to be provided on engine factories, chemical industries further to be specified, shipyards, police-, firebrigade-, airraid precaution and customs organizations (no barracks; small arms). The disarmament in these fields will have to be decisive. However, these measures should not go so far as to prohibit e.g. factories for the production of nitrogen fertilizer for the reason that these could be adapted to the manufacture of explosives. The provisions of the "Plan for reparations and the level of post-war German economy" of March 1946 therefore require to be revised. It will further be advisable for allied control to be exercised on the importation of arms in Germany as well as on the importation of scarce raw materials that may be used by the armament industry. It is to be desired that the Allied powers would mutually agree to exercise control on exports of that nature from their countries to Germany.

8. As German imperialism, industrial expansion and concentration were largely based on a protective tariff policy, only import duties of a fiscal character should be permitted as far as the German trade and customs policy is concerned, without prejudice to the provision sub 14. Dumping and export premiums for industrial products, should be prohibited. It is to be recommended that the occupying powers now prepare such a policy, so as to lay the foundations for the future policy, and to adjust the German administration to that purpose. Thus an aim already laid down at Potsdam will be most effectively realized.

9. Without detriment to the provisions sub 7 it is in principle inadvisable to lay down maximum quota for the production of German industries, including the iron and steel industries. A regulation of this nature as elaborated sub 7 appears out of place in a peace treaty. Nevertheless so long as the Allied powers are responsible for German industrial policy, maximum quota might be set for certain industries. There must, however, be a possibility to revise these quota from time to time. These maximum quota should not *ipso facto* be calculated according to the peace-time demand as existing before the war. Otherwise reference may be made in this matter to paragraph 2.

10. In the discussion of the problem of the decentralization of German industry and the prevention of excessive concentration of economic power (vide sub B) special attention was drawn to the problems of the nationalization of coal-mines and the heavy industries in Germany, as well as the control to be exercised on the industry. In the further study of this problem it seems desirable that the following considerations be kept in mind.

From the point of view of social structure a system might be considered, allowing labour to have a voice in the decision about major problems. In this way it will be possible to combat effectively the aggressive mentality of German industry. In those cases where the industrial plants concerned have no reliable German owners, the property rights or industrial shares, orginally owned by them, should be controlled by an allied authority, with or without total or partial indemnification by the German Government. Such rights of ownership should remain the property of the German community, but will be held as a guarantee for the observance of the stipulations of the peace treaty. In cases where the concessions of certain mines, or the plant in production, are transferred to an allied country, the country concerned shall administer the property rights in consultation with the above-mentioned Allied control authority. In accordance with the observance of the stipulations of the peace treaty, after the lapse of certain pre-arranged periods of time, these rights of ownership might be ceded in part to reliable German private persons or other bodies. Irrespective of these private rights of ownership, however, the Allied control authority should exercize the official controlling functions.

In the peace treaty it shall be laid down what countries are to be represented on the controlling body or bodies, In any case those countries will have to be represented on that body which have the closest economic relations with the undertakings concerned, and which of old have rights of ownership in them, varying in importance and which will have to be respected.

In addition to possessing far reaching rights of supervision and investigation, this body shall have to approve, of certain measures, – to be specified at a later date –, which the German authorities or private bodies would be desirous to take. Finally, the control authority should be granted the right to give certain orders, within the scope of the peace treaty, concerning obligations resulting from reparation clauses, productive capacity, composition of controlled production e.a.

11. Although the food supply in Germany will compel this country to pay the greatest attention to agriculture, it will be necessary that even during the occupation of Germany a policy be followed enabling the neighbouring countries, the Netherlands included, to sell their agricultural products on the German market. It will be necessary to create to that end the conditions needed, so that a healthy reciprocal trade becomes possible. An extreme tariff policy in the agrarian field should be prevented. For this too European co-operation is particularly necessary. It would be a mistake, however, to lay too much stress on the development of agriculture in Germany, as was done at Potsdam. For a country like the Netherlands the export of agricultural products to Germany will always, viewed as a long-term policy, be one of the most important sources of trade. If Germany were allowed complete self-sufficiency in the field of agriculture, one of the pillars of the Netherlands economic life would be endangered.

12. Special attention will have to be paid to German forestry, in order that Germany more than thus far may contribute to the European supply of timber. Considering the depredations committed by the Germans in the Netherlands forests, this is also of great importance to the Netherlands.

13. It is not advisable that in the peace treaty Germany be excluded from high sea-navigation. Nor should shipbuilding for commercial purposes be prohibited. As long, however, as a minimum of reconstruction to be determined later, has not been reached, no iron or steel for shipbuilding on German account should be made available, with the possible exception of small units, e.g. for cabotage.

14. German trade policy should be fitted into the framework of European economic co-operation. In this connection particular attention should be paid to the interests of the neighbouring countries. One of the main principles to be followed is that of non-discrimination. This should be applied to import and export, as well as in the field of customs, quota, and clearing policy. From the very first this should be kept in mind, while due care must be taken lest any *de facto* preferences be created such as might arise from the indemnification for the cost of occupation (vide sub 3). The Netherlands Government are still studying the question whether it is advisable to supplement the peace treaty by a trade agreement in which the foundations for commercial policy are laid down for a long period.

15. It is desirable to put both the German financial and currency systems on a sound basis in the near future. In establishing this basis special attention should be paid to the interests of the neighbouring states and of those countries formerly occupied by Germany. Consultation alone will not suffice; agreement will have to be reached in this field. In this connection it should not be overlooked that the Netherlands have a particularly wide experience of German finance. In view, however, of the fact that in the financial field Germany lacks the organizing machinery necessary to take measures that will at once lead to success, it will in practice not be possible to provide such a basis in the near future. Premature and all-embracing measures should be avoided, the possible breakdown of which would lead to further disruption. A policy of combating the increase of prices by coercive measures cannot be effected in any extreme form because of the lack of adequate organization as well as the impossibility of decisive control, since otherwise the stagnated German economic life will be further disabled. In how far these conditions may lead to the necessity of monetary correction will have to be considered at a later stage.

16. The old internal German mark debts will have to be adjusted to existing possibilities. The social consequences of this will have to be specially considered.

17. In contracting new internal debts the German governing bodies should be subject to control for the duration of the occupation. This control will have to be detailed in the peace treaty. It cannot be terminated until the certainty has been gained that Germany effectively fulfils the obligations to be imposed upon her by the peace treaty.

18. Old debts to the Allies and possibly to neutrals, when expressed in other currency than marks, will not only have to be recognized, but, within the scope of the terms of the peace treaty, attention must be paid as to how these debts can be guaranteed.

19. Bona fide allied holdings of shares in German concerns must be fully respected. In determining the position of such holdings it will be necessary to grant preference to them, not only over German-owned shares, but also over debts to German persons or bodies. In other words, the shares held by Allied owners are to represent a real portion of the possessions of the German concern affected.

20. It will not be possible to use German currency internationally for a long time to come. For this reason the transfer in foreign exchange resulting from trade with Germany should be settled not only in dollars and sterling, but also in the currencies of other allied and neutral states.

21. A new central bank will have to be established in Germany. At the same time a new monetary unit will have to be introduced with a fixed relation to foreign currencies. Should decentralization of the German banking system also be found necessary by the Allied nations, a central reserve bank for Germany would at any rate seem desirable. Due attention should be paid to what has been put forward sub 14.

22. Germany will be allowed to contract foreign loans solely for the purpose of food-supply and the supply of raw materials. As far as the food supply is concerned this holds only for bridging a period, later to be determined and needed to increase German exports sufficiently to finance by this means the import of food-supplies. The supply of raw materials will have to be financed exclusively by short-term credits, based upon the processing trade, a percentage – later to be determined – of the thus added value being used to defray the supply of raw materials for internal German use. Foreign long-term capital investment in German concerns may take place under the supervision of the Allied governments. In this connection the economic interests of the neighbouring states will have to be considered; they should have their full share in the control machinery.

23. The standard of living of the German people will have to be raised to a level, guaranteeing a resaonable measure not only of public health, but also of social order. The attainment of a tolerable standard of living will be a matter dependant on the Germans themselves. Allied policy should be conducted in such a way that the Germans will have no occasion to blame the Allies for an unsatisfactory state of affairs in this field.

24. For conducting a sound economic, financial, agrarian and traffic policy a central organization in Germany is indispensable. Although all concentration of power should here be avoided, coordination for the whole of Germany will be required as regards industrial production, agriculture, food-supply and the price and wage policy, while for foreign trade, traffic and currency as well as for taxation, central direction will be necessary. Similarly a central economic policy will be required in view of the desirability of elaborating plans for guiding German economy.

25. With regard to the domiciliation of aliens and the establishment of foreign industries in Germany, regulations will have to be made going beyond the treatment on a basis of equality with nationals. To this end a uniform policy should be conducted throughout Germany. It could only lead to confusion if for instance a difference of treatment were to be maintained in the various zones of occupation. It is furthermore reasonable to demand that allied nationals domiciled in Germany for *bona fide* reasons shall not be compelled to share in the burden laid upon the German nation as a consequence of the peace treaty. This conception should find expression in the policy of taxation. For industrial and commercial undertakings in Germany similar considerations should apply, with special consideration for companies of which it is known that controlling share holdings are in allied hands. Finally, regulations will have to be made concerning the residence and employment as well as the financial status of Germans in other countries.

III. DEMILITARIZATION AND DISARMAMENT OF GERMANY

It was with great satisfaction that the Netherlands Government learned that the discussion of a draft of a long-term treaty, aiming at the demilitarization and disarmament of Germany, has been placed on the agenda of the ensuing Moscow conference, as well as the consideration of other measures necessary for the economic and military control of Germany.

Like other peace-loving countries, the Netherlands believe that such a treaty should be concluded to cover a long period in which a new generation can grow up in Germany. At present there are already sufficient indications proving that the fall of Hitlerism has not meant the end of Prussian nationalism. The Netherlands Government feel that to eradicate this pernicious mentality there is no better means than to leave the Germans no room for doubt that any renewed attempt at aggression, in whatever form, will be met with immediate opposition on the part of the powers directly concerned, who have clearly defined their common aim in a treaty covering a long period. Such a treaty will not only directly promote the ensurance of peace and security, but also indirectly, as it may prove an important means of re-educating the German people to a democratic and peace-loving way of life. For, since Germany will not be in a position, for the duration of the treaty, to develop its national resources for any but peaceful purposes, the German people will be able to devote their undeniable gifts to the reconstruction of what was destroyed as a result of their aggression; and this does not only include the material destruction in the Allied countries and in Germany, but also the depravation of the German national character. It is obvious that the process of spiritual regeneration will take many years before the world is prepared to bestow its confidence on the German people once more.

The draft treaty published on 29th April 1946 by the Secretary of State of the United States of America contains several references to the Security Council and to its role under the provisions of the draft treaty. The Netherlands Government deem it logical that in the view of the sponsoring power of the draft treaty an important part is allotted to the Security Council of the United Nations. In this connection the Netherlands Government recall the following passage from an address by the President of the United States of America on 27th October 1945:

> "We are convinced that the preservation of peace between nations requires a United Nations Organization composed of all the peace-loving nations of the world, who are willing jointly to use force necessary to ensure peace".

It follows from the above that the draft treaty, in the spirit of the sponsoring power, is conceived as fitting into the framework of the United Nations. Consequently articles 52, 53 and 54 of the Charter concerning regional arrangements, will in particular be applicable. In this connection the Netherlands Government do not overlook the articles of Chapter XVII of the Charter; however, they tend to think it inadvisable to base a treaty of *long duration* on provisions solely intended for transitional security arrangements. They therefore assume that the sponsoring power of the draft treaty for the disarmament and demilitarization of Germany had in mind a treaty in keeping with Chapter VIII of the Charter of the United Nations, the four great powers participating. Such a development would not constitute a precedent. Regional treaties were already drawn up under the Charter of the League of Nations. Outside Europe mention may be made of the Inter-American security system and the Arab League.

The Netherlands Government fully realize that a security system for

Europe can only serve its purpose if the four great powers concerned act in unison. This co-operation is an indispensable condition for an effective European security system. Apart from that the question arises whether a European security system *exclusively* based on the co-operation of these powers may be considered to constitute in every respect a closely integrated entity.

The Netherlands Government are inclined to answer this question in the negative. In their opinion the Allied states neighbouring on Germany should be enabled to partake in such a security system. That the great powers consider the co-operation of other powers in the maintenance of peace and security desirable and necessary, does not only follow from the Charter of the United Nations, but also from the Declaration of Moscow of 30th October 1943.

The Netherlands Government will therefore appreciate it to learn whether they are justified in their view, that besides the Great Powers, all other Allied states neighbouring on Germany, namely Belgium, Czecho-Slovakia, Denmark, Luxemburg, the Netherlands and Poland will, if they so desire, be able to participate in the treaty aiming at the demilitarization and disarmament of Germany.

IV. CULTURAL AND SPIRITUAL ASPECTS OF THE GERMAN PROBLEM

The Netherlands Government are filled with deep concern when realizing the spiritual, moral and cultural degeneration in Germany, which progressed more and more rapidly after 1866 and since 1933 reached its fiendish consequence in National Socialism. This concern is by no means lessened when they visualize the spiritual vacuum which resulted after the collapse of the dream of world domination and which cries out to be filled with positive values. Whatever remnants of "Weltanschauung" are still alive in most Germans with respect to the relation of state to people, the relation of might to right, of community to individual, mind to matter, personal responsibility to social consciousness, need a thorough revision before genuine democratic relations or even normal governing conditions under a régime of occupation can have an effective meaning for them.

The Netherlands Government consider the spread of this nihilism as a threat to the whole world and not only to the neighbouring states.

The cure for this evil is to be sought in the first place in the rousing of the regenerating forces existing in the German people themselves. In this connection attention should be paid to the revival of the religious, humanitarian and other ethical forces suppressed by National Socialism and to the increase of their influence on education, the press, public life and other domains of moral reconstruction. In all this help from abroad will be indispensable.

With the greatest interest the Netherlands Government have already noted numerous ideas and their execution, which aim at the cure of this moral degeneration and the replenishment of these cultural deficiencies. In this connection may be mentioned the selection and training of prisoners of war, started during the war; the high standard of the German press, indicative of the selection of many efficient contributors and reliable information about most of the great powers, – this information is partly lacking as to the smaller countries –, the space allotted to drastic pedagogic experiments, and last but not least the sojourn of teachers, journalists and students in allied countries in order to recuperate and to become acquainted with these countries.

This is all the more appreciated because the Netherlands Government are acquainted with the great difficulties with which the Allied authorities of occupation have to contend, not only in consequence of the intricacy of the spiritual, cultural, social and pedagogic problem itself, but also because of personal and material difficulties such as the exodus and murder of numerous figures from the German religious cultural and social spheres, who might have taken the lead in this task of re-education. Furthermore, the educational system from the elementary school to the University – also owing to the inevitable denazification – is disorganized to such a degree that as far as the staff is concerned, it will have to be partly renewed, while, as the losses owing to destruction and wear and tear have not yet been replenished, material supplies also leave much to be desired.

It is all the more necessary that all the religious, cultural and social forces in and outside Europe should be mobilized in order to bring about this recovery, as otherwise the whole of Europe will be affected, which might form a new threat to the peace of the world.

There is sound ground for the thought that the Netherlands might be able to offer their own important contribution to this recovery. The Netherlands have of old been in touch with the spiritual life of France, England and Germany. They have assimilated the culture of three different nations without lapsing into imitation. They have come to understand the spirit of all thıee. They have also influenced the cultural development of the surrounding countries, be it in various degrees according to place and time.

It would be regrettable if no use were made of the experience gained by the people of the Netherlands during their long history, in order to solve the German question, the more so as it repeatedly appears that a great and keen interest for the solution of this problem by means of the re-education of the German people, is felt in all circles in the Netherlands, ecclesiastical and educational as well as those of the social and cultural organizations. The Netherlands Government are prepared, in case they are called upon to do so, to bring about that Netherlands subjects should also be included in the organizations, which are or will be charged with a spiritual and cultural task in Germany. They urge that the obstructions shall be removed which now stand in the way of the cultural and spiritual intercourse between the Netherlands and the occupied areas. They will appreciate it if facilities are granted to the Netherlands authorities, organizations and institutions active in this domain, necessary and possible for a justifiable exchange of persons as well as publications of a spiritual and cultural character. They further advocate that certain parts of Western Germany, especially those affiliated to the Netherlands by their national character, historical and cultural ties, and dialect, in as far as guidance of cultural and pedagogical recovery is concerned – naturally under the supervision of the central interallied organizations – shall be entrusted to the care of the Netherlands. In this way an important contribution will be made to the re-establishment of personal contacts so urgently needed in a world which is yearning for peace.

Source: Proceedings of the States General, 1946–1947, Annexes, Second Chamber, No 383.

SECTION II OF THE ADDITIONAL MEMORANDUM OF THE
NETHERLANDS GOVERNMENT WITH REGARD TO THE
DEMARCATION OF THE FUTURE NETHERLANDS-GERMAN
FRONTIER AND RELATED PROBLEMS

II. ECONOMIC DESIDERATA

The wishes of Her Majesty's Government in the economic sphere may
be distinguished in desiderata of a general economic character and
demands of a more specified nature.

As to the general desiderata the Netherlands Government do not
deem it necessary, in the present stage of the investigation of the German
problem, to enter into further details. However, they wish to emphasize
that these demands are to be considered of the greatest importance.
These questions are of importance not only for the future peace-treaty;
they also require immediate attention. The questions here referred to
should be taken up at the earliest opportunity in order to ensure that
the régime, now in force in occupied Germany, be adapted as soon as
possible to the system aimed at in the peace-treaty. This applies particularly to sections 2 and 4 of Appendix I of the Memorandum of 5th
November 1946. The problems concerning unfair competition of German
seaports and the monetary régime require immediate attention, whereas
the problems connected with the German canal system are of a less
urgent nature.

For a just appreciation of sections 2 and 4 account should be taken
of the probability that economic activity in Germany, for many years
to come, will be on a low level, considerably lower than in the period
between the two wars. It is especially for this reason that the Netherlands
Government wish to lay particular stress to their claims. For under such
circumstances a system of discrimination regarding the Netherlands
interests will be even less bearable than would be the case in a period of
a relatively high level of prosperity.

This may be illustrated with a few figures. In 1924 the total amount
of goods, transported from and to the Rhine-Ruhr area, was 28.757.600
tons, of which 17.462.000 tons, or 60.7 per cent, passed the Netherlands-
German frontier in transit with transshipment. In 1937 these figures
were respectively 64.207.800 tons, 34.272.600 tons and 53.4 per cent.
From these figures it appears in the first place that in consequence of
the incriminated German measures the Netherlands share of this trade
declined not inconsiderably; but these figures further prove that the
amount of the transit trade was greatly influenced by international
trade fluctuations and the activities of German industry in consequence
of internal German measures, in which rearmament played an important
rôle. As the fixed purpose of the Allied Nations will permanently eliminate
a rearmament policy in Germany and in view of the desolate condition
of German industry, it will be necessary for a considerable time to reckon
with transport figures lying well below the 1924 level.

Consequently the scope and character of one of the great sources of Netherlands prosperity will undergo a permanent change. Therefore, the Netherlands may expect more than ever before that as regards commercial and traffic policy their interests will be fully taken into account.

In times of peace the prosperity of the Netherlands was for a considerable part due to their international position, i.e. overseas traffic and traffic with the hinterland. During the last war German aggression caused the Netherlands to be cut off for five years from their overseas trade, in addition to which severe looting took place. After the unconditional surrender of Germany the Netherlands, mostly as a result of the chaos left by the Hitler régime, are largely shut off from the continent and in particular from the natural hinterland. Although the Netherlands fully realize the difficulties which the Great Powers encounter in the occupation of Germany, yet Her Majesty's Government feel bound to point out the consequences of these elementary facts.

For a reasonable recovery of Netherlands prosperity it is essential that free access to the country's natural hinterland be once more assured, and in particular under conditions excluding all discrimination. This does not mean that the Netherlands demand any preferential treatment; they do demand the free use of the Rhine, not only in a technical sense, but in a manner fitting into the framework of modern economic traffic, i.e. as regards tariffs, and measures of monetary and commercial policy. They are also of opinion that they may claim for the Netherlands railways their due place in international traffic, and the same is expected as regards road traffic. In this connection it may be recalled that the Netherlands hinterland geographically extends to the Danubian countries. For this reason the Netherlands feel justified in their demand that transit-traffic through Germany in both directions should be open to them without any discrimination, and that this be also taken into account in the policy of other than German Northsea ports. In this connection the Netherlands Government trust that in the policy to be applied to the port of Trieste adequate consideration be given to Netherlands interests.

In order to complete this picture it should be recalled that the above does not only refer to traffic problems as such, but also to the multilateral commercial transactions connected therewith. All these questions should be fully considered if the Netherlands are to have a reasonable chance of recovery.

Nevertheless Her Majesty's Government realize that the flow of traffic between their country and Germany has been disrupted and will not soon reach its former level again. They are furthermore convinced that the economic relation between the Netherlands and Germany should not be one of dependence. For that reason more specific demands have been made as well. These mainly amount to the following. In view of the exceptionally rapid increase in population, expansion of the national industry is imperative, requiring in its turn a wider coal-basis. Moreover, a more adequate supply of fertilizer will in future be indispensable for Netherlands agriculture. The more specific claims refer to these two questions.

In the memorandum quoted above it has already been stated that detailed considerations which might arise from a further study of this matter may be submitted at a later date. Without entering at this moment into all the details that require further consideration the Netherlands Government, for the purpose of elucidating their memorandum, deem it desirable at this point to deal more fully with some of these questions.

As regards the mines in actual exploitation, the question at issue is not exclusively concerned with the transfer of the concessions and of the mines themselves, but also with everything connected therewith, such as the plants manufacturing by-products, possible harbour equipment and other traffic apparatus forming part of the concern, while the production of the mines is to include not only the coal, coke and briquettes, but also all by-products. The transfer of the concessions, of the sites of the mines, and of everything connected therewith, is to take place without any compensation.

It has already been pointed out that the capital invested by the Netherlands should be regarded as preferential with respect not only to established shareholders, but to existing creditors as well. Such arrangement would be required pending a settlement with regard to the German owners. In this connection the Netherlands Government wish to refer to paragraphs 10 and 19 of Chapter II of their Memorandum of 14th January 1947. They wish to avail themselves of this opportunity to point out that the Netherlands have a direct financial interest in several of the mines and concessions claimed. Besides these the Netherlands have many other pre-war investments in the German mining industry in general. It might be considered whether these rights could be exchanged for German property rights in the mines referred to in the Memorandum of 5th November, 1946. In this way a definite settlement of this intricate problem could be facilitated. Especially in the case of the mines now in exploitation the question of ownership would be simplified on the expiry of the envisaged period of forty to fifty years, as these mines might as a result of such an exchange, prove to be partly or entirely Netherlands property.

As regards the Netherlands claim that the production of the mines covered by this arrangement will be regarded in all respects as the produce of Netherlands soil, Her Majesty's Government wish to state that, in so far as the coal should prove not to be required to cover Netherlands needs, it will be sold in the world market or in Germany within the limits of possible international coal-agreements.

As the management, economically as well as technically, will be exclusively a Netherlands concern, it should be assured that Germany or any German "Land" concerned shall not in any way use its rights as a sovereign state to discriminate against Netherlands interest. The concessions, not in actual exploitation, are demanded for an indefinite period of time, as only on such a basis it may be expected that the considerable capital investment, necessary for the future, will be justified. For this reason special arrangements will be required for these concessions to the effect that Netherlands interests shall in no way be discriminated against. Moreover, it will have to be stipulated that the Netherlands managing authorities shall be enabled to obtain, on a reasonable basis, all facilities necessary for the exploitation and storage, the transport and sale of the products and by-products. The taxes to be levied in Germany should be imposed on the mines under reference (mines now in exploitation as well as mines not yet in exploitation) only to the extent necessary to make them contribute their reasonable share in the local public expenses; taxes levied to cover German war and reparation debts are to be excluded.

The Netherlands demands regarding the German mining industry will also have to be judged in the light of the recovery and expansion of this industry in Germany itself.

It may finally be recalled that the „Gewerkschaft Sophia Jacoba" is entirely owned by a Netherlands company, viz. the „Nederlandsche Maatschappij tot Ontginning van Steenkolenvelden". The Netherlands property rights in these mines were established in the Credit and Coal Treaty, concluded between the Netherlands and Germany on 11th May, 1920. The question will have to be considered in how far this treaty needs amplification or revision.

Source: Proceedings of the States General, 1946–1947,
Annexes, Second Chamber, No 352.

APPENDIX 9

TREATY BETWEEN BELGIUM, FRANCE, LUXEMBOURG, THE NETHERLANDS AND THE UNITED KINGDOM OF GREAT BRITAIN AND NORTHERN IRELAND

His Royal Highness the Prince Regent of Belgium, the President of the French Republic, President of the French Union, Her Royal Highness the Grand Duchess of Luxembourg, Her Majesty the Queen of the Netherlands, and His Majesty the King of Great Britain, Ireland and the British Dominions beyond the Seas.

Resolved

To reaffirm their faith in fundamental human rights, in the dignity and worth of the human person and in the other ideals proclaimed in the Charter of the United Nations;

To fortify and preserve the principles of democracy, personal freedom and political liberty, the constitutional traditions and the rule of law, which are their common heritage;

To strengthen, with these aims in view, the economic, social and cultural ties by which they are already united;

To cooperate loyally and to coordinate their efforts to create in Western Europe a firm basis for European economic recovery;

To afford assistance to each other, in accordance with the Charter of the United Nations, in maintaining international peace and security and in resisting any renewal of a policy of aggression;

To take such steps as may be held to be necessary in the event of a renewal by Germany of a policy of aggression;

To associate progressively in the pursuance of these aims other States inspired by the same ideals and animated by the like determination;

Desiring for these purposes to conclude a treaty for collaboration in economic, social and cultural matters and for collective self-defence;

Have appointed as their Plenipotentiaries:

. . . .

who, having exhibited their full powers found in good and due form,

have agreed as follows:

Article I

Convinced of the close community of their interests and of the necessity of uniting in order to promote the economic recovery of Europe, the High Contracting Parties will so organize and coordinate their economic activities as to produce the best possible results, by the elimination of conflict in their economic policies, the coordination of production and the development of commercial exchanges.

The cooperation provided for in the preceding paragraph, which will be effected through the Consultative Council referred to in Article VII as well as through other bodies, shall not involve any duplication of, or prejudice to, the work of other economic organizations in which the High Contracting Parties are or may be represented but shall on the contrary assist the work of those organizations.

Article II

The High Contracting Parties will make every effort in common, both by direct consultation and in specialized agencies, to promote the attainment of a higher standard of living by their peoples and to develop on corresponding lines the social and other related services of their countries.

The High Contracting Parties will consult with the object of achieving the earliest possible application of recommendations of immediate practical interest relating to social matters, adopted with their approval in the specialized agencies.

They will endeavour to conclude as soon as possible conventions with each other in the sphere of social security.

Article III

The High Contracting Parties will make every effort in common to lead their peoples towards a better understanding of the principles which form the basis of their common civilization and to promote cultural exchanges by conventions between themselves or by other means

Article IV

If any of the High Contracting Parties should be the object of an armed attack in Europe, the other High Contracting Parties will, in accordance with the provisions of Article 51 of the Charter of the United Nations, afford the Party so attacked all the military and other aid and assistance in their power.

Article V

All measures taken as a result of the preceding Article shall be immediately reported to the Security Council. They shall be terminated as soon as the Security Council has taken the measures necessary to maintain or restore international peace and security.

The present Treaty does not prejudice in any way the obligations of the High Contracting Parties under the provisions of the Charter of the United Nations. It shall not be interpreted as affecting in any way the authority and responsibility of the Security Council under the Charter to take at any time such action as it deems necessary in order to maintain or restore international peace and security.

Article VI

The High Contracting Parties declare, each so far as he is concerned, that none of the international engagements now in force between him and any other High Contracting Party or any third State is in conflict with the provisions of the present Treaty.

None of the High Contracting Parties will conclude any alliance or participate in any coalition directed against any of the other High Contracting Parties.

Article VII

For the purpose of consulting together on all the questions dealt with in the present Treaty, the High Contracting Parties will create a Consultative Council, which shall be so organized as to be able to exercise its functions continuously. The Council shall meet at such times as it shall deem fit.

At the request of any of the High Contracting Parties, the Council shall be immediately convened in order to permit the High Contracting Parties to consult with regard to any situation which may constitute a threat to peace, in whatever area this threat should arise: with regard to the attitude to be adopted and the steps to be taken in case of a renewal by Germany of an aggressive policy: or with regard to any situation constituting a danger to economic stability.

Article VIII

In pursuance of their determination to settle disputes only by peaceful means, the High Contracting Parties will apply to disputes between themselves the following provisions:

The High Contracting Parties will, while the present Treaty remains in force, settle all disputes falling within the scope of Article 36, paragraph 2, of the Statute of the International Court of Justice by referring them to the Court subject only, in the case of each of them, to any reservation already made by that Party when accepting this clause for compulsory jurisdiction to the extent that Party may maintain the reservation.

In addition, the High Contracting Parties will submit to conciliation all disputes outside the scope of Article 36, paragraph 2, of the Statute of the International Court of Justice.

In the case of a mixed dispute involving both questions for which conciliation is appropriate and other questions for which judicial settlement is appropriate, any Party to the dispute shall have the right to insist that the judicial settlement of the legal questions shall precede conciliation.

The preceding provisions of this Article in no way affect the application of relevant provisions of agreements prescribing some other method of pacific settlement.

Article IX

The High Contracting Parties may, by agreement, invite any other State to accede to the present Treaty on conditions to be agreed between them and the State so invited.

Any State so invited may become a Party to the Treaty by depositing an instrument of accession with the Belgian Government.

The Belgian Government will inform each of the High Contracting Parties of the deposit of each instrument of accession.

Article X

The present Treaty shall be ratified and the instruments of ratification shall be deposited as soon as possible with the Belgian Government.

It shall enter into force on the date of the deposit of the last instrument of ratification and shall thereafter remain in force for fifty years.

After the expiry of the period of fifty years, each of the High Contracting Parties shall have the right to cease to be a party thereto provided that he shall have previously given one year's notice of denunciation to the Belgian Government.

The Belgian Government shall inform the Governments of the other High Contracting Parties of the deposit of each instrument of ratification and of each notice of denunciation.

In witness whereof, the above mentioned Plenipotentiaries have signed the present Treaty and have affixed thereto their seals.

Done at Brussels this, 17th day of March, 1948 in English and French, each text being equally authentic, in a single copy which shall remain deposited in the archives of the Belgian Government and of which certified copies shall be transmitted by that Government to each of the other signatories.

Source: Proceedings of the States General, 1947–1948, Annexes, Second Chamber, No 774.

A. COMMUNIQUE ISSUED AT THE END OF THE FIRST SESSION OF THE SIX-POWER CONFERENCE

London, 6 March 1948

The informal discussions of German problems which began in London on 23rd February between the representatives of the United States, United Kingdom and France, and as from February 26th with the representatives of the Benelux countries, went into recess today.

At the request of the other delegations, the meetings were held under the chairmanship of the U.K. representative, Sir William Strang. The U.S. and French delegations were led by Mr. Douglas and M. Massigli, the U.S. and French Ambassadors in London. At the first meeting it was agreed to invite the Benelux countries to take part, on an equal footing, in the discussions of all items on the agenda, except those dealing with administrative matters which are the direct responsibility of the occupying powers controlling the three occupied areas. The chief representatives of the Benelux delegation were Jonkheer Michiels van Verduynen, the Netherlands Ambassador, Vicomte Obert de Thieusies, the Belgian Ambassador, and M. Claessen, the Luxembourg Minister.

Important progress has been made and it has been decided that these discussions will be resumed during April for the purpose of reaching conclusions on the remaining question, so that the delegations may be in a position to submit to their governments, at the end of the next session, their recommendations over the whole field. In the meantime various aspects of certain of these problems will be the subject of more detailed examinations.

The continuous failure of the Council of Foreign Ministers to reach quadripartite agreement has created a situation in Germany which if permitted to continue, would have increasingly unfortunate consequences for western Europe. It was therefore necessary that urgent political and economic problems arising out of this situation in Germany should be solved. The participating powers had in view the necessity of ensuring the economic reconstruction of western Europe including Germany, and of establishing a basis for the participation of a democratic Germany in the community of free peoples. While delay in reaching these objectives can no longer be accepted, ultimate Four Power agreement is in no way precluded.

The various items on the agenda were the subject of a detailed study, with the exception of security questions, which were given preliminary examination and will be considered in detail upon resuming the discussion. Similarly discussion of territorial questions will be held over until the next session.

Discussions took place among the U.S., U.K., and French delegations on certain limited aspects of the question of reparations from Germany relating to internal policy in the zones for which they are responsible as occupying powers.

The relationship of western Germany under the occupying powers to the European Recovery Programme was also discussed by the U.S., U. K., and French delegations. It was agreed that for the political and economic well-being of the countries of western Europe and of a democratic Germany there must be a close association of their economic life. Since it has not proved possible to achieve economic unity in Germany, and since the eastern zone has been prevented from playing its part in the European Recovery Programme, the three western powers have agreed that close cooperation should be established among themselves and among the occupation authorities in western Germany in all matters arising out of the European Recovery Programme in relation to western Germany. Such cooperation is essential if western Germany is to make its full and proper contribution to European recovery. It was also agreed to recommend to the three governments that the combined zone and the French zone should be fully associated in the European Recovery Programme and adequately represented on any continuing organization. Proposals in this sense will be presented at the forthcoming meeting of the C.E.E.C.

Agreement in principle has been reached on recommendations for the association of the Benelux countries in policy regarding Germany. Consideration was given of all delegations to the establishment of an international control of the Ruhr on which Germany would be represented. The purpose of this international control would be to ensure that the economic resources of this area should not again be used for the purposes of aggression and that there should be adequate access to the coal, coke and steel of the Ruhr for the benefit of extensive parts of the European community including Germany. Agreed recommendations in this respect will be submitted to the governments concerned on the scope and form of this control.

A constructive discussion among all the delegations took place on the present situation and the possible evolution of the political and economic organization of Germany in the combined U.S./U.K. zone and the French zone. A wide measure of agreement was reached on a number of controversial points. In particular it was agreed that a federal form of government, adequately protecting the rights of the respective states but at the same time providing for adequate control authority, is best adapted for the eventual reestablishment of German unity, at present disrupted. Moreover, in order to facilitate the association of western Germany with the European Recovery Programme the three delegations concerned further agreed that prompt action should be taken to coordinate as far as possible the economic policies of the three zones, in such matters as foreign and inter-zonal trade, customs, and freedom of movement for persons and goods.

Source: *Documents on International Affairs, 1947–1948*, Royal Institute of International Affairs, 1952, p. 556–558.

B. COMMUNIQUE WITH ANNEX ON INTERNATIONAL CONTROL OF THE RUHR ISSUED BY THE LONDON SIX-POWER CONFERENCE, 7 JUNE 1948

In accordance with an announcement issued on June 2 at the conclusion of informal discussions on Germany between representatives of United States, United Kingdom, France and three Benelux countries (Belgium, Netherlands, Luxembourg) a report containing agreed recommendations on all items discussed was submitted to their respective governments. These recommendations have been submitted as a whole since their main provisions are mutually dependent and form an indivisible program. Principal features of this report are the following:

I. ASSOCIATION OF BENELUX COUNTRIES IN POLICY REGARDING GERMANY

The recommendations include specific provisions for a close association between military governments and Benelux representatives in Germany on matters affecting Benelux interests. Moreover full opportunities will be given the Benelux representatives to be kept informed of developments in the western zones.

II. ROLE OF THE GERMAN ECONOMY IN THE EUROPEAN ECONOMY AND CONTROL OF THE RUHR

(A) As stated in the communiqué of March 6 it had been agreed that for the political and economic well-being of the countries of western Europe and of a democratic Germany, there must be a close association of their economic life. This close association, which will enable Germany to contribute to and participate in European recovery, has been ensured by the inclusion on April 16 of the combined zone and French zone in the organization for European economic cooperation as full members.

(B) It was agreed to recommend the establishment of an international authority for the control of the Ruhr in which United States, United Kingdom, France, Benelux countries and Germany would participate, and which does not involve the political separation of the Ruhr area from Germany. It does, however, contemplate control of distribution of coal, coke and steel of Ruhr in order that on the one hand industrial concentration in that area shall not become an instrument of aggression, and on the other will be able to make its contribution to all countries participating in a European cooperative economic program, including, of course, Germany itself. A draft agreement containing the provisions for its establishment is attached as annex I.

This agreement is to be concluded by the United States, United Kingdom and France as occupying powers. Moreover the Benelux countries are to be fully associated with the preparation of the more detailed agreement provided for in article 12, and are to be consulted as to the time when the authority begins to exercise its functions.

(C) Arising out of the discussions on the Ruhr it has been recommended that the principle of non-discrimination against foreign interests in Germany be reaffirmed, and that each government should promptly study the problem of safeguarding foreign interests in order that there may be subsequently established as soon as possible an inter-governmental group to review the question and make recommendations to their governments.

III. EVOLUTION OF POLITICAL AND ECONOMIC ORGANIZATION OF GERMANY

(A) Further consideration has been given by all delegates to the problem of the evolution of the political and economic organization of Germany. They recognize, taking into account the present situation, that it is necessary to give the German people the opportunity to achieve on the basis of a free and democratic form of government the eventual re-establishment of German unity at present disrupted. In these circumstances they have reached the conclusion that it would be desirable that the German people in the different states should now be free to establish for themselves the political organization and institutions which will enable them to assume those governmental responsibilities which are compatible with the minimum requirements of occupation and control and which ultimately will enable them to assume full governmental responsibility. The delegates consider that the people in the states will wish to establish a constitution with provisions which will allow all the German states to subscribe as soon as circumstances permit.

Therefore the delegates have agreed to recommend to their governments that the military governors should hold a joint meeting with the Ministers-President of the western zone in Germany. At that meeting the Ministers-President will be authorized to convene a Constituent Assembly in order to prepare a constitution for the approval of the participating states.

Delegates to this Constituent Assembly will be chosen in each of the states in accordance with procedure and regulations to be determined by the legislative bodies of the individual states.

The constitution should be such as to enable the Germans to play their part in bringing to an end the present division of Germany not by the reconstitution of a centralized Reich but by means of a federal form of government which adequately protects the rights of the respective states, and which at the same time provides for adequate central authority and which guarantees the rights and freedoms of the individual.

If the constitution as prepared by the Constituent Assembly does not conflict with these general principles the military governors will authorize its submission for ratification by the people in the respective states.

At the meeting with the military governors the Ministers-President will also be authorized to examine the boundaries of the several states in order to determine what modification might be proposed to the military governors for the purpose of creating a definitive system which is satisfactory to the peoples concerned.

(B) Further discussions have taken place between the United States, United Kingdom and French delegations on measures for coordinating economic policies and practices in the combined zone and the French zone. Agreed recommendations have been reached on the joint conduct and control of the external trade of the whole area. It has been recognized that a complete economic merger of the two areas cannot effectively take place until further progress has been made in establishing the necessary German institutions common to the entire area.

IV. PROVISIONAL TERRITORIAL ARRANGEMENTS

The delegations have agreed to submit for the consideration of their governments proposals for dealing with certain minor provisional territorial adjustments in connection with the western frontiers of Germany.

V. SECURITY

This problem was considered in three aspects: (A) General Provisions, (B) Measures during the period in which the occupying powers retain supreme authority in Germany. (C) Measures after the period in which the occupying powers retain supreme authority in Germany.

General Provisions

The United States, United Kingdom and French Delegates reiterated the firm views of their governments that there could not be any general withdrawal of their forces from Germany until the peace of Europe is secured and without prior consultation. During this period there should be no general withdrawal of the forces of occupation of the United States, France, or the United Kingdom without prior consultation. It was further recommended that the governments concerned should consult if any of them should consider that there was a danger of resurgence of German military power or of the adoption by Germany of a policy of aggression.

Measures during the period in which the occupying powers retain supreme authority in Germany.

The prohibitions on the German armed forces and the German General Staff as contained in 4-power agreements were reaffirmed, as well as the exercise of controls by the military governors with respect to disarmament and demilitarization, level of industry and certain aspects of scientific research. To ensure the maintenance of disarmament and demilitarization in the interests of security, the three military governors should set up a military security board in the western zones of Germany to carry out the proper inspections and make the necessary recommendations to the military governors, who decide the action to be taken.

Measures after the period in which the occupying powers retain supreme authority in Germany.

It was affirmed that Germany must not again be permitted to become an aggressive power and that prior to general withdrawal of the forces of occupation agreement will be reached among the governments concerned with respect to necessary measures of demilitarization, disarmament and control of industry and with respect to occupation of key areas. Also there should be a system of inspection to ensure the maintenance of the agreed provisions of German disarmament and demilitarization.

The present recommendations, which in no way preclude and on the contrary should facilitate eventual 4-power agreement on the German problem, are designed to solve the urgent political and economic problems arising out of the present situation in Germany. Because of the previous failure to reach comprehensive 4-power decisions on Germany, the measures recommended mark a step forward in the policy which the powers represented at these talks are determined to follow with respect to the economic reconstruction of western Europe, including Germany, and with respect to the establishment of a basis for the participation of a democratic Germany in the community of free peoples.

Annex I

Whereas international security and general economic recovery require: – that the resources of the Ruhr shall not in the future be used for the purpose of aggression but shall be used in the interests of peace; – that access to the coal, coke and steel of the Ruhr, which was previously subject to the exclusive control of Germany, be in the future guaranteed without discrimination to the countries of Europe cooperating in the common economic good;

Whereas it is desirable for the political and economic well-being of these countries and a democratic Germany that there be close association of their economic life;

Whereas it is important that trade between the countries mentioned in the preceding paragraph should be facilitated by lowering trade barriers and by any other means,

The Governments of the United States, United Kingdom and France, after consultation with the Governments of the Netherlands, Belgium and Luxembourg, have agreed as follows:

1. An international control shall be set up in the Ruhr and exercised by an International Authority for the Ruhr (hereinafter called the International Authority); the International Authority shall be organized forthwith and shall begin to exercise its functions at a time to be determined by the contracting Governments, and in any case before the establishment of a provisional German Government.

2. The International Authority shall be composed of representatives of the United States, United Kingdom, France, Netherlands, Belgium, Luxembourg and Germany.

3. The International Authority shall take its decisions by majority vote. The United States, United Kingdom, France and Germany shall have three votes each, and the Netherlands, Belgium and Luxembourg one vote each.

4. Until the contracting Governments decide otherwise, the representative of Germany shall be designated and the vote for Germany exercised by those Powers which share the responsibility for the economic administration of that part of Germany which includes the Ruhr (hereinafter called "the Occupying Powers concerned").

5. The functions of the International Authority shall, subject to existing or future international agreements among the contracting governments concerning the allocation of coal, coke and steel, be as follows:

(a) subject to the provisions of Article 6 below, to make the division of coal, coke and steel from the Ruhr as between German consumption and export, in order to ensure adequate access to supplies of these products, taking into account the essential needs of Germany.

(b) to ensure that the German authorities do not institute, carry out or permit artificial measures or discriminatory practices which would distort the movement of Ruhr coal, coke and steel in international trade, except for measures of protection approved by the International Autority.

(c) to exercise, in the circumstances envisaged in Article 10 (b) below, the powers described in Article 9 (b) below.

(d) During the period in which the Occupying Powers concerned exercise supreme authority (which period is hereinafter called "The Control Period") to bring to the attention of the occupation authorities concerned measures which would ensure, and thereafter itself to ensure, safeguard and protection for coal, coke and steel enterprises in the Ruhr involving foreign interests, within the framework of existing or future agreements between the Allied Governments represented on the Authority.

6. (a) The findings of the International Authority under the provisions of Article 5 (a) shall be consistent with the programmes of the O.E.E.C. for the recovery of the participating countries.

(b) During the Control Period, or until such earlier time as may be agreed upon by the contracting Governments, the findings of the International Authority under the provisions of Article 5 (a) will be transmitted to the Military Governors for implementation. The Military Governors will proceed with the implementation of these findings (1) to the extent consistent with any agreements relative to the provision of financial assistance to Germany which are now or may come in effect between any two or more of the contracting Governments; and (2) in accordance with the terms of any existing international agreement among the contracting Governments, or extension thereof, with respect to the allocation of coal and coke.

7. The International Authority shall have the right:

(a) to receive regular reports on production, distribution and consumption of Ruhr coal, coke and steel;

(b) to demand additional reports on these subjects whenever necessary;

(c) to verify the information at its disposal by enquiries on the spot and by subpoena and examination of witnesses;

(d) to call for information about supplies of coal, coke and steel from sources other than the Ruhr.

8. During the Control Period the occupation authorities concerned will maintain adequate control over the management in the Ruhr coal and coke industry.

9. During the Control Period, or until such earlier time as may be agreed upon by the contracting Governments, the occupation authorities concerned will maintain

(a) such powers in respect of the coal, coke and steel industries of the Ruhr as will enable the International Authority to perform the functions and exercise the rights assigned to it in Articles 5 and 7 above, and as may be necessary to ensure that the decisions with respect to the export of these products from Germany are carried out;

(b) such further powers as may be necessary to enforce the disarmament of Germany, including power to control the supply of Ruhr coal, coke and steel to any industries which may be prohibited or limited in the interests of security by agreement among the contracting Governments or under the terms of any international agreement to which they shall become party.

10. (a) When the occupation authorities concerned relinquish the powers referred to in Article 9 (a) the German authorities shall be responsi-

ble to the International Authority for enabling it to perform the functions and exercise the rights assigned to it in Articles 5 and 7 above and shall take such measures as may be necessary to ensure that the decisions of the International Authority are carried out.

(b) When the occupation authorities concerned relinquish the further powers referred to in Article 9 (b) these powers shall be transferred to such international body as may be designated for these purposes by the Peace Settlement or by any international agreement to which the Allied Governments represented on the Authority are parties, and the Authority shall cooperate with that international body in such ways as shall be prescribed by the Peace Settlement or by such international agreement. If no such international body is set up, these powers shall be transferred to the Authority but shall be exercised only by the Allied representatives on the Authority.

11. Should the German Government not carry out the decisions of the International Authority, the latter may, by a majority vote of the Allied representatives, find that the German Government is in default on its obligations and recommend, to the occupation authorities during the Control Period, and thereafter to the Allied Governments represented on the Authority, the application of the necessary enforcement measures, provided however that before such enforcement measures are applied the German Government shall be given a reasonable opportunity for a hearing. At the expiry of the Control Period, these enforcement measures shall be applied in accordance with the relevant provisions of the Peace Settlement or any international agreement to which the Allied Governments represented on the Authority are parties.

12. This Agreement constitutes a statement of principles which shall form the basis for a more detailed agreement setting up the International Authority.

Source: *Documents on American Foreign Relations,* Vol. X, 1948, Princeton University Press, pp. 109–114.

ORDRE DU JOUR ADOPTÉ PAR L'ASSEMBLÉE À L'ISSUE DU DÉBAT SUR LES RECOMMANDATIONS DE LONDRES

L'Assemblée nationale,

Ayant entendu les déclarations du gouvernement sur les recommandations issues des entretiens de Londres sur l'Allemagne.

Constate, d'une part, que si ces recommandations marquent un progrès certain des positions anglaises et américaines vers les thèses constamment affirmées par la France, elles ne tiennent compte que partiellement, sur des points importants, des requêtes françaises;

Considère d'autre part, qu'un rejet des recommandations de Londres entrainerait le relâchement regrettable d'une entente entre des puissances amies dont la coopération soutenue est aujourd'hui la plus sûre garantie de paix;

Prenant acte de la déclaration du ministre des affaires étrangères selon laquelle les recommandations de Londres constituent un résumé des points de vue sur lesquels les Alliés se sont mis d'accord et qu'en conséquence sur les autres points les négociations restent ouvertes;

Invite le gouvernement à participer à l'application des recommandations de Londres:

1. en réaffirmant la position française sur la nécessité d'une internationalisation des mines et des industries de base de la Ruhr;

2. en assurant la participation effective de la France au contrôle du potentiel industriel allemand en vue de réaliser l'expropriation des anciens magnats et d'obtenir l'extension du contrôle de l'autorité internationale à la gestion des richesses minières et industrielles de cette région-clé;

3. en assurant la sécurité de la France et les réparations qui lui sont dues, spécialement par l'occupation de l'Allemagne pendant une longue periode et en subordonnant le retrait des troupes alliées à un accord précis sur les garanties du maintien de la paix et les conditions d'occupation des régions-clés;

4. en faisant écarter tous risques de reconstitution d'un Reich autoritaire et centralisé;

5. en continuant de rechercher un accord final à quatre sur le problème allemand;

6. en accentuant son action en vue de l'organisation économique et politique de l'Europe;

Donne acte au gouvernement des engagements qu'il a pris de s'élever contre toute décision qui s'écarterait de ces principes;

Et, repoussant toute addition,

Passe à l'ordre du jour.

Source: *L'Année Politique, 1948,* Paris, 1949, pp. 335–336.

NORTH ATLANTIC TREATY

Washington D.C., 4th April, 1949

The Parties to this Treaty reaffirm their faith in the purposes and principles of the Charter of the United Nations and their desire to live in peace with all peoples and all governments.

They are determined to safeguard the freedom, common heritage and civilisation of their peoples, founded on the principles of democracy, individual liberty and the rule of law.

They seek to promote stability and well-being in the North Atlantic area.

They are resolved to unite their efforts for collective defence and for the preservation of peace and security.

They therefore agree to this North Atlantic Treaty:

Article 1

The Parties undertake, as set forth in the Charter of the United Nations, to settle any international dispute in which they may be involved by peaceful means in such a manner that international peace and security and justice are not endangered, and to refrain in their international relations from the threat or use of force in any manner inconsistent with the purposes of the United Nations.

Article 2

The Parties will contribute toward the further development of peaceful and friendly international relations by strengthening their free institutions by bringing about a better understanding of the principles upon which these institutions are founded, and by promoting conditions of stability and well-being. They will seek to eliminate conflict in their international economic policies and will encourage economic collaboration between any or all of them.

Article 3

In order more effectively to achieve the objectives of this Treaty, the Parties, separately and jointly, by means of continuous and effective self-help and mutual aid, will maintain and develop their individual and collective capacity to resist armed attack.

Article 4

The Parties will consult together whenever, in the opinion of any of them, the territorial integrity, political independence or security of any of the Parties is threatened.

Article 5

The Parties agree that an armed attack against one or more of them in Europe or North America shall be considered an attack against them all; and consequently they agree that, if such an armed attack occurs, each of them, in exercise of the right of individual or collective self-defence recognised by Article 51 of the Charter of the United Nations, will assist the Party or Parties so attacked by taking forthwith, individually and in concert with the other Parties, such action as it deems necessary, including the use of armed force, to restore and maintain the security of the North Atlantic area.

Any such armed attack and all measures taken as a result thereof shall immediately be reported to the Security Council. Such measures shall be terminated when the Security Council has taken the measures necessary to restore and maintain international peace and security.

Article 6

For the purpose of Article 5 an armed attack on one or more of the Parties is deemed to include an armed attack on the territory of any of the Parties in Europe or North America, on the Algerian Departments of France, on the occupation forces of any Party in Europe, on the islands under the jurisdiction of any Party in the North Atlantic area north of the Tropic of Cancer or on the vessels or aircraft in this area of any of the Parties.[1]

Article 7

This Treaty does not affect, and shall not be interpreted as affecting, in any way the rights and obligations under the Charter of the Parties which are members of the United Nations, or the primary responsibility of the Security Council for the maintenance of international peace and security.

Article 8

Each Party declares that none of the international engagements now in force between it and any other of the Parties or any third State is in conflict with the provisions of this Treaty, and undertakes not to enter into any international engagements in conflict with this Treaty.

Article 9

The Parties hereby establish a council, on which each of them shall be represented, to consider matters concerning the implementation of this Treaty. The Council shall be so organized as to be able to meet promptly at any time. The Council shall set up subsidiary bodies as may be necessary; in particular it shall establish immediately a defence committee which shall recommend measures for the implementation of Articles 3 and 5.

[1] Modified by the Greece-Turkey Protocol.

Article 10

The Parties may, by unanimous agreement, invite any other European State in a position to further the principles of this Treaty and to contribute to the security of the North Atlantic area to accede to this Treaty. Any State so invited may become a Party to the Treaty by depositing its instrument of accession with the Government of the United States of America. The Government of the United States of America will inform each of the Parties of the deposit of each such instrument of accession.

Article 11

This Treaty shall be ratified and its provisions carried out by the Parties in accordance with their respective constitutional processes. The instruments of ratification shall be deposited as soon as possible with the Government of the United States of America, which will notify all the other signatories of each deposit. The Treaty shall enter into force between the States which have ratified it as soon as the ratifications of the majority of the signatories, including the ratifications of Belgium, Canada, France, Luxembourg, the Netherlands, the United Kingdom and the United States, have been deposited and shall come into effect with respect to other States on the date of the deposit of their ratifications.

Article 12

After the Treaty has been in force for ten years, or at any time thereafter, the Parties shall, if any of them so requests, consult together for the purpose of reviewing the Treaty, having regard for the factors then affecting peace and security in the North Atlantic area, including the development of universal as well as regional arrangements under the Charter of the United Nations for the maintenance of international peace and security.

Article 13

After the Treaty has been in force for twenty years, any Party may cease to be a Party one year after its notice of denunciation has been given to the Government of the United States of America, which will inform the Governments of the other Parties of the deposit of each notice of denunciation.

Article 14

This Treaty, of which the English and French texts are equally authentic, shall be deposited in the archives of the Government of the United States of America. Duly certified copies will be transmitted by that Government to the Governments of the other signatories.

Source: Proceedings of the States General, 1948–1949,
Annexes, Second Chamber, No. 1237.

SPEECH OF THE NETHERLANDS MINISTER OF FOREIGN AFFAIRS IN WASHINGTON

"The Treaty we are about to sign marks the end of an illusion: the hope that the United Nations would, by itself, ensure international peace. Regretfully we were driven to the conclusion that the Charter though essential, is not enough in the world as it is, to protect those vital principles for which we of the Western world who have gathered here, stand. Therefore we felt it our duty to make this Treaty. So far from merely marking the end of an illusion, it most especially marks the birth of a new hope of enduring peace.

Its opponents are clamoring that this Treaty aims at war. That is a lie. Its aim is peace – peace, not after a new war but peace now, and from now on. We who are vitally interested in the security of the North Atlantic area, henceforth stand united in our resolve to repel aggression just as we stand united in our resolve not to attack others.

Such, then, is the Treaty's unshakable moral basis. We shall sign with a clear conscience in the face of God.

Various aspects of the new Treaty are being explained by my fellow speakers. Let me add and stress this:

Together we are determined in our mutual interest to gird the North Atlantic with a chain of strength. That chain is necessarily as strong as its weakest link. Let us then strive together, on a basis of equal treatment for all, to uphold the strength of the strongest links and to increase that of the weakest, for weak links are a common peril. This is a dictate of plain common sense.

Here, as in so many other fields of international cooperation and integration, the Netherlands will not be found wanting. As we have participated in making and implementing the Brussels Pact, and Benelux and O.E.E.C. and a Western European Federation (to mention only these), so shall we participate in making the Treaty now before us a living and inspiring reality. We know that you all in turn will not fail us.

We rejoice at the thought that at last the truth prevails that the North Atlantic is a highway that unites, not a barrier that divides. We rejoice at the thought that North Americans and Western Europeans have found each other in a common edifice dedicated to peace. Freedom from fear is being brought nearer to all of us today.

Let me close with a word of Netherlands gratitude to all those who have laboured towards bringing us here together. In saying this I am not thinking merely of the negotiators whom I thank most warmly, but also and no less, of those enlightened men who built that massive pedestal of popular support on which this Treaty now securely stands: members of Congress, parliamentarians, moulders and interpreters of public opinion in all our countries.

And so, with a humble prayer for Gods merciful blessing, I declare the Netherlands Government's readiness to sign this Treaty for Peace".

Source: See, p. 263.

STATUTE OF THE COUNCIL OF EUROPE

The Governments of the Kingdom of Belgium, the Kingdom of Denmark, the French Republic, the Irish Republic, the Italian Republic, the Grand Duchy of Luxembourg, the Kingdom of the Netherlands, the Kingdom of Norway, the Kingdom of Sweden and the United Kingdom of Great Britain and Northern Ireland;

Convinced that the pursuit of peace based upon justice and international co-operation is vital for the preservation of human society and civilisation;

Reaffirming their devotion to the spiritual and moral values which are the common heritage of their peoples and the true source of individual freedom, political liberty and the rule of law, principles which form the basis of all genuine democracy;

Believing that, for the maintenance and further realisation of these ideals and in the interests of economic and social progress, there is need of a closer unity between all like-minded countries of Europe;

Considering that, to respond to this need and to the expressed aspirations of their peoples in this regard, it is necessary forthwith to create an organisation which will bring European States into closer association;

Have in consequence decided to set up a Council of Europe consisting of a Committee of representatives of Governments and of a Consultative Assembly, and have for this purpose adopted the following Statute:

Chapter I

AIM OF THE COUNCIL OF EUROPE

Article 1

(*a*) The aim of the Council of Europe is to achieve a greater unity between its Members for the purpose of safeguarding and realising the ideals and principles which are their common heritage and facilitating their economic and social progress.

(*b*) This aim shall be pursued through the organs of the Council by discussion of questions of common concern and by agreements and common action in economic, social, cultural, scientific, legal and administrative matters and in the maintenance and further realisation of human rights and fundamental freedoms.

(*c*) Participation in the Council of Europe shall not affect the collaboration of its Members in the work of the United Nations and of other international organisations or unions to which they are parties.

(*d*) Matters relating to National Defence do not fall within the scope of the Council of Europe.

Chapter II

MEMBERSHIP

Article 2

The Members of the Council of Europe are the Parties to this Statute.

Article 3

Every Member of the Council of Europe must accept the principles of the rule of law and of the enjoyment by all persons within its jurisdiction of human rights and fundamental freedoms, and collaborate sincerely and effectively in the realisation of the aim of the Council as specified in Chapter I.

Article 4

Any European State, which is deemed to be able and willing to fulfil the provisions of Article 3, may be invited to become a Member of the Council of Europe by the Committee of Ministers. Any State so invited shall become a Member on the deposit on its behalf with the Secretary-General of an instrument of accession to the present Statute.

Article 5

(a) In special circumstances, a European country, which is deemed to be able and willing to fulfil the provisions of Article 3, may be invited by the Committee of Ministers, to become an Associate Member of the Council of Europe. Any country so invited shall become an Associate Member on the deposit on its behalf with the Secretary-General of an instrument accepting the present Statute. An Associate Member shall be entitled to be represented in the Consultative Assembly only.

(b) The expression "Member" in this Statute includes an Associate Member except when used in connexion with representation on the Committee of Ministers.

Article 6

Before issuing invitations under Articles 4 or 5 above, the Committee of Ministers shall determine the number of representatives on the Consultative Assembly to which the proposed Member shall be entitled and its proportionate financial contribution.

Article 7

Any Member of the Council of Europe may withdraw by formally notifying the Secretary-General of its intention to do so. Such withdrawal shall take effect at the end of the financial year in which it is notified, if the notification is given during the first nine months of that financial year. If the notification is given in the last three months of the financial year, it shall take effect at the end of the next financial year.

Article 8

Any Member of the Council of Europe, which has seriously violated Article 3, may be suspended from its rights of representation and requested by the Committee of Ministers to withdraw under Article 7. If such Member does not comply with this request, the Committee may decide that it has ceased to be a Member of the Council as from such date as the Committee may determine.

Article 9

The Committee of Ministers may suspend the right of representation on the Committee and on the Consultative Assembly of a Member, which has failed to fulfil its financial obligation, during such period as the obligation remains unfulfilled.

Chapter III

GENERAL

Article 10

The organs of the Council of Europe are:
(i) the Committee of Ministers;
(ii) the Consultative Assembly;
Both these organs shall be served by the Secretariat of the Council of Europe.

Article 11

The seat of the Council of Europe is at Strasbourg.

Article 12

The official languages of the Council of Europe are English and French. The rules of procedure of the Committee of Ministers and of the Consultative Assembly shall determine in what circumstances and under what conditions other languages may be used.

Chapter IV

COMMITTEE OF MINISTERS

Article 13

The Committee of Ministers is the organ which acts on behalf of the Council of Europe in accordance with Articles 15 and 16.

Article 14

Each Member shall be entitled to one representative on the Committee of Ministers and each representative shall be entitled to one vote. Representatives on the Committee shall be the Ministers for Foreign Affairs. When a Minister for Foreign Affairs is unable to be present or in other circumstances where it may be desirable, an alternate may be nominated to act for him, who shall, whenever possible, be a member of his Government.

Article 15

(*a*) On the recommendation of the Consultative Assembly or on its own initiative, the Committee of Ministers shall consider the action requied to further the aim of the Council of Europe, including the conclusion of conventions or agreements and the adoption by Governments of a common policy with regard to particular matters. Its conclusions shall be communicated to Members by the Secretary-General.

(*b*) In appropriate cases, the conclusions of the Committee may take the form of recommendations to the Governments of Members, and the Committee may request the Governments of Members to inform it of the action taken by them with regard to such recommendations.

Article 16

The Committee of Ministers shall, subject to the provisions of Articles 24, 28, 30, 32, 33 and 35, relating to the powers of the Consultative Assembly, decide with binding effect all matters relating to the internal organisation and arrangements of the Council of Europe. For this purpose the Committee of Ministers shall adopt such financial and administrative regulations as may be necessary.

Article 17

The Committee of Ministers may set up advisory and technical committees or commissions for such specific purposes as it may deem desirable.

Article 18

The Committee of Ministers shall adopt its rules of procedure which shall determine amongst other things:

(i) the quorum;

(ii) the method of appointment and term of office of its President;

(iii) the procedure for the admission of items to its agenda, including the giving of notice of proposals for resolutions; and

(iv) the notifications required for the nomination of alternates under Article 14.

Article 19

At each session of the Consultative Assembly the Committee of Ministers shall furnish the Assembly with statements of its activities, accompanied by appropriate documentation.

Article 20

(a) Resolutions of the Committee of Ministeıs relating to the following important matters, namely:

(i) recommendations under Article 15 (*b*);

(ii) questions under Article 19;

(iii) questions under Article 21 (*a*) (i) and (*b*);

(iv) questions under Article 33;

(v) recommendations for the amendment of Articles 1 (*d*), 7, 15, 20 and 22; and

(vi) any other question which the Committee may, by a resolution passed under (d) below, decide should be subject to a unanimous vote on account of its importance.

require the unanimous vote of the representatives casting a vote, and of a majority of the representatives entitled to sit on the Committee.

(b) Questions arising under the rules of procedure or under the financial and administrative regulations may be decided by a simple majority vote of the representatives entitled to sit on the Committee.

(c) Resolutions of the Committee under Articles 4 and 5 require a two-thirds majority of all the representatives entitled to sit on the Committee.

(d) All other resolutions of the Committee, including the adoption of the Budget, of rules of procedure and of financial and administrative regulations, recommendations for the amendment of articles of this Statute, other than those mentioned in paragraph (a) (v) above, and deciding in case of doubt which paragraph of this Article applies, require a two-thirds majority of the representatives casting a vote and of a majority of the representatives entitled to sit on the Committee.

Article 21

(a) Unless the Committee decides otherwise, meetings of the Committee of Ministers shall be held:

(i) in private, and

(ii) at the seat of the Council.

(b) The Committee shall determine what information shall be published regarding the conclusions and discussions of a meeting held in private.

(c) The Committee shall meet before and during the beginning of every session of the Consultative Assembly and at such other times as it may decide.

Chapter V

THE CONSULTATIVE ASSEMBLY

Article 22

The Consultative Assembly is the deliberative organ of the Council of Europe. It shall debate matters within its competence under this Statute and present its conclusions, in the form of recommendations. to the Committee of Ministers.

Article 23

(a) The Consultative Assembly shall discuss, and may make recommendations upon, any matter within the aim and scope of the Council of Europe as defined in Chapter I, which (i) is referred to it by the Committee of Ministers with a request for its opinion, or (ii) has been approved by the Committee for inclusion in the Agenda of the Assembly on the proposal of the latter.

(b) In taking decision under (a), the Committee shall have regard to the work of other European inter-governmental organisations to which some or all of the Members of the Council are parties.

(c) The President of the Assembly shall decide, in case of doubt, whether any question raised in the course of the Session is within the Agenda of the Assembly approved under (*a*) above.

Article 24

The Consultative Assembly may, with due regard to the provisions of Article 38 (*d*), establish committees or commissions to consider and report to it on any matter which falls within its competence under Article 23, to examine and prepare questions on its agenda and to advise on all matters of procedure.

Article 25

(*a*) The Consultative Assembly shall consist of representatives of each Member appointed in such a manner as the Government of that Member shall decide. Each representative must be a national of the Member whom he represents, but shall not at the same time be a member of the Committee of Ministers.

(*b*) No representative shall be deprived of his position as such during a session of the Assembly without the agreement of the Assembly.

(*c*) Each representative may have a substitute who may, in the absence of the representative, sit, speak and vote in his place. The provisions of paragraph (*a*) above apply to the appointment of substitutes.

Article 26

The following States, on becoming Members, shall be entitled to the number of representatives given below:

Belgium	6
Denmark	4
France	18
Irish Republic	4
Italy	18
Luxembourg	3
Netherlands	6
Norway	4
Sweden	6
United Kingdom	18

Article 27

The conditions under which the Committee of Ministers collectively may be represented in the debates of the Consultative Assembly, or individual representatives on the Committee may address the Assembly, shall be determined by such rules of procedure on this subject as may be drawn up by the Committee after consultation with the Assembly.

Article 28

(*a*) The Consultative Assembly shall adopt its rules of procedure and shall elect from its members its President, who shall remain in office until the next ordinary session.

(*b*) The President shall control the proceedings but shall not take part in the debate or vote. The substitute of the representative who is President may sit, speak and vote in his place.

(c) The rules of procedure shall determine *inter alia:*

(i)   the quorum;

(ii) the manner of the election and terms of office of the President and other officers;

(iii) the manner in which the Agenda shall be drawn up and be communicated to representatives; and

(iv) the time and manner in which the names of representatives and their substitutes shall be notified.

Article 29

Subject to the provisions of Article 30, all resolutions of the Consultative Assembly, including resolutions:

(i)   embodying recommendations to the Committee of Ministers;

(ii) proposing to the Committee matters for discussion in the Assembly;

(iii) establishing committees or commissions;

(iv) determining the date of commencement of its sessions;

(v)   determining what majority is required for resolutions in cases not covered by (i) to (iv) above or determining cases of doubt as to what majority is required,

shall require a two-thirds majority of the representatives casting a vote.

Article 30

On matters relating to its internal procedure, which includes the election of officers, the nomination of persons to serve on committees and commissions and the adoption of rules of procedure resolutions of the Consultative Assembly shall be carried by such majorities as the Assembly may determine in accordance with Article 29 (v).

Article 31

Debates on proposals to be made to the Committee of Ministers that a matter should be placed on the Agenda of the Consultative Assembly shall be confined to an indication of the proposed subject matter and the reasons for and against its inclusion in the Agenda.

Article 32

The Consultative Assembly shall meet in ordinary session once a year, the date and duration of which shall be determined by the Assembly so as to avoid as far as possible overlapping with parliamentary sessions of Members and with sessions of the General Assembly of the United Nations. In no circumstances shall the duration of an ordinary session exceed one month unless both the Assembly and the Committee of Ministers concur.

Article 33

Ordinary sessions of the Consultative Assembly shall be held at the seat of the Council unless both the Assembly and the Committee of Ministers concur that it should be held elsewhere.

Article 34

The Committee of Ministers may convoke an extraordinary session of the Consultative Assembly at such time and place as the Committee, with the concurrence of the President of the Assembly, shall decide.

Article 35

Unless the Consultative Assembly decides otherwise, its debates shall be conducted in public.

Chapter VI

THE SECRETARIAT

Article 36

(a) The Secretariat shall consist of a Secretary-General, a Deputy Secretary-General and such other staff as may be required.

(b) The Secretary-General and Deputy Secretary-General shall be appointed by the Consultative Assembly on the recommendation of the Committee of Ministers.

(c) The remaining staff of the Secretariat shall be appointed by the Secretary-General, in accordance with the administrative regulations.

(d) No member of the Secretariat shall hold any salaried office from any Government or be a member of the Consultative Assembly or of any national legislature or engage in any occupation incompatible with his duties.

(e) Every member of the staff of the Secretariat shall make a solemn declaration affirming that his duty is to the Council of Europe and that he will perform his duties conscientiously, uninfluenced by any national considerations, and that he will not seek or receive instructions in connexion with the performance of his duties from any Government or any authority external to the Council and will refrain from any action which might reflect on his position as an international official responsible only to the Council. In the case of the Secretary-General and the Deputy Secretary-General this declaration shall be made before the Committee, and in the case of all other members of the staff, before the Secretary-General.

(f) Every Member shall respect the exclusively international character of the responsibilities of the Secretary-General and the staff of the Secretariat and not seek to influence them in the discharge of their responsibilities.

Article 37

(a) The Secretariat shall be located at the seat of the Council.

(b) The Secretary-General is responsible to the Committee of Ministers for the work of the Secretariat. Amongst other things, he shall, subject to Article 38 (d), provide such secretarial and other assistance as the Consultative Assembly may require.

Chapter VII

FINANCE

Article 38

(*a*) Each Member shall bear the expenses of its own representation in the Committee of Ministers and in the Consultative Assembly.

(*b*) The expenses of the Secretariat and all other common expenses shall be shared between all Members in such proportions as shall be determined by the Committee on the basis of the population of Members.

The contributions of an Associate Member shall be determined by the Committee.

(*c*) In accordance with the financial regulations, the budget of the Council shall be submitted annually by the Secretary-General for adoption by the Committee.

(*d*) The Secretary-General shall refer to the Committee requests from the Assembly which involve expenditure exceeding the amount already allocated in the budget for the Assembly and its activities.

Article 39

The Secretary-General shall each year notify the Government of each Member of the amount of its contribution and each Member shall pay to the Secretary-General the amount of its contribution, which shall be deemed to be due on the date of its notification, not later than six months after that date.

Chapter VIII

PRIVILEGES AND IMMUNITIES

Article 40

(*a*) The Council of Europe, representatives of Members and the Secretariat shall enjoy in the territories of its Members such privileges and immunities as are reasonably necessary for the fulfilment of their functions. These immunities shall include immunity for all representatives in the Consultative Assembly from arrest and all legal proceedings in the territories of all Members, in respect of words spoken and votes cast in the debates of the Assembly or its committees or commissions.

(*b*) The Members undertake as soon as possible to enter into an agreement for the purpose of fulfilling the provisions of paragraph (*a*) above. For this purpose the Committee of Ministers shall recommend to the Governments of Members the acceptance of an Agreement defining the privileges and immunities to be granted in the territories of all Members. In addition a special Agreement shall be concluded with the Government of the French Republic defining the privileges and immunities which the Council shall enjoy at its seat.

Chapter IX

AMENDMENTS

Article 41

(*a*) Proposals for the amendment of this Statute may be made in the Committee of Ministers or, in the conditions provided for in Article 23, in the Consultative Assembly.

(*b*) The Committee shall recommend and cause to be embodied in a Protocol those amendments which it considers to be desirable.

(*c*) An amending Protocol shall come into force when it has been signed and ratified on behalf of two-thirds of the Members.

(*d*) Notwithstanding the provisions of the preceding paragraph of this Article, amendments to Articles 23–35, 38 and 39 which have been approved by the Committee and by the Assembly, shall come into force on the date of the certificate of the Secretary-General, transmitted to the Governments of Members, certifying that they have been so approved. This paragraph shall not operate until the conclusion of the second ordinary session of the Assembly.

Chapter X

FINAL PROVISIONS

Article 42

(*a*) This Statute shall be ratified. Ratifications shall be deposited with the Government of the United Kingdom of Great Britain and Northern Ireland.

(*b*) The present Statute shall come into force as soon as seven instruments of ratification have been deposited. The Government of the United Kingdom shall transmit to all signatory Governments a certificate declaring that the Statute has entered into force, and giving the names of the Members of the Council of Europe on that date.

(*c*) Thereafter each other signatory shall become a party to this Statute as from the date of the deposit of its instrument of ratification.

In witness whereof the undersigned, being duly authorised thereto, have signed the present Statute.

Done at London, this 5th day of May, 1949, in English and French, both texts being equally authentic, in a single copy which shall remain deposited in the archives of the Government of the United Kingdom which shall transmit certified copies to the other signatory Governments.

Source: Proceedings of the States General, 1948–1949,
Annexes, Second Chamber, No. 1247.

SIX-POWER COMMUNIQUÉ REGARDING PROVISIONAL RECTI-
FICATIONS OF THE WESTERN GERMAN FRONTIER

Issued in Paris, 26 March, 1949

It was announced at the conclusion of the London talks on Germany on
June 7, 1948, that proposals were being submitted to the Governments of
the United States, France, the United Kingdom, and the Benelux
countries for bringing about provisionally certain minor territorial
adjustments in the western boundary of Germany.

The six governments, taking into account the unforeseen delays to
which the conclusion of a final peace settlement with Germany has been
subjected, consider it necessary to proceed to a preliminary examination
of the problem of frontiers and to put into effect the minor adjustments
justified by administrative necessities and by conditions affecting
communications along Germany's western frontier. The problem of
Germany's frontiers will be re-examined and settled definitively in its
entirety at the time of final peace settlement.

After detailed study, the six governments have approved the proposals
for provisional adjustments of the frontier which have been submitted to
them by a working-party meeting in Paris.

The six governments have also examined the frontiers of the Saar
territory and have agreed that, pending confirmation or modification by
the terms of the final peace settlement, the present frontier shall be maintained with the minor modifications.

The areas affected by the adjustments will be placed under the administration of the countries adjacent to Germany.

These adjustments may be confirmed or modified by the terms of the
final settlement concerning Germany.

The London recommendations fixed a very restricted frame of reference
for the working party. Only those proposals might be examined which
involved no appreciable loss to the German economy and which, being of
minor character only, could be regarded as desirable to eliminate local
anomalies and improve communications.

This limited frame of reference did not permit the working party to
take into consideration certain major territorial claims of Germany's
western neighbours.

Within the limits thus defined, 31 minor rectifications will be effected
at a date to be announced later, along the frontier between Germany, on
the one hand and the Netherlands, Belgium, Luxembourg, the Saar, and
France, on the other.

These will affect a total area of approximately 135 square kilometers
(approximately 52 square miles) and a population of some 13,500 persons.

These modifications have been defined in general outline. Their exact
limits will be fixed by delimitation commissions. These commissions will
make their decision after having heard, if this appears desirable, the local

authorities and persons in the area capable of giving information or explanations necessary for the accomplishment of the commission's task.

All measures will be taken with a view to safeguarding the interests of the inhabitants, as regards both their personal status and their movable and real property. No one will be forced to accept the nationality of the country to which the area is attached. Persons not desiring to accept this nationality will enjoy the protection accorded to persons and property by the laws of the country and no discrimination will be exercised against them. They will have the right to settle in Germany, in which case they will be allowed to take with them their movable property, either retaining ownership of their real property or selling it and being permitted to transfer the funds to Germany under the special regulations which will be prescribed. They will, on the other hand, have the right to continue to reside in the area concerned, if they so desire.

Source: *Documents on Germany under Occupation,*
1945–1954, Royal Institute of International
Affairs, 1955, pp. 368–369.

MEMORANDUM ON THE NETHERLANDS-GERMAN ECONOMIC RELATIONS [1]

I. INTRODUCTION

Sound relations to the German hinterland are of great importance to the economic life of the Netherlands. These relations have always been mutual, as Germany also had a great interest in good economic relations with the Netherlands. The economic intercourse between the Netherlands and Germany, two countries linked up by natural traffic-routes, was in normal times among the greatest between any two European countries. The autarchic policy, which Germany pursued to the detriment of the Netherlands during the period of National-Socialism was directly contrary to the natural economic and geographic conditions.

The development of the economic relations with Germany after the German capitulation has been a source of great disappointment to the Netherlands. The Netherlands Government, however, fully realise that the Allied Authorities have been confronted with an extremely difficult task during the past few years in Germany. In their note on the situation with regard to the German problem presented to the Netherlands States General on 19th July 1949 the Government drew attention to the difficulties confronting the Allied Authorities and to the large financial sacrifices which the Occupying Powers have made for the recovery of Germany.

The Netherlands Government do not now wish to go too deeply into the past. But they do wish to draw attention to the fact that already in the memorandum of January 14th, 1947, presented to the United Kingdom, the United States, and the U.S.S.R., they emphasized the necessity of admitting Germany to the European economic co-operation.

It was particularly the Netherlands delegation which insisted on Germany's participation in the European economic co-operation at the Paris conference in the summer of 1947 to prepare the report on European economic co-operation presented on 22nd September 1947 to the American Secretary of State, Mr. Marshall.

It was expected that participation of the three Western zones of Germany in the work of the O.E.E.C. would intensify the co-operation between Germany and the other participating countries. The development of the Netherlands-German economic relations, however, remained unsatisfactory in many respects; the volume of trade continued to be very limited. While on the whole trade between the other participating countries has already reached the pre-war level and in many cases has even greatly exceeded it, the Netherlands-German trade in the period from 1st July 1948 – 30th June 1949 had resumed only some 25 percent

[1] Kindly made available by the Netherlands Ministry of Foreign Affairs.

of its pre-war volume. This stagnation is partly the result of the economic difficulties in which Germany found itself after the war. Partly however, it is due to obstacles to trade imposed by the responsible authorities in Germany. The almost complete adjustment of Germany's commercial policy to the dollar and the dollar area, ignoring other possibilities and diverting the flow of trade from its natural channels has led in practice to measures which have a disquieting similarity to the autarchic measures which Germany used to take before the war, albeit based on other considerations.

The Netherlands Government consider it extremely gratifying that the inter-dependence of the economies of the Netherlands and Germany in the field of exchange of goods has now been fully recognised. The Netherlands-German trade agreement for the period 1st September 1949–31st August 1950 which was initialled in Frankfurt on 7th September 1949 offers great possibilities for a sound development of trade.

The exchange of goods from which in the past both countries always derived great benefit can again take place on a satisfactory scale.

To ensure that the Netherlands and Germany will profit to the fullest extent from the agreement which has been concluded, it will be necessary that the desire to liberalize Inter-European trade and to abolish the obstacles with which it has to contend will also be borne in mind in the implementation of this trade agreement.

In the sphere of trade, therefore, the main obstacles to sound development would seem to have been removed, although it may still take considerable time for the German-Netherlands trade to reach anything like the pre-war level.

In some other sectors of economic intercourse, however, practically no progress has been made. The Netherlands Government may therefore be allowed to subjoin an enumeration of the impediments which in their opinion still hamper the desired restoration of sound economic relations in the interest of both countries.

II. SHIPPING SERVICES AND TRANSIT TRADE

The economic and geographical position of the Netherlands makes this country peculiarly fitted for the fulfilment of a very important function in transit traffic and transit trade with respect to the German hinterland. Transit-traffic embraces the services of the Netherlands ports, international navigation on the Rhine and furthermore the Netherlands participation in German internal navigation. To this must be added the services of Netherlands ocean-going vessels, carrying goods destined for Germany and goods of German origin.

As regards transit-trade mention should be made of the voluminous German imports and exports which used to be handled by the Netherlands intermediate trade.

Since the war the recovery of these shipping services and the transit-trade has been highly disappointing. Not only did it undergo the detrimental influence of the difficult economic situation in Germany, but it was also hindered by artificial intervention by the responsible authorities in Germany.

A number of obstacles which have assumed the character of serious discrimination, are referred to below.

a. Discrimination with regard to ports

Since the war an artificial diversion of traffic via the North-West German ports has taken place to the detriment of the Benelux-ports, which constitute the natural and cheapest routes for a considerable part of the German traffic. This diversion has been promoted by the initially existing central control on the entire German foreign trade, which caused the decision as to routing to be taken by a central body, so that free competition was entirely precluded. It is, however, very alarming that even though foreign trade is gradually being entrusted to the German importers and exporters, central control on the choice of port has in many cases been maintained. This is true in particular for a great part of bulk traffic, which has always been of paramount importance to Rotterdam. The consequences of this policy are illustrated by the following comparison between the traffic in the North-West German ports and transit traffic in the principal Benelux-ports:

	1938		1948	
	mill. tons	% total traffic	mill. tons	% total traffic
Benelux-ports (transit) . .	35	51	5,3	26
N.W. German ports . . .	33,5	49	15	74
	68,5	100	20,3	100

These figures show that the share of the Benelux-ports in the greatly diminished total of Germany's overseas traffic has shrunk very considerably, even relatively.

The Netherlands Government wish to draw attention to the fact that the necessity of saving foreign exchange cannot justify this autarchic policy. For the Netherlands-German balance of payments shows a continual tendency to form an adverse balance for the Netherlands. It is specially the falling off of the Netherlands revenues from these services, which constitutes one of the principal causes of the lack of equilibrium which exercises such a harmful influence on the whole of Netherlands-German economic relations.

During discussions held at Frankfurt in September 1948 between Netherlands and Belgian representatives on the one hand and the J.E.I.A. on the other hand it was agreed that the currency argument should no longer play a part with reference to the choice of port.

The Netherlands Government regret to observe that the artificial diversion of traffic has been continued. Although some traffic has passed through Netherlands ports the participation of these ports in the available traffic is still unsatisfactory.

Although the Netherlands Government are not unmindful of the difficulties with which the North-West German ports, especially Hamburg, have to contend they do not consider the present onesided traffic policy in aid of these ports compatible with European economic co-operation. They feel justified in demanding that the existing obstacles to the Netherlands ports obtaining a reasonable share in the available traffic on a strictly competitive basis, should be removed.

b. Inland water-traffic

Traditionally the Netherlands inland water-traffic craft were largely employed on the German waterways, particularly on the Rhine. Since the war the resumption of this traffic has met with a number of obstacles, and this to an extent unknown before the war.

The strongest obstacles have been met with in respect of the participation in German inland water-traffic. In fact, Netherlands ships have been entirely excluded from this traffic. The expectation had arisen that this situation might improve as a result of the agreement reached in September 1948 to admit again on the one hand German craft to the Netherlands and on the other hand to allow Netherlands craft to participate in German internal traffic. This expectation has, however, not been fulfilled. Although the Netherlands frontier has been opened to German vessels, the understanding with respect to participation in German internal traffic has not materialised. In Germany the view is held that Netherlands vessels should only be considered when no German craft are available. The result has been that the Netherlands fleet is entirely excluded just as before.

The traffic crossing the frontier is also a source of grave concern. In September 1948 it was agreed that the German fleet would be limited to 20% in the up-stream traffic. The German authorities no longer consider this percentage to be binding and are endeavouring to secure an increasing German participation in international traffic. It is characteristic that this aim is not pursued by allowing free competition, but through the intervention of government bodies who endeavour to enforce a minimum percentage of participation by the German fleet in big shipping contracts. This autarchic policy has been very pronounced of late, now that the control of shipping contracts has been entrusted to the German authorities.

The legal basis for the intervention of the German authorities is formed by the J.E.I.A. instructions. Nos. 30 and 31. In instruction No. 30 the principle is laid down that the use of foreign tonnage can only be considered when no German shipping-space is available. J.E.I.A. instruction No. 31, which has only recently been amended, provides that the previous approval of the Verwaltung für Verkehr is required for the chartering of foreign vessels both in the case of German internal traffic and, if entire cargoes are concerned, also for the traffic crossing the frontier. The Netherlands Government are of opinion that the protectionist control on navigation on the Rhine and other German waterways entrusted to the German authorities by these instructions, is unacceptable. They consider it necessary that these instructions should be altered in such a manner as again to offer equal opportunities to the Netherlands fleet for participation both in German internal and in international traffic. The result of this principle of freedom is a pre-condition for future co-operation in this field.

c. Maritime shipping

The existing foreign exchange regulations in Germany embodied in J.E.I.A.-instruction No. 29 tend to give preference to German maritime shipping to the detriment of foreign shipping. As Germany's fleet is being expanded, the effect of this regulation will grow more serious. It is desirable that this regulation be altered so as to allow participation of foreign shipping on a free competitive basis.

d. Transit trade

Netherlands transit trade is still practically paralysed as a result of the numerous restrictions in the exchange of goods and payments. The Netherlands Government regard as a matter of the greatest importance the restoration of the traditional function of the Netherlands as an intermediary in the international trade of Germany.

III. CAPITAL INTERESTS

The Netherlands capital interests in Germany have been estimated at abt. RM. 1.700.000.000 based on 1938 values. The greater part of these extensive assets consists of participations in productive concerns. These important investments have steadily accumulated in the course of many years and by no means bear the character of speculative capital. They originated in the intensive economic intercourse between the Netherlands and Germany, whilst they in their turn formed the basis for the development of further economic relations. With a view to European economic co-operation the rehabilitation of Dutch investments in Germany is therefore of the utmost importance. A number of obstacles which still impede such rehabilitation are referred to below:

a. Blocking of Netherlands assets

All Netherlands assets in Germany are still blocked under laws 52 and 53. The restrictions thus imposed on Netherlands nationals and on Netherlands-owned companies in Germany do not apply to Germans and therefore constitute a serious discrimination. The Netherlands Government do not know of any reasons which might justify the continuation of this discrimination which has already done such great damage to Netherlands interests, in particular in connection with the monetary reform. On 18th October 1948 at a meeting with the U.S. and U.K. Military Governors a document (BIB/P(49)/122/3) was handed to the Netherlands representatives. It contained a proposal by the Bipartite Board to the British and United States Government for the deblocking of foreign assets. This proposal on which the Governments of the Benelux countries commented on 9th November 1948, has not yet been put into effect. It is urgently requested that this deblocking should take place within a shortest possible time.

The Netherlands Government rely on deblocking being carried out in such a manner that the existing discrimination between Netherlands and German assets will be removed. They wish to point out in advance that this end would not be attained if a system of licences were maintained, under which each separate transaction requires approval. In respect of Netherlands companies in Germany in particular this would mean that they would remain subject to special controls and restrictions not appplicable to German concerns. Should special restrictions with reference to foreign capital in Germany prove necessary in connection with foreign exchange, they should on no account exceed what is customary in Western European countries.

b. Netherlands capital interests in the Ruhr-industry

Since the beginning of the occupation Netherlands capital interests in German coalmines and iron and steel-industries have been adversely affected by the reorganisation measures taken by the occupation authorities. These measures prevent Netherlands shareholders from exercising their rights, with the result that so far the existing Netherlands participations in these industries have been practically eliminated.

Law No. 75, which was promulgated in November 1948 simultaneously by the United States and the British Military Governors, held out a prospect of a satisfactory arrangement only for the Sophia-Jacoba mine, which is 100% Netherlands owned. In all other cases the rights of the Netherlands shareholders remain suspended, whilst no provision is made for any ultimate satisfactory arrangement.

The Netherlands Government have repeatedly urged that the Netherlands interests concerned should be respected. The question was last broached in the memorandum presented to the Foreign Office in London on 10th June 1949. A memorandum of same tenor was presented to the State Department at Washington whilst the Ministry of Foreign Affairs in Paris was informed of this action.

The Netherlands Government adopt the standpoint that in so far as certain modifications in the Netherlands interests are necessary in connection with the reorganisation of the Ruhr-industry, equivalent participations in Ruhr coalmines or iron- and steel-industries should be received in exchange. In any case a reduction of the Netherlands overall-share in the Ruhr-industry as a result of the reorganisation should be avoided, in accordance with the principle laid down in recommendation No. 12 of the Intergovernmental Group on Protection of Foreign Interests in Germany. To this end a number of concrete proposals and desiderata are put forward in the above-mentioned memorandum. On 22nd of July 1949 the Foreign Office replied that the discussion of this question with Netherlands representatives was not yet considered opportune.

The Netherlands Government regret the further delay thus entailed. Firstly because it means that the rights of the Netherlands shareholders remain suspended. In consequence thereof nothing can be done to protect them.

Secondly it should be taken into account that the protection of the Netherlands interests depends not only on fundamental decisions, but also on the finding of practical solutions. The taking of fundamental decisions without adequate investigation of the practical possibilities would be bound to lead to difficulties in their application.

The Netherlands Government therefore consider it essential that an opportunity should be provided in the near future to discuss practical solutions for the safe-guarding of the Netherlands interests concerned. They are of opinion that these discussions could best take place between Netherlands experts and the competent Allied authorities in Germany. An essential condition for such discussions is the recognition by the Allied Governments that it is desirable to seek practical solutions for the preservation of the Netherlands interests and to instruct the Allied authorities in Germany to this effect. The latter should not be tied to the present text of law No. 75, implementation of which is under consideration. In the opinion of the Netherlands Government there is the less objection to this since the discussions referred to above need not prejudice the ultimate decisions which would be reserved to the Governments.

The Netherlands Government would highly appreciate the co-operation of the United Kingdom Government to bring about such discussions as soon as possible. They would suggest to the United Kingdom Government to instruct the British authorities in Germany accordingly.

c. Acceptance of the recommendations of the Intergovernmental Group in Paris

The report and the recommendations of the Inter-Governmental Group on the Protection of Foreign Interests in Germany which met in Paris in October/November 1948 were communicated to the other Governments concerned by the French Government in January 1949. These recommendations have now been accepted by the Netherlands Government as well as by the other Governments concerned, with the exception, however, of the Government of the United States. The Netherlands Government have repeatedly urged the United States Government to make known their decisions in this matter. The Netherlands Ambassador in Washington has again received instructions to present to the Department of State a memorandum on this subject, drafted in concert with the Belgian and Luxembourg Governments. Also in connection with the formation of the German Federal Government the Netherlands Government consider it of great importance that the United States Government should now express their opinion on these recommendations as soon as possible.

The Netherlands Government would like to draw special attention to the following recommendations, to the execution of which they attack great importance.

A. Recommendation No. 6: Equalisation of burdens

The Netherlands Embassy in Washington took up with the Department of State the question of the interpretation of the term "qualifying shares" (§ 1-c). To the Netherlands Government's surprise the Bipartite Board approved Economic Council Ordinance No. 71 A "to Alleviate Social Hardships" before these discussions were concluded. This law contained a narrow interpretation of the term, unfavourable to the Netherlands interests. According to article 6 § 1–2 of the above law by qualifying shares are exclusively meant shares which must be held by members of the board of directors or members of the board of management according to the statute. In practise such provisions do not occur in Germany, so that this provision is valueless. The Netherlands Government trust that this law will be implemented with due consideration for the Netherlands interests..

B. Recommendation No. 23: Prewar Treaties

The Netherlands Government are desirous of discussing with the Allied Governments at an early date the question of pre-war treaties in general and the Netherlands-German treaty of 1920 and its consequences for the mine Sophia-Jacoba in particular.

d. Transfer of proceeds of capital invested

The Netherlands Government are of the opinion that for a true rehabilitation of Netherlands capital interests facilities will necessarily have to be granted in the near future for the transfer of capital proceeds. For in the long run value can only be accorded to investments if it is possible to enjoy the proceeds.

Should no possibility of transfer be forthcoming and this essential condition thus remain unfulfilled, the Dutch investor would find himself at a disadvantage as compared with his German counterpart.

If the existing productive capital investments should continue to be deprived of the possibility of transfer this would undoubtedly exercise a very prejudicial influence on the restoration of confidence which is essential for the attraction of new capital.

Transfer of capital proceeds is furthermore considered necessary by the Netherlands Government in order to restore the equilibrium of the balance of payments between the Netherlands and Germany, in which such proceeds have always played an important part. Resumption of transfer would not lead to an increase of the total European dollar shortage, since the proceeds would enable the Netherlands to buy goods in Germany which must now to a large extent be bought in the dollar area.

Therefore the Netherlands Government again urge a restoration of the possibility of the transfer of capital proceeds.

IV. RESTITUTION OF SHIPS

Whereas the restitution to the Netherlands of most categories of goods has been all but concluded, a large number of Netherlands claims for the restitution of vessels still remains unsettled.

Protracted negotiations in Germany yielded no definite solution.

The primary object of the Netherlands Government with respect to the restitution of craft is to effect a definite settlement of the whole matter as soon as possible. They remain of opinion that they are entitled to the ships claimed. In view of the altered situation however, they are prepared to make considerable concessions concerning the still unsettled claims, in particular with respect to N.V.-craft.

By N.V.-craft are understood those ships which belong to Netherlands companies, the capital of which was German-owned before the war. The vast majority of the still unsettled claims in the American zone of occupation relates to this category.

It is for this reason that the Netherlands Government urgently request discussions to be opened as soon as possible concerning all Netherlands claims including those to N.V.-craft, in order to finalize this question as soon as possible.

They would highly appreciate the United Kingdom Government's co-operation in bringing about such negotiations, which in the opinion of the Netherlands Government would be most fruitful if the British and United States Governments jointly participated in them.

V. RESTITUTION OF SECURITIES

The request is made for an early release of securities claimed by the Netherlands. Thus the last obstacle would be removed to transfer of securities located in Germany, which have accrued as reparations to the Allied Governments.

VI. NOTES ON SOME ARRANGEMENTS RENDERED NECESSARY BY THE DELAY
IN CONCLUDING A PEACE TREATY

As no peace treaty with Germany is likely to be concluded in the near future, the Netherlands Government consider it necessary to proceed without delay to the settlement of a number of matters normally settled by peace treaties. The Netherlands Government attaches the greatest importance to Germany's participation in the European cultural, political and economic co-operation. They hope that further steps to this end can be taken in the near future. To minimize the difficulties which may arise they consider it essential that settlements should be made in certain sectors.

They have in mind, for instance, arrangements to preclude the possibility that the Allied measures in connection with reparations and restitutions should lead to difficulties between the Allies and the German Federal Republic at some future date. In particular the legal consequences of these Allied measures should be embodied in German law and recognised by the German authorities. If no adequate provision is made in the near future, this may cause conflicts of different nature which would adversely affect the relations between the new Federal Republic and the Allied Governments.

In this connection the Netherlands Government has noted with interest the Agreed Minute on Claims against Germany, drawn up by the Foreign Ministers of France, the United Kingdom and the United States in Washington on 8th April last. The Netherlands Government consider it important that negotiations should take place shortly regarding the matters referred to in the above-mentioned Agreed Minute. The most suitable form for such discussions is considered to be a conference attended by the six powers which took part in the Talks on Germany in London in 1948.

ECONOMIC COOPERATION AGREEMENT BETWEEN THE GOVERNMENTS OF THE KINGDOM OF THE NETHERLANDS AND THE UNITED STATES OF AMERICA

The Governments of the Netherlands and the United States of America:

Recognizing that the restoration or maintenance in European countries of principles of individual liberty, free institutions, and genuine independence rests largely upon the establishment of sound economic conditions, stable international economic relationships, and the achievement by the countries of Europe of a healthy economy independent of extraordinary outside assistance;

Recognizing that a strong and prosperous European economy is essential for the attainment of the purposes of the United Nations;

Considering that the achievement of such conditions calls for a European recovery plan of self-help and mutual cooperation, open to all nations which cooperate in such a plan, based upon a strong production effort, the expansion of foreign trade, the creation or maintenance of internal financial stability and the development of economic cooperation, including all possible steps to establish and maintain valid rates of exchange and to reduce trade barriers;

Considering that in furtherance of these principles the Government of the Netherlands has joined with other like-minded nations in a Convention for European Economic Cooperation signed at Paris on April 16, 1948 under which the signatories of that Convention agreed to undertake as their immediate task the elaboration and execution of a joint recovery program, and that the Government of the Netherlands is a member of the Organization for European Economic Cooperation created pursuant to the provisions of that Convention;

Considering also that, in furtherance of these principles, the Government of the United States of America has enacted the Economic Cooperation Act of 1948, providing for the furnishing of assistance by the United States to nations participating in a joint program for European recovery, in order to enable such nations through their own individual and concerted efforts to become independent of extraordinary outside economic assistance;

Taking note that the Government of the Netherlands has already expressed its adherence to the purposes and policies of the Economic Cooperation Act of 1948;

Desiring to set forth the understandings which govern the furnishing of assistance by the Government of the United States of America under the Economic Cooperation Act of 1948, the receipt of such assistance by the Netherlands, and the measures which the two Governments will take individually and together in furthering the recovery of the

Netherlands as an integral part of the joint program for European recovery;

Have agreed as follows:

Article I

(Assistance and Cooperation)

1. The Government of the United States of America undertakes to assist the Netherlands, by making available to the Government of the Netherlands or to any person, agency or organization designated by the latter Government such assistance as may be requested by it and approved by the Government of the United States of America. The Government of the United States of America will furnish this assistance under the provisions, and subject to all of the terms, conditions and termination provisions, of the Economic Cooperation Act of 1948, acts amendatory and supplementary thereto and appropriation acts thereunder, and will make available to the Government of the Netherlands only such commodities, services and other assistance as are authorized to be made available by such acts.

2. The Government of the Netherlands, acting individually and through the Organization for European Economic Cooperation, consistently with the Convention for European Economic Cooperation signed at Paris on April 16, 1948, will exert sustained afforts in common with other participating countries speedily to achieve through a joint recovery program economic conditions in Europe essential to lasting peace and prosperity and to enable the countries of Europe participating in such a joint recovery program to become independent of extraordinary outside economic assistance within the period of this Agreement. The Government of the Netherlands reaffirms its intention to take action to carry out the provisions of the General Obligations of the Convention for European Economic Cooperation, to continue to participate actively in the work of the Organization for European Economic Cooperation, and to continue to adhere to the purposes and policies of the Economic Cooperation Act of 1948.

3. With respect to assistance furnished by the Government of the United States of America to the Netherlands and procured from areas outside the United States of America, its territories and possessions, the Government of the Netherlands will cooperate with the Government of the United States of America in ensuring that procurement will be effected at reasonable prices and on reasonable terms and so as to arrange that the dollars thereby made available to the country from which the assistance is procured are used in a manner consistent with any arrangements made by the Government of the United States of America with such country.

Article II

(General Undertakings)

1. In order to achieve the maximum recovery through the employment of assistance received from the Government of the United States of America, the Government of the Netherlands will use its best endeavors:

(*a*) to adopt or maintain the measures necessary to ensure efficient and practical use of all the resources available to it, including

(i) such measures as may be necessary to ensure that the commodities and services obtained with assistance furnished under this Agreement are used for purposes consistent with this Agreement and, as far as practicable, with the general purposes outlined in the schedules furnished by the Government of the Netherlands in support of the requirements of assistance to be furnished by the Government of the United States of America;

(ii) the observation and review of the use of such resources through an effective follow-up system approved by the Organization for European Economic Cooperation; and

(iii) to the extent practicable, measures to locate, identify and put into appropriate use in furtherance of the joint program for European recovery, assets, and earnings therefrom which belong to nationals of the Netherlands and which are situated within the United States of America, its territories or possessions. Nothing in this clause imposes any obligation on the Government of the United States of America to assist in carrying out such measures or on the Government of the Netherlands to dispose of such assets;

(*b*) to promote the development of industrial and agricultural production on a sound economic basis; to achieve such production targets as may be established through the Organization for European Economic Cooperation; and when desired by the Government of the United States of America, to communicate to that Government detailed proposals for specific projects contemplated by the Government of the Netherlands to be undertaken in substantial part with assistance made available pursuant to this Agreement, including whenever practicable projects for increased production of coal, steel, transportation facilities and food;

(*c*) to stabilize its currency, establish or maintain a valid rate of exchange, balance its governmental budget as soon as practicable create or maintain internal financial stability, and generally restore or maintain confidence in its monetary system; and

(*d*) to cooperate with other participating countries in facilitating and stimulating an increasing interchange of goods and services among the participating countries and with other countries and in reducing public and private barriers to trade among themselves and with other countries.

2. Taking into account Article 8 of the Convention for European Economic Cooperation looking toward the full and effective use of manpower available in the various participating countries, the Government of the Netherlands will accord sympathetic consideration to proposals made in conjunction with the International Refugee Organization directed to the largest practicable utilization of manpower available in any of the participating countries in furtherance of the accomplishment of the purposes of this Agreement.

3. The Government of the Netherlands will take the measures which it deems appropriate, and will cooperate with other participating countries to prevent, on the part of private or public commercial enterprises, business practices or business arrangements affecting international trade which restrain competition, limit access to markets or foster monopolistic control whenever such practices or arrangements have the effect of interfering with the achievement of the joint program of European recovery.

Article III

(Guaranties)

1. The Governments of the Netherlands and of the United States of America will, upon the request of either Government, consult respecting projects in the Netherlands proposed by nationals of the United States of America and with regard to which the Government of the United States of America may appropriately make guaranties of currency transfer under section 111 (*b*) (3) of the Economic Cooperation Act of 1948.

2. The Government of the Netherlands agrees that if the Government of the United States of America makes payment in United States dollars to any person under such a guaranty, any guilders, or credits in guilders, assigned or transferred to the Government of the United States of America pursuant to that section shall be recognized as property of the Government of the United States of America.

Article IV

(Local Currency)

1. The provisions of this Article shall apply only with respect to assistance which may be furnished by the Government of the United States of America on a grant basis.

2. The Government of the Netherlands will establish a special account in The Netherlands Bank in the name of the Government of the Netherlands (hereinafter called the Special Account) and will make deposits in guilders to this account as follows:

(*a*) The unencumbered balances of the deposits made by the Government of the Netherlands pursuant to the exchange of notes between the two Governments dated April 20, 1948;

(*b*) Amounts commensurate with the indicated dollar cost to the Government of the United States of America of commodities, services and technical information (including any costs of processing, storing, transporting, repairing or other services incident thereto) made available to the Netherlands on a grant basis by any means authorized under the Economic Cooperation Act of 1948, less, however, the amount of the deposits made pursuant to the exchange of notes referred to in subparagraph (*a*). The Government of the United States of America shall from time to time notify the Government of the Netherlands of the indicated dollar cost of any such commodities, services and technical information, and the Government of the Netherlands will thereupon deposit in the Special Account a commensurate amount of guilders computed at a rate of exchange which shall be the par value agreed at such time with the International Monetary Fund. The Government of the Netherlands may at any time make advance deposits in the Special Account which shall be credited against subsequent notifications pursuant to this paragraph.

3. The Government of the United States of America will from time to time notify the Government of the Netherlands of its requirements for administrative expenditures in guilders within the Netherlands incident to operations under the Economic Cooperation Act of 1948, and the Government of the Netherlands will thereupon make such sums available

out of any balances in the Special Account in the manner requested by the Government of the United States of America in the notification.

4. Five percent of each deposit made pursuant to this Article in respect of assistance furnished under authority of the Foreign Aid Appropriation Act, 1949, shall be allocated to the use of the Government of the United States of America for its expenditures in the Netherlands, and sums made available pursuant to paragraph 3 of this Article shall first be charged to the amounts allocated under this paragraph.

5. The Government of the Netherlands will further make such sums of guilders available out of any balances in the Special Account as may be required to cover costs (including port, storage, handling and similar charges) of transportation from any point of entry in the Netherlands to the consignee's designated point of delivery in the Netherlands of such relief supplies and packages as are referred to in Article VI.

6. The Government of the Netherlands may draw upon any remaining balance in the Special Account for such purposes as may be agreed from time to time with the Government of the United States of America. In considering proposals put forward by the Government of the Netherlands for drawings from the Special Account, the Government of the United States of America will take into account the need for promoting or maintaining internal monetary and financial stabilization in the Netherlands and for stimulating productive activity and international trade and the exploration for and development of new sources of wealth within the Netherlands, including in particular:

(a) expenditures upon projects or programs, including those which are part of a comprehensive program for the development of the productive capacity of the Netherlands and the other participating countries, and projects or programs the external costs of which are being covered by assistance rendered by the Government of the United States of America under the Economic Cooperation Act of 1948 or otherwise, or by loans from the International Bank for Reconstruction and Development;

(b) expenditures upon the exploration for and development of additional production of materials which may be required in the United States of America because of deficiencies or potential deficiencies in the resources of the United States of America; and

(c) effective retirement of the national debt, especially debt held by the central bank or other banking institutions.

7. Any unencumbered balance other than unexpended amounts allocated under paragraph 4 of this Article remaining in the Special Account on June 30, 1952, shall be disposed of within the Netherlands for such purposes as may hereafter be agreed between the Governments of the Netherlands and the United States of America, it being understood that the agreement of the United States of America shall be subject to approval by Act or joint resolution of the Congress of the United States of America.

Article V

(Access to Materials)

1. The Government of the Netherlands will facilitate the transfer to the United States of America, for stockpiling or other purposes, of materials originating in the Netherlands which are required by the United

States of America as a result of deficiencies or potential deficiencies in its own resources, upon such reasonable terms of sale, exchange barter, or otherwise, and in such quantities, and for such period of time, as may be agreed to between the Governments of the Netherlands and the United States of America, after due regard for the reasonable requirements of the Netherlands for domestic use and commercial export of such materials. The Government of the Netherlands will take such specific measures as may be necessary to carry out the provisions of this paragraph, including the promotion of the increased production of such materials within the Netherlands, and the removal of any hindrances to the transfer of such materials to the United States of America. The Government of the Netherlands will, when so requested by the Government of the United States of America, enter into negotiations for detailed arrangements necessary to carry out the provisions of this paragraph.

2. Recognizing the principle of equity in respect to the drain upon the natural resources of the United States of America and of the participating countries, the Government of the Netherlands will, when so requested by the Government of the United States of America, where applicable negociate (a) a future schedule of minimum availabilities to the United States of America for future purchase and delivery of a fair share of materials originating in the Netherlands which are required by the United States of America as a result of deficiencies or potential deficiencies in its own resources at world market prices so as to protect the access of United States industry to an equitable share of such materials either in percentages of production or in absolute quantities from the Netherlands, (b) arrangements providing suitable protection for the right of access for any citizen of the United States of America or any corporation, partnership, or other association created under the laws of the United States of America or of any State or Territory thereof and substantially beneficially owned by citizens of the United States of America, in the development of such materials on terms of treatment equivalent to those afforded to the nationals of the Netherlands, and (c) an agreed schedule of increased production of such materials where practicable in the Netherlands and for delivery of an agreed percentage of such increased production to be transferred to the United States of America on a long-term basis in consideration of assistance furnished by the United States of America under this Agreement.

3. The Government of the Netherlands, when so requested by the Government of the United States of America, will cooperate, wherever appropriate, to further the objectives of paragraphs 1 and 2 of this Article in respect of materials originating outside of the Netherlands.

Article VI

(Travel Arrangements and Relief Supplies)

1. The Government of the Netherlands will cooperate with the Government of the United States of America in facilitating and encouraging the promotion and development of travel by citizens of the United States of America to and within participating countries.

2. The Government of the Netherlands will, when so desired by the Government of the United States of America enter, into negotiations for

agreements (including the provision of duty-free treatment under appropriate safeguards) to facilitate the entry into the Netherlands of supplies of relief goods donated to or purchased by United States voluntary non-profit relief agencies and of relief packages originating in the United States of America and consigned to individuals residing in the Netherlands.

Article VII

(Consultation and Transmittal of Information)

1. The two Governments will, upon the request of either of them consult regarding any matter relating to the application of this Agreement or to operations or arrangements carried out pursuant to this Agreement.

2. The Government of the Netherlands will communicate to the Government of the United States of America in a form at intervals to be indicated by the latter after consultation with the Government of the Netherlands:

(a) detailed information of projects, programs and measures proposed or adopted by the Government of the Netherlands to carry out the provisions of this Agreement and the General Obligations of the Convention for European Economic Cooperation:

(b) full statements of operations under this Agreement, including a statement of the use of funds, commodities and services received thereunder, such statements to be made in each calendar quarter;

(c) information regarding its economy and any other relevant information, necessary to supplement that obtained by the Government of the United States of America from the Organization for European Economic Cooperation, which the Government of the United State of America may need to determine the nature and scope of operations under the Economic Cooperation Act of 1948, and to evaluate the effectiveness of assistance furnished or contemplated under this Agreement and generally the progress of the joint recovery program.

3. The Government of the Netherlands will assist the Government of the United States of America to obtain information relating to the materials originating in the Netherlands referred to in Article V which is necessary to the formulation and execution of the arrangements provided for in that Article.

Article VIII

(Publicity)

1. The Governments of the Netherlands and the United States of America recognize that it is in their mutual interest that full publicity be given to the objectives and progress of the joint program for European recovery and of the actions taken in furtherance of that program. It is recognized that wide dissemination of information on the progress of the program is desirable in order to develop the sense of common effort and mutual aid which are essential to the accomplishment of the objectives of the program.

2. The Government of the United States of America will encourage the dissemination of such information and will make it available to the media of public information.

3. The Government of the Netherlands will encourage the dissemination of such information both directly and in cooperation with the Organization for European Economic Cooperation. It will make such information available to the media of public information and take all practicable steps to ensure that appropriate facilities are provided for such dissemination. It will further provide other participating countries and the Organization for European Economic Cooperation with full information on the progress of the program for economic recovery.

4. The Government of the Netherlands will make public in the Netherlands in each calendar quarter, full statements of operations under this Agreement, including information as to the use of funds, commodities and services received.

Article IX

(Missions)

1. The Government of the Netherlands agrees to receive a Special Mission for Economic Cooperation which will discharge the responsibilities of the Government of the United States of America in the Netherlands under this Agreement.

2. The Government of the Netherlands will, upon appropriate notification from the Ambassador of the United States of America in the Netherlands, consider the Special Mission and its personnel, and the United States Special Representative in Europe, as part of the Embassy of the United States of America in the Netherlands for the purpose of enjoying the privileges and immunities accorded to that Embassy and its personnel of comparable rank. The Government of the Netherlands will further accord appropriate courtesies to the members and staff of the Joint Committee on Foreign Economic Cooperation of the Congress of the United States of America and grant them the facilities and assistance necessary to the effective performance of their responsibilities.

3. The Government of the Netherlands, directly and through its representatives on the Organization for European Economic Cooperation, will extend full cooperation to the Special Mission, to the United States Special Representatives in Europe and his staff, and to the members and staff of the Joint Committee. Such cooperation shall include the provision of all information and facilities necessary to the observation and review of the carrying out of this Agreement, including the use of assistance furnished under it.

Article X

(Settlement of Claims of Nationals)

1. The Government of the Netherlands and the United States of America agree to submit to the decision of the International Court of Justice any claim espoused by either Government on behalf of one of its nationals against the other Government for compensation for damage arising as a consequence of governmental measures (other than measures concerning enemy property or interests) taken after April 3, 1948, by the other Government and affecting property or interest of such national, including contracts with or concessions granted by duly authorized authorities of such other Government. It is understood that the undertaking of each Govern-

ment in respect to claims espoused by the other Government pursuant to this paragraph is made in the case of each Government under the authority of and is limited by the terms and conditions of such effective recognition as that heretofore given to the compulsory jurisdiction of the International Court of Justice under Article 36 of the Statute of the Court. The provisions of this paragraph shall be in all respects without prejudice to other rights of access, if any, of either Government to the International Court of Justice or to the espousal and presentation of claims based upon alleged violations by either Government of rights and duties arising under treaties, agreements or principles of international law.

2. The Governments of the Netherlands and the United States of America further agree that such claims may be referred in lieu of the Court, to any arbitral tribunal mutually agreed upon.

3. It is further understood that neither Government will espouse a claim pursuant to this Article until its national has exhausted the remedies available to him in the administrative and judicial tribunals of the country in which the claim arose.

Article XI

(Definitions)

As used in this Agreement:

(a) the Netherlands means the Kingdom of the Netherlands consisting of its territory in Europe, the Netherlands Indies, Surinam and Curaçao;

(b) the term "participating country" means

(i) any country which signed the Report of the Committee of European Economic Cooperation at Paris on September 22, 1947, and territories for which it has international responsibility and to which the Economic Cooperation Agreement concluded between that country and the Government of the United States of America has been applied, and

(ii) any other country (including any of the zones of occupation of Germany, and areas under international administration or control, and the Free Territory of Trieste or either of its zones) wholly or partly in Europe, together with dependent areas under its administration;

for so long as such country is a party to the Convention for European Economic Cooperation and adheres to a joint program for European recovery designed to accomplish the purposes of this Agreement.

Article XII

(Entry into Force, Amendment, Duration)

1. This Agreement shall become effective on this day's date. Subject to the provisions of paragraphs 2 and 3 of this Article it shall remain in force until June, 1953, and, unless at least six months before June 30, 1953, either Government shall have given notice in writing to the other of intention to terminate the Agreement on that date, it shall remain in force thereafter until the expiration of six months from the date on which such notice shall have been given.

2. If, during the life of this Agreement, either Government should consider there has been a fundamental change in the basic assumptions underlying this Agreement, it shall so notify the other Government in

writing and the two Governments will thereupon consult with a view to agreeing upon the amendment, modification or termination of this Agreement. If, after three months from such notification, the two Governments have not agreed upon the action to be taken in the circumstances, either Government may give notice in writing to the other of intention to terminate this Agreement. Then, subject to the provisions of paragraph 3 of this Article, this Agreement shall terminate either:

(*a*) six months after the date of such notice of intention to terminate, or

(*b*) after such shorter period as may be agreed to be sufficient to ensure that the obligations of the Government of the Netherlands are performed in respect of any assistance which may continue to be furnished by the Government of the United States of America after the date of such notice;

provided, however, that Article V and paragraph 3 of Article VII shall remain in effect until two years after the date of such notice of intention to terminate, but not later than June 30, 1953.

3. Subsidiary agreements and arrangements negotiated pursuant to this Agreement may remain in force beyond the date of termination of this Agreement and the period of effectiveness of such subsidiary agreements and arrangements shall be governed by their own terms. Article IV shall remain in effect until all the sums in the currency of the Netherlands required to be deposited in accordance with its own terms have been disposed of as provided in that Article. Paragraph 2 of Article III shall remain in effect for so long as the garanty payments referred to in that Article may be made by the Government of the United States of America.

4. This Agreement may be amended at any time by agreement between the two Governments.

5. The Annex to this Agreement forms an integral part thereof.

6. This Agreement shall be registered with the Secretary-General of the United Nations.

In witness whereof the respective representatives, duly authorized for the purpose, have signed the present Agreement.

Done at the Hague, in duplicate, in the Dutch and English languages, both texts authentic, this second day of July, 1948.

ANNEX

(Interpretative Notes)

1. It is understood that the requirements of paragraph 1 (*a*) of Article II, relating to the adoption of measures for the efficient use of resources, would include, with respect to commodities furnished under the Agreement, effective measures for safeguarding such commodities and for preventing their diversion to illegal or irregular markets or channels of trade.

2. It is understood that the obligation under paragraph 1 (*c*) of Article II to balance the budget as soon as practicable would not preclude deficits over a short period but would mean budgetary policy involving the balancing of the budget in the long run.

3. It is understood that the business practices and business arrangements referred to in paragraph 3 of Article II mean:

(*a*) fixing prices, terms or conditions to be observed in dealing with others in the purchase, sale or lease of any product;

(b) excluding enterprises from, or allocating or dividing, any territorial market or field of business activity, or allocating customers, or fixing sales quotas or purchase quotas;

(c) discriminating against particular enterprises;

(d) limiting production or fixing production quotas;

(e) preventing by agreement the development or application of technology or invention whether patented or unpatented;

(f) extending the use of rights under patents, trademarks or copyrights granted by either country to matters which, according to its laws and regulations, are not within the scope of such grants, or to products or conditions of production, use or sale which are likewise not the subjects of such grants; and

(g) such other practices as the two Governments may agree to include.

4. It is understood that the Government of the Netherlands is obligated to take action in particular instances in accordance with paragraph 3 of Article II only after appropriate investigation or examination.

5. It is understood that the phrase in Article V "after due regard for the reasonable requirements of the Netherlands for domestic use" would include the maintenance of reasonable stocks of the materials concerned and that the phrase "commercial export" might include barter transactions. It is also understood that arrangements negotiated under Article V might appropriately include provision for consultation, in accordance with the principles of Article 32 of the Havana Charter for an International Trade Organization, in the event that stockpiles are liquidated.

6. It is understood that the Government of the Netherlands will not be requested, under paragraph 2 (a) of Article VII, to furnish detailed information about minor projects or confidential commercial or technical information the disclosure of which would injure legitimate commercial interests.

7. It is understood that the Government of the United States of America in making the notifications referred to in paragraph 2 of Article IX would bear in mind the desirability of restricting, so far as practicable, the number of officials for whom full diplomatic privileges would be requested. It is also understood that the detailed application of Article IX would, when necessary, be the subject of intergovernmental discussion.

8. It is understood that any agreements which might be arrived at pursuant to paragraph 2 of Article X would be subject to ratification by the Senate of the United States of America.

9. It is understood that the definitions contained in Article XI imply no restriction upon the Government of the Netherlands with regard to the carrying forward of contemplated changes in the structure of the Kingdom of the Netherlands. It is further understood that if while this Agreement is in effect arrangements are made for a change in status of territories presently a part of the Kingdom of the Netherlands, the relation of such territories to this Agreement will be the subject of future consultation.

Source: *Road to Recovery*, Ministry of Foreign Affairs, The Hague, 1954, Annex B, pp. 184–195.

CUSTOMS CONVENTION BETWEEN THE NETHERLANDS AND THE ECONOMIC UNION OF BELGIUM AND LUXEMBURG

The Government of Her Majesty the Queen of the Netherlands on the one hand;

The Government of His Majesty the King of the Belgians and of Her Royal Highness the Grand Duchess of Luxemburg on the other hand,

Desiring, at the moment of liberation of the Territories of the Netherlands and the Economic Union of Belgium and Luxemburg, to create the most favourable conditions for the ultimate formation of a complete and durable Customs Union and for the restoration of economic activity, have decided to further these ends by establishing a common tariff of import duties, and granting mutual exemptions from those duties and to this end, have agreed to the following articles:

Article 1

The Netherlands and the Economic Union of Belgium and Luxemburg shall impose identical Customs duties on the importation of goods according to the appended tariff which forms an integral part of this agreement.

Apart from the duties provided for in this tariff. they shall be entitled to levy excise duties on alcohol, wine, beer, sugar and tobacco, as well as any other taxes according to the system in force in the Netherlands and in the Economic Union of Belgium and Luxemburg; they shall reserve their right to modify the rates.

Article 2

No Customs duty shall be levied on goods entering the Netherlands from the Economic Union of Belgium and Luxemburg and on goods entering the Economic Union of Belgium and Luxemburg from the Netherlands. The Netherlands and the Economic Union of Belgium and Luxemburg shall be entitled to levy entry duties on alcohol, wine, beer, sugar and tobacco, and other taxes according to the system in force in their respective territories; they reserve their right to modify the rates.

Article 3

An Administrative Council on Customs duties shall be constituted; this shall be composed of three delegates of the Netherlands and three delegates of the Economic Union of Belgium and Luxemburg. The chairmanship of the Administrative Council on Customs Duties shall be exercised in turn by the first delegate of the Netherlands and the first delegate of the Economic Union of Belgium and Luxemburg.

The Administrative Council on Customs Duties shall without prejudice to the provisions of the annexed tariff propose measures aimed at the unification of the legislative provisions and regulations governing the collection of import and excise duties in the Netherlands and in the Economic Union of Belgium and Luxemburg and the adjustment of the latter to the provisions of this agreement.

Article 4

The Administrative Council on Customs Duties shall be assisted by a Commission on Customs Disputes, composed of two delegates of the Netherlands and two delegates of the Economic Union of Belgium and Luxemburg.

The Commission on Customs Disputes shall make a binding award in the case of disputes concerning decisions taken in last resort by the competent instances in the Netherlands or in the Economic Union of Belgium and Luxemburg in matters of the application of the legal provisions and regulations resulting from this agreement.

The Commission shall communicate its decisions to the competent ministers, who shall be responsible for carrrying them out within the limits of their respective competence.

Article 5

An Administrative Council for the Control of Foreign Trade shall be constituted, composed of three delegates of the Netherlands and three delegates of the Economic Union of Belgium and Luxemburg. The chairmanship of the Administrative Council for the Control of Foreign Trade shall be exercised in turn by the first delegate of the Netherlands and the first delegate of the Economic Union of Belgium and Luxemburg.

The functions of the Administrative Council for the Control of Foreign Trade shall consist of:

a. giving its views to the competent authorities in the Netherlands and the Economic Union of Belgium and Luxemburg concerning any measures which they might intend to take for the purpose of regulating imports, exports and transit either with or without accessory duties or dues in particular by imposing restrictions of an economic character, such as licences, quotas, or special licence fees and administrative charges;

b. coordinating the above measures for the purpose of establishing a regime common to the Netherlands and the Economic Union of Belgium and Luxemburg;

c. administering the import, export and transit quotas common to the Netherlands and the Economic Union of Belgium and Luxemburg;

d. informing the competent authorities in the Netherlands and the Economic Union of Belgium and Luxemburg of its views concerning all measures relating to production bounties or subsidies which the Contracting Parties intend to take.

Article 6

A commercial Agreements Council shall be constituted, composed of three delegates of the Netherlands and three delegates of the Economic

Union of Belgium and Luxemburg. The chairmanship of the Commercial Agreements Council shall be exercised in turn by the first delegate of the Netherlands and by the first delegate of the Economic Union of Belgium and Luxemburg.

The Commercial Agreements Council shall whenever possible ensure the coordination of measures in respect of relations established with third States.

Article 7

The joint measures mentioned under Articles 3, 5 and 6 of this Agreement shall be decided upon by the competent ministers on behalf of the Netherlands on the one hand and of the Economic Union of Belgium and Luxemburg on the other and shall be referred to the competent governmental or legal authorities for approval.

Article 8

The present Convention shall be ratified and shall come into force eight days after the exchange of the instruments of ratification.

It may be cancelled at any time provided that one year's notice is given.

It shall in any case cease to be operative on the implementation of the long term Economic Union which the contracting parties intend to conclude.

Article 9

Pending the exchange of instruments of ratification, the Convention shall come into force as soon as the Netherlands and Belgian Governments reintegrate their respective territories.

Either Government however shall have the right to cancel the Convention at any time provided that six months notice is given.

In witness whereof, the Ministers Plenipotentiary, provided with the necessary powers to this end, have signed the present Convention and fixed their seals thereto.–

Signed in London on September 5, 1944, in triplicate, in the Dutch and French languages both of which texts have force of law.–

Source: *Report on the Ministerial discussions between the Netherlands, Belgium and Luxemburg, March 10–13, 1949*, Secretariat-General of the Benelux Customs Convention, 1949, Brussels, Annex 2.

PROTOCOL ESTABLISHED BY THE GOVERNMENTS OF THE NETHERLANDS, BELGIUM AND LUXEMBURG AT THE CONFERENCE OF CABINET MINISTERS,

held at The Hague on March 10, 11, 12 and 13, 1949

The three Governments, having taken cognizance of the report submitted by the Presidents of the Customs Union Councils in pursuance of the Protocol of June 8, 1948, and of the results obtained at the Ministerial Conference at The Hague, believe that the conditions enumerated in the said Protocol as essential to an Economic Union between the three countries can be fulfilled by July 1, 1950.

It will be possible to initiate a Pre-Union system on July 1, 1949. They further find with satisfaction that good progress has been made on the road towards the realization of the Economic Union since their meeting at Château d'Ardenne.

They have more particularly noted the effects of the steps already taken in the three countries towards the re-establishment of free consumption and the reduction of production and consumption subsidies. They also appreciate the efforts made and the results achieved as regards unifying indirect taxes, harmonizing commercial policies and coordinating investments.

In order to reach the ends in view and ensure that the economies of the three countries are integrated as well as possible immediately the Union comes into force, the three Governments have adopted the following resolutions:

I. THE REMOVAL OF CONTROLS AND SUBSIDIES

They will pursue a co-ordinated policy of free production, distribution and consumption of goods, and will abolish subsidies, so as to remove obstacles in the way of free exchange of goods between the two economies.

II. MONETARY AND COMMERCIAL POLICY

Action taken in the budgetary, fiscal, financial and monetary fields towards equilibrium between the two economies shall be in accordance with the spirit of the recommendations made by the O.E.E.C. Consultative Group on March 8, 1949.[1]

In view of the essential role which the exceptional aid from the United States under the Marshall Plan plays in the recovery of their economy, the three Governments believe that the successive stages in the realization of the Union must be adapted to the annual allocations under the European Recovery Program (July 1–June 30).

[1] These recommendations were later approved by the O.E.E.C. Council on March 26, 1949.

They have therefore chosen the first of July for the commencement of the Pre-Union period, which will be characterized by the gradual freeing of trade between their territories, the systematic co-ordination of the commercial and monetary policies of the partners with respect to third countries, and by the preparation of a regime whereby the partners can jointly enter into agreements with third parties. A Ministerial Commission will be set up to supervise the systematic co-ordination of external trade and monetary policies.

In order to enable the Netherlands to introduce this Pre-Union regime, the B.L.E.U. is prepared to grant the Netherlands Government adequate credits on the understanding that the amount of such credits shall be adjusted to the importance of the steps taken by the Netherlands towards freeing trade subject to the agreement of the Belgian and Luxemburg Governments. In determining the degree of priority to be assigned to the various categories of de-controlled goods, special attention will be paid, on the one hand, to products of importance to the employment policy of the Belgo-Luxemburg Economic Union and, on the other, to the conditions required for abolishing rationing and restrictions on the Dutch home market.

Should present conditions remain unchanged and a global balance in the international payments of the two economies be achieved, the three Governments will pass from the Pre-Union stage to that of the Economic Union proper on July 1, 1950.

A common system of financial settlements with third countries will be established on the same date. Further proposals will be made regarding the way in which the Union must function in the monetary field. These will have to establish, in particular:

a. The conditions governing mutual currency convertibility;
b. Safety measures to detect the fundamental differences liable to arise between the balance-of-payments in the two economies, as well as any disturbances of the balance between the Union and third countries;
c. Steps to be taken in the case of such disturbances. These will be sought particularly in the field of commerce.

In agreeing upon the foregoing, the three Governments have based themselves on expectations regarding E.R.P. aid and the Benelux countries' share of this aid. They also think that the objectives of the O.E.E.C. will be attained. Should these expectations fail to materialize, the three Governments will have to consult together and reconsider the whole problem.

III. AGRICULTURAL POLICY

The three Governments adopt the following principles as bases for the gradual harmonization of the three agricultural policies:

a. agricultural policy should ensure that farmers and agricultural labourers in the three countries enjoy security in well-managed enterprises which are justified from the economic and social points of view;
b. agricultural policy should aim at increasing the agricultural productive capacity in the three countries to the maximum.

To attain these ends, the three countries propose:

— to encourage, increase and direct their agricultural production;
— to plan measures likely to suit the production to the marketing of
  agricultural commodities.

The Governments charge the Commission on Agriculture, Food Supply
and Fisheries to submit proposals based on the above principles before
the Economic Union comes into effect.

The three Governments appreciate the happy results of the implementation of the Protocol of May 9, 1947, which will facilitate the harmonization of the agricultural policies of the three countries.

IV. SOCIAL POLICY

They will co-ordinate their wage policies and their social policies as
far as necessary.

V. INVESTMENTS

They will co-ordinate their investments according to O.E.E.C. principles taking account of the increase of population and possibilities of
adapting existing enterprises, in order to ensure the highest and most
balanced level of employment in each country and attain optimal conditions of production.

VI. FISCAL QUESTIONS

They will complete the unification of excise duties and will unify road
taxes on motor vehicles as far as necessary.

Regarding purchase tax, they will adopt the recommendations formulated by the Administrative Customs Council for the unification of
collecting methods. As regards the rate of the tax, they recognize that
the recommendations submitted by the said Council have due regard
to the respective interests but find that budgetary considerations prevent
them from making final decisions at the moment. They will immediately
appoint experts who will decide to what extent the budgetary consequences could be offset, without prejudice to competitive conditions or
the free circulation of goods; this could be done by maintaining certain
differences in the rates of taxation after the Economic Union takes effect.
These experts will issue a report within three months.

They will establish a certain harmonization in the field of direct
taxation which is considered indispensable. Their aim will be to complete
the adaptation of fiscal systems wherever these would present differences
liable to affect competitive conditions to an appreciable degree.

VII. CUSTOMS FORMALITIES

Measures aiming at a gradual simplification of frontier control on
passenger traffic between the Netherlands and the B.L.E.U. will be
taken as from to-day.

VIII. WATERWAYS AND PORT PROBLEMS

The three Governments agree to recognize:
1. a. that major problems exist between the three countries as regards
       waterways and ports;

b. that a solution to these problems should be found which is satis-
    factory to all three countries;
        The study of these problems will be entrusted to a special com-
    mission composed of representatives of the countries concerned.
    This commission will set to work at once.
2. that questions of minor importance exist in the same field.
    On this point, the Governments note the results attained by the Com-
mission for Transport and Ports, find that several questions still remain
unsettled, and charge the said Commission to settle these in the common
interest as soon as possible.

IX. PARTICIPATION OF TRADE AND INDUSTRY REPRESENTATIVES

An Advisory Committee drawn from circles interested in the preparation and functioning of the Economic Union will be set up in each
of the three countries. Regular contacts will be established between these
Committees and the national delegations to the various organs of the
Customs Convention.

X. SPECIAL DIFFICULTIES

Those problems arising from commercial and financial relations between the three countries which cannot be satisfactorily solved by normal
administrative methods will be referred to the Board of the Presidents
of the Councils, in cases where the existing situation is such that it might
disturb the good economic relations between the three countries.
    The Presidents will examine every possible solution for such difficulties.

XI. ADMINISTRATIVE PROVISIONS

In order to carry out this program, the three Governments charge the
Board of Presidents to submit a detailed scheme of execution before July
1, 1949; this will be systematically put into operation during the Pre-
Union period from July 1, 1949 to July 1, 1950.
    In addition, a special commission will be appointed to prepare the
document implementing the Economic Union between the three countries,
and providing for the institution of organizations to ensure its proper
functioning.

Signed at The Hague in triplicate on March 13, 1949.

> Source: *Report on the Ministerial discussions between
> the Netherlands, Belgium and Luxemburg,
> March 10–13, 1949*, Secretariat-General of the
> Benelux Customs Convention, 1949, Brussels,
> II.

INDEX